A
HISTORY
OF IDEAS
IN
SCIENCE
EDUCATION

IMPLICATIONS
FOR PRACTICE

A
HISTORY
OF IDEAS
IN
SCIENCE
EDUCATION
IMPLICATIONS
FOR PRACTICE

GEORGE E. DeBOER

Teachers College, Columbia University
New York and London

Published by Teachers College Press, 1234 Amsterdam Avenue
New York, NY 10027

Library of Congress Cataloging-in-Publication Data

DeBoer, George E.
    A history of ideas in science education : implications for
practice / George E. DeBoer.
      p.   cm.
    Includes bibliographical references (p.) and index.
    ISBN 0-8077-3054-8 (alk. paper).—ISBN 0-8077-3053-X (pbk. :
alk. paper)
      1. Science—Study and teaching—United States—History—19th
century.   2. Science—Study and teaching—United States—
History—20th century.   3. n-us.   I. Title.
    Q183.3.A1D4   1991
    507'.073—dc20   90-46958
                                                                        CIP

Printed on acid-free paper

Manufactured in the United States of America

10   09   12 11 10

In Memory of
Judith Ann DeBoer
1948-1990

Contents

Preface   xi

CHAPTER 1   **Science versus Classical Studies**   **1**

The Contributions of Science Study to Mental   4
    Discipline
The Utility of Science Study   8
Summary   17

CHAPTER 2   **Educational Thought and Practice in the**   **18**
Nineteenth Century

The Role of the Academy   18
The Influence of European Educators   21
American Influences   30
Summary   37

CHAPTER 3   **The Turn of the Century and the Committee**   **39**
of Ten

The Committee of Ten   40
The Committee on College-Entrance   50
    Requirements
Science Education at the Turn of the Century   53
Summary   62

CHAPTER 4   **The Reorganization of Science Education**   **64**

Commission on the Reorganization of Secondary   67
    Education
Science Committee   69
Reactions to Reorganized Science   80
Summary   83

CHAPTER 5 **Social Relevance and the Organized Disciplines**   **85**

General Science   86
Biology   92
Physics   99
Chemistry   104
Summary   106

CHAPTER 6 **School Science Seeks Its Own Identity**   **108**

The Laboratory   108
College Domination of the High School   116
    Curriculum
The Scientific Study of the Curriculum   121
Summary   127

CHAPTER 7 **World War II and the Beginnings of Change**   **128**

War-Related Issues   129
Science Education at the End of the   138
    Progressive Era
Life Adjustment Education   142
Summary   146

CHAPTER 8 **Curriculum Reform**   **147**

Curriculum Projects Supported by the National   147
    Science Foundation
Theoretical Support for the Curriculum Reform
    Movement   158
How Successful Were the New Programs?   166
Summary   171

CHAPTER 9 **Scientific Literacy and the New Progressivism**   **173**

Scientific Literacy   174
The Science-Technology-Society Theme   178
Controversy About Social Issues as Organizing   184
    Themes
Summary   189

CHAPTER 10 **Process and Product in Science Education**   **190**

Developing the Scientific Mind   192
The Nature of Science   198

	Concept Learning	200
	Inquiry Teaching	206
	Summary	214

Chapter 11	**What We Hâve Learned and Where We Are Headed**	**215**
	Why Science Is Part of the School Curriculum	216
	The Teaching of Science: What Does It Mean?	217
	Science as a Structured Body of Knowledge	219
	The Scientific Way of Thinking	226
	Science for Social Relevance	233
	A Composite Model of Science Teaching	237
	Conclusion	240

References		245
Index		257
About the Author		269

Preface

There has been a great deal of concern recently about the crisis in science education and in education in general. The declining status of the United States in world economic markets is being blamed on a lack of rigor in the educational system, just as 30 years ago education was blamed for our failure to win the space race with the Soviet Union. Science education is particularly vulnerable to such attacks because scientific and technical knowledge is thought to be key to success in these areas and because there is a body of evidence that suggests that American youth are falling short when it comes to learning science. International comparisons of science knowledge place U.S. students in the lower ranks, and our own internal assessments demonstrate a generally inadequate level of science literacy among youth and adults. In addition, there is a declining interest in science teaching as a career and, most recently, a precipitous drop in higher education enrollments in science. These problems in science education come at a time when a new crisis is upon us, one that is potentially more serious than Cold War competition with the Soviets or economic competition with the Japanese. We are now in a struggle to save the planet Earth from what some think may be its ultimate destruction, a task that will take as much scientific and technological creativity as we can generate.

This book does not try to analyze the reasons for our failings in science education, nor does it try to resolve them. Rather, it offers a perspective on the science education enterprise that individuals can use as they attempt to understand what takes place in science classrooms and what should take place. It is a historical account of *ideas* in science education that covers the time period from approximately the middle of the nineteenth century to the present.

Most of the ideas that we recognize in science education today had their origins at least a hundred years ago, during a time when science was struggling for a place in the school curriculum. In fact, many of our modern ideas in science education were very well elaborated in the nineteenth century. A few, such as the recently intensified concern for the environment, are truly new. Others, such as the belief in mental discipline, are for the most part passé. But between the new and the old are many ideas that have been shared by science educators over the years.

To many educators the past seems quaint and irrelevant. This may be as much the case for science educators as for anyone. The present is what matters. The latest idea is what counts. It is rare for science educators to discuss in any depth early twentieth-century science education, let alone the ideas of the nineteenth century. For science educators who were trained during the 1960s and 1970s, there is the pre-curriculum-reform period, which they perceive to be characterized by rote memorization and meaningless cookbook laboratory exercises, and the post-curriculum-reform period, characterized by inquiry, conceptual understanding, and, more recently, societal and technological concerns. For science educators being prepared today, many do not even know in any depth the significance of the curriculum reforms of the 1960s. A paper that I recently reviewed dealt with inquiry teaching as if it were an idea just invented by the author.

A study of history reveals that most ideas have had their origins in other times and other places. The validity of ideas over time gives them a legitimacy for today, and this makes us less likely to treat them as trivial—in vogue today, out of vogue tomorrow. It makes our decisions about curriculum and instructional strategies more intelligent and our evaluation of those strategies more cautious.

We are also more likely to realize that what we may accomplish on one front may produce a significant loss on another front. We can look back and see what has been lost and gained by each major shift in the past. I think here of some current efforts to head with greater vigor in the direction of social responsibility and socially relevant instruction in science. Will this be at the expense of the development of basic conceptual understanding or perhaps the development of fundamental inquiry skills? Is this a price we are willing to pay? Or what about efforts to achieve *excellence* in science education through special programs for the gifted and the highly motivated science students? Will these efforts lead to increased differentiation in the curriculum, perhaps starting the selection process at the middle school or elementary level? Will the cost be the lowering of the quality of the educational experience for the average or below-average student? Is this a cost we are willing to accept? What have been the results of such choices in the past?

This book is an attempt to identify the goals of science education in the United States from the early nineteenth century to the present and to show how these goals have competed with one another for our attention. Another purpose is to examine how important each of these goals is for us today and the ways that we try to accomplish them. Science instruction has been part of the education of American youth in some form or another since the early days of this country. Why is science included in the curriculum? What have educators felt would be accomplished by instruction in science? This book will discuss the origins of science teaching in the United States and at the same time will pay particular attention to the larger educational goals that science instruction was supposed to accomplish and the strategies that were used to accomplish those goals.

Most of the goals that science teaching has been expected to accomplish over the years remain with us today. We may use different language to express them and they may take on more or less importance at the present moment, but most of them persist. They include the intellectual goals of thinking and reasoning, the personal goals of appreciation and understanding, the practical goals that will help us in our life's work and in our role as intelligent citizens, and the futuristic goals of innovation and creativity. Creativity is particularly important because it enables us to look ahead to a new day, characterized by new technology and by a new understanding of the world. Science is one of the few areas of human understanding where we truly believe that frontiers can be conquered, that there are natural laws that can be discovered and new forces that can be put to our use. Instilling a sense of optimism about innovation is an essential ingredient in any science education program.

Progress in science has produced a new area of interest in science education, and that is the area of science ethics. As new discoveries are made, we are faced with new ethical dilemmas concerning our overall well-being. We live in a moral world. We have established standards of right and wrong for ourselves over the ages. As scientific knowledge and technological applications progress rapidly, these standards are tested. This prompts many to say that our youth need to know how to deal with value dilemmas that arise out of the context of science, and they need to learn how to deal with them in the context of science instruction. Genetic engineering, nuclear energy, environmental conservation, and euthanasia are just a few of the issues that are both related to science and have ethical dimensions. How should these be handled in the context of school science?

This book is intended for all those who are interested in science education. It is for classroom teachers and those who are planning to become classroom teachers. It is for parents faced with the task of assessing the wisdom of some particular approach to science instruction that is being used in their schools. And it is for science education leaders who are concerned about the historical justification of the goals and strategies that are proposed for science education.

The approach that I have taken is to rely on the published accounts of key scientists, science education researchers, professors of science education, classroom teachers, and others that appear in the professional literature. Their *ideas* about what is best for science education is what constitutes this book. I have tried to treat the ideas of those key individuals with thoroughness and to let their own words speak for them as much as possible. The book is not an account of school *practices* except as information about schooling is presented by the writers themselves. Thus it represents our best thinking about what is good for science education, whether that educational goal ever reached the stage of implementation or not. In this regard, I believe that a major task of science educators is to document and compare what actually happens in schools with the best thinking about what should happen there and to resolve the discrepancies that arise out of that study.

I would like to thank a number of people who have contributed to the production of this work. Thanks first to the students in my Seminar on Science Teaching, who over the years encouraged me to synthesize the materials that I had accumulated on science education into a work of my own. In addition, two of my graduate students, Walter Peck and Jennifer Jacobs, helped enormously in gathering materials, checking references, and discussing ideas for the book. Thanks also to Joan Thompson, who provided invaluable secretarial and word-processing assistance. Finally, I would like to thank my family for their generous support and love.

Chapter 1

Science versus Classical Studies

The nineteenth century was a time of important scientific discovery and of profound change in our way of looking at the world. It began with primitive sanitation and horse-drawn carriages, but also with a faith in the certainty of the laws of nature and the inevitable progress of the human race. The century ended with the discovery of previously unimagined forces—radioactive emission, the internal combustion engine, and the great dynamos of industry—and with uncertainty. Fixed principles no longer held. The laws of nature, which were considered to be certain and a revelation of the unfolding truths of God's universe, were open to question. By the end of the nineteenth century, the methods of science had pervaded the world to produce a new way of thinking and a new power to understand and to control the forces of nature.

In his autobiography Henry Adams (1918/1973) poignantly expressed the impact of these changes on himself and the failure of nineteenth-century education to prepare him for that changing world. Writing in the early years of the twentieth century as a man in his 60s and speaking in the third person, Adams reflected on his own schoolboy days:

> On looking back, fifty years later, at his own figure in 1854, and pondering on the needs of the twentieth century, he wondered whether, on the whole, the boy of 1854 stood nearer to the thought of 1904, or to that of the year 1. He found himself unable to give a sure answer. The calculation was clouded by the undetermined values of twentieth-century thought, but the story will show his reasons for thinking that, in essentials like religion, ethics, philosophy; in history, literature, art; in the concepts of all science, except perhaps mathematics, the American boy

1

of 1854 stood nearer the year 1 than to the year 1900. The education he
had received bore little relation to the education he needed. Speaking as
an American of 1900, he had as yet no education at all. He knew not
even where or how to begin. (p. 53)

Although his education did not prepare Adams for life as he
found it in the twentieth century, the changes that took place in education during the nineteenth century were fundamental, similar in
magnitude to the changes that took place in science, religion, and
politics. The century began with an educational system that had been
inherited from the Middle Ages. It consisted at the primary level of
reading, writing, and arithmetic, while at the upper levels it was dominated by the study of the classical languages. But by the end of the
century, the elementary curriculum had been expanded and modern
subjects had to a great extent replaced Greek and Latin in both secondary schools and in higher education.

During colonial times and the early nineteenth century, the ability to read, write, and manage simple accounts separated the educated from the uneducated. A classical education was functional only
for those who entered the clergy and for some literary careers, but
for most who attained it, it was simply an adornment of their social
class. The ability to read and recite the classics did little more than
separate the wealthy from the masses. By the end of the century, however, a broad and practical education was increasingly seen as essential for life in a world that was becoming dominated by science, technology, and industry.

The fundamental changes that took place in the educational system during the nineteenth century were the gradual but unrelenting
infusion of the sciences and other modern studies into the curriculum
at all levels and the gradual but certain diminishing of the study of
the classical languages. The new scientific studies also brought with
them independent inquiry and self-discovery to replace the unques-
tioned authority of classical learning. Debates about the relative merits of the classical studies and newer courses in science, history, English literature, and modern languages raged throughout the
century, and the wisdom of this move away from the classics and toward modern studies was the theme of countless educational treatises
of the day.

The debate between science and classical studies took a number
of directions. Advocates of change said that the educational system
was outmoded and needed to be modernized. They argued that there
were urgent questions that citizens of the nineteenth century faced

that were not being addressed in a classical education—questions of the treatment of the poor, sanitation and public health, universal education, the management of criminals, and religious freedom. The critics said that the true purpose of education was to prepare people to deal with these socially relevant questions—to equip them for the age in which they lived. It was not to dwell on the ancient past. Modern citizens needed experience with those things that would help them live in the realities of the present world—a world that was being increasingly dominated by scientific discovery and technological development. As John Tyndall (1867) said: "Let the gleaned wealth of antiquity be showered into the open breast; but while we 'unsphere the spirit of Plato' and listen with delight to the lordly music of the past, let us honour by adequate recognition the genius of our own time" (p. 85).

Related to the modernization argument was the claim that the world had changed in ways that required the development of independent judgment, not passive acceptance of authority. The prevailing educational system was dominated by a faith in the authority of the words written in textbooks and spoken by teachers. In the larger society, however, independent thought had replaced the authoritarian dictates of church and government, and it was time for education to reflect this change.

A counterargument introduced by the classicists was that the true purposes of a liberal education were the development of one's intellectual faculties through the study of ancient classics and mathematics, and the growth of personal pleasure that results from this study. The learning of science was seen by some classicists as narrowly utilitarian and debased, aimed, as they said it was, at the making of money through vocational and professional preparation. According to the classicists, their own motives were humanizing and would lead to feelings that were refined and generous, whereas the scientists' motives could be viewed as crass and materialistic.

Perhaps the most well known defense of classical education came from the faculty of Yale College in 1828. "The Yale Report" was written in reply to critics of the classical college curriculum who were pressing for a more practical form of education. Their report was not an attack on science but rather a statement of the value of ancient studies. The following excerpts from the report make the point:

> The study of the classics is useful, not only as it lays the foundations of a correct taste, and furnishes the student with those elementary ideas which are found in the literature of modern times, and which he no

where so well acquires as in their original sources;—but also as the study itself forms the most effectual discipline of the mental faculties. . . . Every faculty of the mind is employed; not only the memory, judgment, and reasoning powers, but the taste and fancy are occupied and improved. . . . (p. 289)

The proper question is,—what course of discipline affords the best mental culture, leads to the most thorough knowledge of our own literature, and lays the best foundation for professional study. The ancient languages have here a decided advantage. (Yale Corporation, 1828/1961, pp. 289–290)

Advocates of science replied in turn that it was science study that provided the best mental discipline, not classical studies. Three writers in particular represent the efforts that were typical of nineteenth-century scientists to increase the attention paid to science in the schools and to decrease the amount of time and energy spent on the classical languages. The first was Edward Livingston Youmans, a mid-nineteenth-century science textbook writer and science lecturer in the United States. The other two were the respected and popular British scientists and essayists Herbert Spencer and Thomas Huxley, both of whom were vitally interested in school science in both England and the United States.

The Contributions of Science Study to Mental Discipline

It was the relative contributions of science and the classical languages to intellectual development that Edward Livingston Youmans addressed in his book *The Culture Demanded by Modern Life* (1867). Youmans wrote and lectured extensively on topics of popular interest in science and was personally acquainted with most of the leading scientists of the day. He was especially interested in evolutionary theory and became a great supporter of Herbert Spencer's work on social evolution. In fact, it was Youmans who was responsible for having Spencer's essays on education published in the United States. In addition to writing a well received textbook on chemistry, Youmans also published a book on household chemistry and established *The Popular Science Monthly* in 1872. (For a discussion of the contribution of Youmans to American science education, see Fiske, 1899.)

The Culture Demanded by Modern Life was a collection of essays by American and British scientists and educators arguing for the inclusion of the sciences in the school and college curriculum. Youmans's introductory chapter on "Mental Discipline in Education" was a clear statement of mid-nineteenth-century thinking about the process of mental development and the advantages of science instruction as part of that development.

Youmans argued that science study was actually superior to the study of languages and mathematics for mental discipline because of the broader range of mental abilities to which science study was related. For example, it was widely believed by educators that memory could be strengthened through difficult memory exercises, that this was an important goal of education, and that language study was an effective means of developing the memory. Youmans and other proponents of science said in response: If you want memory exercises, science provides all the detailed facts you could ever need for exercising the powers of memory. In addition, science facts can be related in organized ways to produce generalizations that are easier to remember. Youmans argued that language study, on the other hand, was less valuable because it tended to deal with the memorization of unrelated and, in his opinion, often meaningless rules.

While language study was defended by the classicists because of its power to discipline the memory, they defended the study of mathematics because of its ability to develop reasoning power. Youmans claimed, however, that mathematics study fell short when it came to the kind of reasoning that humans engaged in every day, namely, inductive thought. Speaking of mathematicians, he said;

> They begin with axioms, self-evident truths, established principles, and proceed to their conclusions along a track each step of which is an intuitive certainty. But it so happens that in our mental dealings with the experiences of life, the first, the most important, and most difficult thing is to get the data or premises from which to reason. The primary question is, What are the facts, the pertinent facts, and all the facts, which bear upon the inquiry? This is the supreme step; for, until this is done, reasoning is futile, and it may be added that, when this is done, the formation of conclusions is a comparatively simple process. (p. 11)

Mathematics study dealt with reasoning, to be sure, but it was deductive reasoning, not the essential component of everyday practical thought, which was induction.

Classicists and scientists differed not only in the kind of mental discipline that they claimed for their subject areas but also in their views of the nature of mind and the way in which mental development occurred. Many scientists were beginning to view learning as a process by which neural connections were built and strengthened by means of organized sense impressions. According to this model, sense impressions and the verbal generalizations that are derived from them had to be presented to the learner in an organized fashion, repeated many times to strengthen them, and repeated in varying contexts and in higher and more complex combinations to make them broadly useful. Thus the key to education was the *specific* way in which knowledge drawn from sense impressions was organized for the learner. It was not effort alone that was responsible for the strengthening of mental capacity, but also the way in which the knowledge was organized. In Youmans's words:

> The simple elements of mind are built up into complex knowledge by the law of association of ideas; and the mental associations are formed by combinations of currents in the brain, and are made permanent by the growth and modification of cells at the points of union. When a child associates the sight, weight, and ring of a dollar, with the written word and verbal sound that represent it so firmly together in its mind that any one of these sensations will instantly bring up the others, it is said to "learn" it. But the real fact of the case is, that the currents formed by visible impressions, vocal movements and sounds, are often repeated together, and are thus combined in the brain, and fixed by specific growths at their points of union, and in this way the mental associations are cemented by cerebral nutrition. And thus the child goes on multiplying its experiences of the properties of objects and of localities, persons, actions, conduct; he observes, compares, contrasts, infers, and judges, and all this growing and complex mass of acquisition is definitely combined in the growing and perfecting organ of the mind. (p. 14)

In contrast to this material view of organized mind that required a specific ordering of knowledge for its development, classical educators argued for a generalized form of mental exercise that would in some undetermined way lead to improved mental power. Since the process was not related to a physical concept of mind, the order and organization of presented material were not important. Effort at memorizing a list of words or at working through a complex mathematical proof would reap its own rewards in a strengthened mental capacity. The specific exercises did not matter. One mental activity was as good as another, as long as it was thought to improve one's mental strength.

According to Youmans, prevailing educational practice focused too much on useless facts as a way of increasing a generalized mental capacity. What was needed instead was a process that produced both useful knowledge and improved mental power at the same time. This was the contribution that science could make. Through the study of science, useful knowledge could be gained for the work of life, while the faculties of the mind were being developed simultaneously.

Youmans's plan for science education would begin science teaching at the earliest age, when children have "a vast capability of accumulating simple facts." Youmans said:

> When curiosity is freshest, and the perceptions keenest, and memory most impressible, before the maturity of the reflective powers, the opening mind should be led to the art of noticing the aspects, properties, and simple relations of the surrounding objects of Nature. (p. 26)

The focus of this instruction was the accumulation of sense impressions and simple relationships between them. Skill in observation and acquisition of impressions of nature were the key components of science education at this age.

This early phase of science education would lead naturally into a more systematic observation of nature for older children and the systematic development of both their inductive and deductive reasoning powers. The physical sciences were the best place to start because they dealt with systems of relationship that were the least complicated and the most certain. Biological study had its own value, but should be taught later because of its complexity and uncertainty. Dealing with this uncertainty demanded "a subtler exercise of the reason, . . . more circumspection in weighing evidence and checking conclusions, and a severer necessity for suspension of judgment" (p. 34). If it were attempted at the right time, the study of difficult biological systems would lead to important attitudes such as tentativeness and careful objectivity. A second quality of biological study for mental development was that which came from the "comprehensiveness and perfection of their *classifications*" (p. 35). As Youmans said: "Not only do they furnish inexhaustible material for the exercise of memory, but by the presentation of facts in their natural relations, they exercise it in its highest and most perfect form" (p. 35). Finally, in addition to its ability to strengthen the mind, biological study provided a person with important knowledge about sanitation, hygiene, health, and disease, essential knowledge for a healthy life in the mid-nineteenth century.

Science study provided knowledge of useful facts and the relationships among those facts, and it strengthened the intellect by offering an effective way of thinking about the natural world. Both of these were important to educators, but it was the strengthening of the intellect that was the more important function of science teaching. To make this point, Youmans drew upon John Stuart Mill's inaugural address to the University of St. Andrew in 1867:

It is surely no small part of education to put us in intelligent possession of the most important and most universally interesting facts of the universe, so that the world which surrounds us may not be a sealed book to us, uninteresting because unintelligible. This, however, is but the simplest and most obvious part of the utility of science. . . . It is more important to understand the value of scientific instruction as a training and disciplining process, to fit the intellect for the proper work of a human being. (cited in Youmans, 1867, p. 30)

According to Mill, science instruction provides us with a method for arriving at truth through observation, experimentation, and reasoning that has utility in everyday life. In fact, the process of arriving at the nature of things through observation, and judging the significance of those observations, is what separates one human intellect from another. The ability to weigh evidence, to determine what is relevant and what is not—these are the things that make for intellectual strength, and it is these things that science instruction can provide.

The Utility of Science Study

Many noted scientists of the nineteenth century joined the campaign to make science teaching a part of the school curriculum both in Europe and in the United States. John Tyndall, Thomas Huxley, James Paget, Claude Bernard, Michael Faraday, Herbert Spencer, Justus Von Liebig, John Herschel, Charles Lyell, Joseph Hooker, and many others wrote essays, gave lectures, and presented testimony before government commissions on the value of science education. But two who stand out because of the vigor of their support and the passion of their arguments are Thomas Huxley and Herbert Spencer, both respected scientists as well as popular essayists. Their writings were published in the United States as well as in England and were widely read by both educational leaders and the lay public. Huxley and Spencer were effusive in their claims of the importance of science both as a practical, utilitarian study and as a superior form of intellectual training, and their writings provide rich sources of insight into both the content and method of science teaching as it was developing in the nineteenth century.

Thomas Huxley

Huxley made several arguments in favor of science study, one of which was the modernization argument mentioned earlier. Huxley felt that science should be a major branch of school and university study because it dealt with such an enormous portion of the totality of human knowledge. But, in fact, the curriculum was dominated by the study of Greek and Roman civilization and the Greek and Latin languages. The humanists had won their victory during the Renaissance 300 years earlier with the incorporation of the rediscovered Greek civilization into the curriculum. This was a major improvement over the ecclesiastical scholasticism of the Middle Ages, but in Huxley's view the humanists of the nineteenth century were acting as if the study of the Greek classics was to be the permanent character of education. What the classicists were forgetting was that there was now a modern world whose literature, painting, music, and science could compete with the great works of the Greek civilization. In Huxley's (1899) words:

> There is one feature of the present state of the civilised world which separates it more widely from the Renascence, than the Renascence was separated from the middle ages. This distinctive character of our own times lies in the vast and constantly increasing part which is played by natural knowledge. Not only is our daily life shaped by it, not only does the prosperity of millions of men depend upon it, but our whole theory of life has long been influenced, consciously or unconsciously, by the general conceptions of the universe, which have been forced upon us by physical science. (p. 149)

The study of science was essential for understanding this modern world. Studying biology, for example, would provide knowledge of one's body and the ways to avoid disease and maintain good health. In his essay "On the Study of Biology," Huxley talked about the emerging germ theory of infectious disease and the practical measures that must be taken by people to avoid infection. He said: "It may be well that the general, as well as the professional, public would have a sufficient knowledge of biological truths to be able to take a rational interest in the discussion of such problems" (pp. 280–281). Huxley also spoke about the usefulness of biology study to farmers, who could obtain the knowledge needed to improve crop yields and to avoid plant disease.

To Huxley, a person involved in virtually any trade or profession could make good use of science knowledge because of the way science was being implicated in virtually all of nineteenth-century society. Among the professions he felt would be aided by an early study of science were medicine, engineering, and the clergy. For the first two, science study was traditionally begun too late, requiring that the first year of professional study be spent studying basic science. An earlier study of science would alleviate this problem. For the clergy, he felt that a study of science would give them a greater sensitivity to the person who had studied science and thus may have a different view of the world.

The most important of Huxley's arguments concerning the value of science study had to do with the power of science to affect the direction of one's intellectual development. Science could develop the mind in ways that the classical studies could not. The uniqueness of science to Huxley lay in its direct contact with the natural world— direct observations of physical objects and conclusions based on these observations. No other studies in the school curriculum could claim to develop these observational and inductive abilities. Like Youmans, Huxley pointed out that mathematics was taught almost entirely as a deductive science, beginning as it did with simple, self-evident propositions and drawing inferences from them. Languages were studied in the same deductive way, starting from a set of authoritative linguistic rules and proceeding from that authority. Only science was an attempt to discover relationships based on direct observations of the natural world, and only the study of science would help one deal more intelligently with the everyday world of observable fact.

Huxley, like Youmans, recommended the teaching of science in the schools at as early an age as possible. The first course should provide children with a general, panoramic view of their natural world. It would answer the questions that curious children have about the weather, the sky, the sea, animals, and themselves. Huxley felt that such a course, "accompanied by a strong infusion of the scientific habit of mind" could be taught to every child of 9 or 10 (p. 123). As a child's ability to reason grew, the general course would be followed by science courses that dealt both with the knowledge of natural forms and the relations among those forms, as well as courses that dealt with causes and their effects. Huxley used systematic botany as an example of a study of form, and physics as a study of cause and effect.

These studies should not rely on the textbook as their source of information. According to Huxley: "If scientific education is to be dealt with as mere bookwork, it will be better not to attempt it, but to stick to the Latin Grammar which makes no pretence to be anything but bookwork" (p. 125). To Huxley, the source of knowledge was to be the physical objects themselves. Only through the direct observation and classification of natural objects and direct study of natural phenomena would science retain its uniqueness and its role in developing the kind of mental discipline that other school subjects could not provide. As Huxley put it:

> The great peculiarity of scientific training, that in virtue of which it cannot be replaced by any other discipline whatsoever, is this bringing of the mind directly into contact with fact, and practising the intellect in the completest form of induction; that is to say, in drawing conclusions from particular facts made known by immediate observation of Nature. (p. 126)

Mind was to be brought into direct contact with fact by placing before the child the objects that were being studied. If explanations were merely verbal abstractions, they would not be meaningful to the child and the point of the instruction would be lost. In addition, explanations had to be made real to the child and related to what the child had personally experienced. Huxley said:

> In teaching him botany, he must handle the plants and dissect the flowers for himself; in teaching him physics and chemistry, you must not be solicitous to fill him with information, but you must be careful that what he learns he knows of his own knowledge. Don't be satisfied with telling him that a magnet attracts iron. Let him see that it does; let him feel the pull of the one upon the other for himself. And, especially, tell him that it is his duty to doubt until he is compelled, by the absolute authority of Nature, to believe that which is written in books. (p. 127)

This view of the proper way to acquire meaningful understanding of the natural world provided the major justification for the emerging science laboratory. The laboratory would provide the opportunity for students to develop "a clear and definite conception" (p. 285) of natural phenomena. Laboratory study would allow the student to develop "a definite image in his mind" (p. 285) of the names encountered in books. Reading would then move beyond "mere repetition of words" (p. 285). Huxley said that book study without direct experience with the objects of science leads to knowing in a "dilettante paper-philosopher" way (p. 282). What is needed in order to read with understanding are "definite images which can only be acquired through the operation of [the] observing faculties on the phenomena of nature" (p. 283).

Such teaching, whether in the classroom or in the laboratory, also contained important implications for the preparation of the teacher. The teacher would be required to know the subject in the same practical way that the subject was to be taught. A teacher who understood the subject in that practical way would be able to talk about it comfortably. But if not, Huxley said, this teacher "will be afraid to wander beyond the limits of the technical phraseology which he has got up; and a dead dogmatism" would result (p. 129).

Herbert Spencer

Herbert Spencer, who also used a variety of utilitarian arguments to make his case, was another strong advocate for increasing the study of science in the educational program. His ideas were delineated in four essays that comprise his *Education: Intellectual, Moral, and Physical* (1864). The essays were originally published as four separate articles, and following some difficulty in publishing these as a single work in Britain, Spencer was able to have them published in the United States. The most well known of these essays is entitled "What Knowledge Is of Most Worth?" In this essay he pointed to the great variety of ways in which science study was superior to a study of the classics.

Besides his work of popularizing science education, Spencer was a prominent nineteenth-century evolutionist. Spencer was primarily interested in the notion of evolution as an explanation for the development of society and social phenomena. His ideas concerning education reflected his belief in the spontaneous development of human mind in relation to the external environment and the importance of individual human progress.

In "What Knowledge Is of Most Worth?" Spencer (1864) set out to determine the relative value of the various areas of education. The measure of value he used was the impact that knowledge had on human welfare, taken in its widest sense. Spencer classified human activity into several major categories. These included both direct and indirect attempts at self-preservation, the rearing and disciplining of offspring, the maintenance of social and political relations, and leisure activities "devoted to the gratification of the tastes and feelings" (p. 32). The knowledge that was considered most important for self-preservation was the knowledge of the functions of the human body—the principles of human physiology—so that we may put this knowledge to work to ensure our good health. Spencer believed that health and good spirits were "larger elements of happiness than any other things" and therefore teaching how to maintain one's health "yields in moment to no other whatever" (p. 43). Thus, the study of physiology and its relation to good health was an essential part of his plan for education.

Spencer described indirect self-preservation as that which came through the gaining of a livelihood. Reading, writing, and arithmetic were important skills for most employment, but beyond those subjects most of what was taught in schools had little relevance for one's life work according to Spencer. Since most people were involved in the production, preparation, and distribution of commodities, it was the properties of these commodities and their distribution that should be taught in schools. Modern manufacture was dependent on the use of machines that operated according to the laws of mechanics—the lever, the wheel, and the axle. Physics had given us the steam engine and ways of increasing the productivity of smelting furnaces. Chemistry was involved in the activities of gunpowder manufacture, sugar refining, bleaching, and dyeing. Biology was essential for an understanding of agricultural production, and sociology, the science of society, was essential for an understanding of supply and demand, the money market, and profit and loss.

But science was not what nineteenth-century youth were learning. Spencer said that this "vital knowledge" that had created the great industrialized nations was being ignored while the schools were "mumbling little else but dead formulas" (p. 54). Arguing against the supporters of a classical education, Spencer said: "While anxious that their sons should be well up in the superstitions of two thousand years ago, they care not that they should be taught anything about the structure and functions of their own bodies—nay, would even disapprove such instruction" (p. 43).

Another division of human activities that was benefited by the study of science was the rearing of children by their parents. Spencer was astonished that schools offered no instruction at all in the principles of childrearing. The very life and death as well as moral welfare of children depended on how they were cared for by their parents, yet future parents were given no help in that essential life work. Spencer discussed the physical, moral, and intellectual development of children and argued that, among other things, parents must have instruction in physiology and the laws of psychological development if they were to help their children to grow as they should.

The final division of human experience that Spencer addressed in the context of science was the pleasure that filled a person's leisure hours, especially the enjoyment of art, music, and poetry. According to Spencer, an appreciation of the arts depended on an understanding of science. Spencer argued that proportion, balance, and physical form were all physical concepts that were important in the arts and that both the construction of these works and the appreciation of them was enhanced by an understanding of science. Finally, he believed that science itself was an art form.

> Think you that what is carelessly looked upon by the uninitiated as a mere snow-flake, does not suggest higher associations to one who has seen through a microscope the wondrously varied and elegant forms of snow-crystals? Think you that the rounded rock marked with parallel scratches calls up as much poetry in an ignorant mind as in the mind of a geologist, who knows that over this rock a glacier slid a million years ago? The truth is, that those who have never entered upon scientific pursuits know not a tithe of the poetry by which they are surrounded. (p. 83)

Spencer, like Youmans and Huxley, also described the effects that science study had on mental development and the proper way to achieve that development through the teaching of science. We noted earlier in our discussion of Huxley that one of the important roles of the science laboratory was to move beyond book learning so that words would have meaning to the reader. Spencer pointed out that there is another important role of the laboratory besides giving precise mental images to go along with verbal abstractions—and that is the ability to draw conclusions from observations, what Spencer called "judgment."

> No extent of acquaintance with the meaning of words, can give the power of forming correct inferences respecting causes and effects. The constant habit of drawing conclusions from data, and then of verifying those conclusions by observation and experiment, can alone give the power of judgment correctly. And that it necessitates this habit is one of the immense advantages of science. (p. 88)

Science, Spencer argued, was also important for developing what was referred to as moral discipline. Moral discipline included the development of independence of thought, perseverence, sincerity, and a willingness to abandon any preconceived notion that proved to be incorrect. In contrast, the study of language increased one's dependence on authority, as Spencer explained:

> Such and such are the meanings of these words, says the teacher or the dictionary. So and so is the rule in this case, says the grammar. By the pupil these dicta are received as unquestionable. His constant attitude of mind is that of submission to dogmatic teaching. And a necessary result is a tendency to accept without inquiry whatever is established. Quite the

opposite is the attitude of mind generated by the cultivation of science. By science, constant appeal is made to individual reason. Its truths are not accepted upon authority alone; but all are at liberty to test them— nay, in many cases, the pupil is required to think out his own conclusions. Every step in a scientific investigation is submitted to his judgment. He is not asked to admit it without seeing it to be true. (p. 89)

To Spencer, the changes that were occurring in education, including the increased presence of science in the curriculum, were part of an evolutionary development of all social institutions. Spencer believed that systems of education and educational methods tended to match the other social systems that existed at the time. Since the Reformation, for example, the emphasis in Protestant churches had switched from a dependence on the strict, authoritarian commands of the clergy to a respect for personal judgment and responsibility in matters of faith. In politics, harsh and sometimes despotic rulers and authoritarian forms of government were replaced by democratic forms that gave broad rights and responsibilities to the individual. These changes in society were also beginning to be seen in less authoritarian forms of education. Schooling was starting to focus on the development of personal understanding instead of on rote memorization, often accompanied by harsh punishment for failure. The changes in education represented a natural movement away from authority, formality, and dogmatism and toward understanding, meaning, and freedom.

These new methods in education were in large part applications of the ideas of Johann Heinrich Pestalozzi and his followers. They focused on developing an understanding of generalizations or principles that were derived from an acquaintance with the facts on which those principles depended. Those facts would not be presented dogmatically, but in a spirit of discovery and inquiry. When explanations were made by the teacher and principles were developed, they would be taught inductively. As Spencer said: "The mind should be introduced to principles through the medium of examples, and so should be led from the particular to the general—from the concrete to the abstract" (pp. 121–122).

The advantages of such a system were very clear to Spencer. Not only would the generalizations that were discovered by the learner be remembered longer than would be the isolated facts or rules, but the process of inquiry used to discover these relationships would be useful because it would make that learner forever independent of the authority of the teacher. An inductive approach to teaching would give the child the power of inquiry, of discovery, and of independent thought.

The development of independent learners was essential to Spencer. He said that the process of self-development should be encouraged to the fullest extent possible. "Children should be led to make their own investigations, and to draw their own inferences. They should be *told* as little as possible, and induced to *discover* as much as possible" (pp. 124–125). He said that if we watch children we can see a constant process of observation, inquiry, and inference going on in their minds. We can very well expect that if these natural powers were brought to bear on studies within their range of comprehension, they would readily master them without help. He said our need for "perpetual telling is the result of our stupidity, not of the child's" (p. 126). He said we drag the child away from the facts that the child is interested in and capable of learning. Instead, the child is presented with material that is far too complex to understand, and therefore distasteful. When we find that the child resists, Spencer said, then we try to impose the material on the child "by force of threats and punishment" (p. 126).

Spencer supported the growing belief that the child's mind was spontaneously unfolding as it interacted with the surrounding environment. If the child showed pleasure in learning, it was because the child's mind had developed to the stage where it was able to comprehend what was being placed before it. If the child felt disgust toward learning, it was because the knowledge had been presented prematurely. The spontaneous development of the mind in its relation to the environment was consistent with Spencer's overall view of the progressive evolutionary development of the world, both in its physical forms and in its social institutions. Mental development was just another aspect of the natural development of the physical and social world. The key to education, then, was to present the child with materials that were at a level the child could understand.

The failure to fully utilize this method Spencer blamed on the limited understanding of the developing mind and on the inability of teachers to apply what little knowledge they had. By the mid-nineteenth century little was known in detail about the sequence of development of mental abilities outside of the widespread observation that young children did not comprehend abstract relationships as older children and adults did and therefore needed to operate on a more concrete level. For teachers to perceive the level of mental development of each child, given such limited knowledge, required a skill that most did not have.

Summary

By the second half of the nineteenth century, a number of prominent scientists had begun to wage a lively assault on the existing classical curriculum. In addition to Huxley, Spencer, and Youmans, others, such as Charles Lyell, Michael Faraday, and John Tyndall, argued that science should replace the study of the classical languages in the school curriculum. The particular kind of science teaching that the scientists supported focused on the meaningful learning of science concepts derived from direct contact with the natural world. The laboratory was to be a place where skills in observation and inductive reasoning powers would be developed. Proficiency in scientific reasoning would free individuals from the dominance of authoritarian teaching and empower them to derive truth independently. It was a spirited attack and one that successfully opened the way for the widespread inclusion of science in the school curriculum.

Chapter 2

Educational Thought and Practice in the Nineteenth Century

During the eighteenth and nineteenth centuries, opinion in America concerning education was affected largely by European ideas. Our colonial textbooks came from England, and our most important educational leaders went abroad to study European educational theory. As noted in Chapter 1, most colonial and early nineteenth-century practices were based on European traditions that emphasized the classical languages and ecclesiastical authority. But as we also saw there, another force that had its origins in European thought was especially well adapted to American thinking. The scientific discoveries, the technological apparatus, and the complexities of a new social order were emerging as the essential ingredients of an education for the practical man and woman in the nineteenth century. Education was to be a useful activity.

The Role of the Academy

The first American institution to provide this utilitarian education as a substitute for the established educational system was the American academy. A curriculum that included surveying, navigation, agriculture, and accounting provided an alternative form of education for the person with a practical interest. Academies began as early as 1750, with Benjamin Franklin's Philadelphia Academy, and grew steadily in number and importance until about 1850. By the

1880s the more recently formed and rapidly growing public high schools had surpassed the academies in number, but they retained much of the academy's pragmatic character (Cubberley, 1919).

Theodore Sizer, in *The Age of the Academies* (1964a), identified the role that the academies played in eighteenth- and nineteenth-century America in comparison to the classical curriculum of the Latin grammar school. Speaking first of the grammar schools, he said:

> The narrow classical curriculum was simply out of step with the ideas of the this-worldly, commercial, optimistic American, who often associated traditional learning with the social distinctions he wished America to avoid. . . . Americans were interested in supporting studies, if not wholly vocational in the modern sense, at least useful in Franklin's sense. The academies, which provided both the classics and the more modern subjects, met their desires. (p. 9)

As Sizer suggested, this practical aim was not a vocational aim but rather was meant to be preparation for life broadly conceived. In fact, any practical utility that was claimed for these courses could be seriously questioned, since most of them, including navigation, surveying, and all the sciences, did not provide practice in developing skill but rather were book-taught intellectual exercises. But, even so, the new curriculum was an important change from the classical curriculum because it represented a movement toward a study of the affairs and language of the present rather than of the ancient past.

As the new academies increased in number, so did the number of subjects that became available for study. According to Cubberley (1919), 149 new subjects appeared in the academies of New York between 1787 and 1870, with half of them appearing between 1825 and 1828. Most common among the new subjects were algebra, astronomy, botany, chemistry, general history, U.S. history, English literature, surveying, intellectual philosophy, declamation, and debating. Sizer (1964a) referred to such course lists as "pretentious curricula . . . taught by one or two teachers to a constantly changing group of students, most of whom lacked a sound grasp of the rudimentary studies" (p. 29). He called the curriculum of the academies "optimistic and laissez-faire in the extreme. . . . Anything and everything could be put into a course" (p. 28), and most were as short as six weeks in length. Of the programs in New York State, he said they ranged from "acoustics to Greek, Chaldee to needlework, English to phrenology, waxwork, conchology, and optics" (p. 28).

With such a large number of offerings, the academies appealed to a wide range of interests and increasingly large numbers of students. The academies acted as a continuation of the common schools and provided an extension of an elementary education to those students who did not wish to enter the grammar schools and the elitist colleges. The academies in fact competed with the colleges as a form of higher education in the early nineteenth century. Speaking of this competition, Sizer (1964a) said that many of the colleges "smacked of aristocracy" (p. 17) and had a difficult task justifying their curriculum to the public. "The academy offered a more flexible and useful course of study and became a strong competitor to the college, for most fledgling colleges were taking students as young and as untutored as were the academies" (pp. 17–18).

Thus the academy became the first important nineteenth-century institution to promote the study of science. It did so because of its mission of providing a practical education to American youth who had utilitarian interests. Science was one of the modern studies with obvious practical applications, and the academy was one place where it could be taught without having first to compete for a position in the curriculum with more traditional subjects. For the most part, however, science teaching in the academies was not of high quality. In addition to the short courses, often only six weeks in length, textbooks were inadequate, teachers were poorly prepared to teach the wide range of subjects, and demonstration materials were in short supply and in poor repair. Only occasionally were such things as rocks and animal specimens used to assist in that instruction. Consistent with early nineteenth-century educational practice, the courses were primarily book-taught, with the recitation of memorized texts the mode of instruction. In an address delivered at Williston Seminary in 1845, Edward Hitchcock, a scientist and president of Amherst College, spoke about the condition of science teaching in the academies and the need for improvements.

> With perhaps a few exceptions, our Academies do not possess the means of giving [an] elevated course of scientific instruction. The recitation of limited and imperfect text books, with now and then an experiment clumsily performed, and the exhibition of a battered, poorly characterised specimen, will by no means answer the purpose. And not much more than this can be done in most of our Academies for want of means. They do not possess, and cannot obtain, the requisite apparatus, nor afford to their instructors the time necessary to classify specimens and prepare experiments that shall be elegant, satisfactory, and full. (cited in Sizer, 1964a, pp. 117–118)

The Influence of European Educators

Pestalozzi

The academies reached the peak of their influence around 1850 and then began to decline as public secondary schools rose to take their place. As was the case with colonial and early nineteenth-century American schooling, the public schools that grew up during the mid and late nineteenth century were also influenced by European educational ideas. One of the most respected educational thinkers of the nineteenth century was the Swiss educator Johann Heinrich Pestalozzi. As noted earlier, Spencer, Huxley, and other scientists who wrote about education in the nineteenth century advocated a system of education that was derived in large part from the ideas of Pestalozzi. Pestalozzi, in turn, had received much of his inspiration from Jean-Jacques Rousseau. Rousseau's *Emile*, (1762/1979) called for a return to the "state of nature." The aim of education, according to Rousseau, was to prepare a child for life by developing the child's natural, inborn capacities. The natural state is good as it comes to us and degenerates because of what humans do to it. Rousseau's education of the boy, Emile, was intended to show how the study of nature within the limits of the naturally developing mind of the boy was superior to the formal, authoritarian, ecclesiastical methods in use at the time. It was in plans like this that we see the early stages of a changing belief in the importance of natural phenomena as objects of study in education.

Pestalozzi studied Rousseau's writings and applied them in the creation of a residential school for fifty abandoned children on his farm in Neuhoff in 1774. Here he taught reading, writing, and arithmetic and provided practical experience in farming, cheese-making, and gardening. In 1798, Pestalozzi was put in charge of an orphanage in the Swiss town of Stanz, and in 1800 he opened a school at Burgdorf that was later expanded by the government to include a teacher-training component. In 1805 he opened an institute at Yverdon, where he stayed for the next 20 years. It was at Yverdon that the great educators of Europe, such as Froebel and Herbart, came to study and where many of the ideas that influenced educational trends in the nineteenth century were developed. The work of Pestalozzi was first brought to the United States around 1820 through the writings of John Griscom, William Woodbridge, and other American educators who observed and wrote about European educational practices during the early nineteenth century (Cubberley, 1919).

Pestalozzi was interested in study that was based on sense impressions, experimentation, and reasoning. He was opposed to meaningless verbal learning and what he called the "empty chattering of mere words" (cited in Cubberley, 1919, p. 264). Education was to be based on the natural development of the child's mental faculties. The job of the educator was to determine the way in which the mental faculties developed and to teach the child in harmony with that natural development. To a large extent this included the study of natural objects themselves in place of the words that symbolized those objects. Investigation and experimentation were more important than memorization, and activity was more important than passive listening. The ultimate objective of education was the development of independent self-activity. Classroom instruction was to involve the discussion of ideas with a goal of personal understanding. It was not to be recitation of memorized lessons. The teacher's role was changed from one of listening to and evaluating the quality of the memorized recitations to one of presenting the child with materials and ideas that were important, meaningful, and in harmony with the natural mental growth of the child. Finally, Pestalozzi vigorously opposed the severe discipline that often characterized schools, preferring instead a strict but loving guidance of the child. (For a discussion of Pestalozzi's life and work, see Pinloche, 1901).

One way that Pestalozzian ideas spread to England and the United States was through the writings of people who had visited the Pestalozzian institute at Yverdon or who had visited Pestalozzian-based schools in Europe. These articles, which appeared in the American educational literature beginning in the early 1820s, however, had only a minor impact in a few isolated locations. A more powerful influence was a book of object lessons written by Elizabeth Mayo after her brother, the Reverend Charles Mayo, an early visitor to the institute, returned home to England and with her began a Pestalozzian school. The book was widely used in England as educators attempted to implement the ideas of Pestalozzi. According to Cubberley (1919), however, the Mayos seemed to have missed the Pestalozzian spirit, for the lessons and the manual for teachers "were formal, scientific, far too detailed and analytical, and much beyond the comprehension of children" (p. 270).

Cubberley provided an example of how common table salt would be used as the object for a lesson under this formal approach. He said:

The children would be expected to learn its chemical composition, its uses, how and where found in nature, how mined and refined, that its crystalline form is cubical, that it varies in color from white to bluish and reddish, that it is transparent to translucent, that it is soluble in water and saline in taste, that it imparts a yellow color to a flame, etc. without more contact with a piece of real salt than seeing the "specimen" passed around by the teacher. (p. 270)

According to Cubberley, this kind of object teaching soon became an educational fad in England and later in the United States, but because of its formality, it was not consistent with the Pestalozzian spirit. In Cubberley's words: "The effect of this instruction was to 'formalize' the Pestalozzian movement in England, and in consequence much of the finer spirit and significance of Pestalozzi's work was lost" (p. 270).

It was about 1860 when Edward A. Sheldon, Superintendent of Schools in the city of Oswego, New York, came across a display of Pestalozzian instructional materials in a museum in Toronto, Canada. The materials, which had been designed in the formal style popularized by the Mayos in England, had been adopted by the English Home and Colonial Infant Society. Sheldon acquired a set of these materials from England for use in the training of teachers in the Oswego school system. The next year the board of education in Oswego created a city normal school for the training of their teachers, and it was from that vantage point that Sheldon spread the doctrine of Pestalozzian object lessons. During the 1860s and most of the 1870s, object lessons and the Oswego Movement received national recognition in the educational journals and at educational conferences.

Although many of the object lessons that were developed were too technical to be appreciated by children, they did place an emphasis on the study of natural objects of all types. Thus object lessons became an early form of science education in the elementary schools. Also, many of the ideas that had been developed by Pestalozzi and associated with the Oswego Movement were in such contrast to the prevailing methods of instruction that, even in their distorted form, they represented a substantial change in direction for American education.

Through the influence of Pestalozzi and his followers, teaching became an active process that required teachers to interact with the subject matter and with the children in a way they had not been accustomed to doing. It was no longer a matter of telling the children to read and memorize pages from a textbook; the teacher had to be an active participant in the process. The old practice of "keeping school" involved listening to memorized recitations of individual children who had prepared their work at home, or listening to the singsong chorus of responses that children had learned through repeated drill. As teaching became a more personally engaging activity, the teacher had to have considerably greater knowledge of his or her subject, greater skill in selecting materials of interest to the child, and greater skill in managing the variety of interactions that developed in the classroom. Thus, for science teaching, not only were concepts introduced through the study of natural objects, but the approach was one that focused on the active, thinking child.

Herbart and the Herbartians

If Pestalozzian theory and Sheldon's object lessons were popular in the 1860s, it was Herbartian pedagogy that captured the attention of American educators in the 1890s and gave added support to the teaching of science and other practical studies. Johann Friedrich Herbart had died 50 years earlier in 1841, and his *General Pedagogy* (1806/1893) had been published 35 years earlier, but it was not until late in the century that his work became known and valued in the United States. Delays like this of several decades were common in the nineteenth century, and it was not at all unusual for theories to arrive as much as 50 years after they had been introduced in Europe.

Herbart's ideas were brought to the United States from Germany by a number of American educators who had studied at the University of Jena, where Herbartian ideas were being taught. One of the most important disciples of Herbart in the United States was Charles DeGarmo. DeGarmo translated several of Herbart's works, published articles on Herbartian pedagogy in educational journals, and wrote a number of books on Herbartian pedagogy. The pedagogy of Herbart and the Herbartians became so popular in the United States in the 1890s that William T. Harris, U.S. Commissioner of Education, said: "There are more adherents of Herbartian pedagogy to-day in America than in Germany itself" (U.S. Bureau of Education, 1896, p. 322).

Herbart taught philosophy at the universities of Göttingen and Königsberg, and from 1810 to 1832 he held the chair of philosophy previously occupied by Immanual Kant at Königsberg. Herbart's intellectual interest throughout his career was in developing a science of education. He had visited Pestalozzi at Burgdorf and like Pestalozzi he took direct sense perception as the beginning of education. From this starting point he developed a theory of instruction whose purpose was the creation of mind—mind composed of ideas that could guide a person in all phases of life.

To Herbart, mind was a set of ideas or concepts that were built upon each other and richly interconnected. The purpose of instruction, and therefore education, was to construct for each person this arrangement of ideas. Since Herbart began with sense perception, rather than an inherited biological capacity, as the starting point for the development of mind, he believed that all knowledge must be *acquired* by the individual. Thus each person developed his or her mind according to the efforts extended throughout that person's entire life. The process was continuous and theoretically without bounds.

In his discussion of Herbart, Gabriel Compayre (1907) claimed that this conception of mind put Herbart in direct conflict with the traditional notion that education could be used to discipline mental faculties such as memory or rational thought. When mind is viewed as a set of functional capacities or faculties that can be strengthened through exercise, the nature of the content loses much of its significance. The most important consideration under the "development of the faculties" view was that a particular mental ability could be exercised regardless of the content that was used. Under Herbart's conception of mind, the concept was most important. Ideas were considered to be the fundamental building blocks of mind, and the utility of the idea or concept to a broadly functioning person was the justification for its inclusion in the curriculum. The purpose of education was not to exercise the mind but to create conceptual structures that would enable a person to live a well-rounded, moral life.

Herbart made several contributions to educational thought that were significant in the development of a systematic approach to teaching, but perhaps the most important were to show how instruction could be used to build *conceptual understanding* and how *interest* operates in relation to the development of new ideas. Both of these were aimed by Herbart at instruction in general, but they were particularly important for the way science teaching came to be viewed. Each of these is discussed here in the context of Herbart's four-step model of teaching.

THEORY OF INTEREST.   According to Herbart, the first condition of successful instruction was that it stimulate the pupil's interest—the pleasure derived from or positive feelings toward something. There were two main types of interest according to Herbart. The first came from direct experience with the natural world, and the second, from our social interactions. He viewed observations of natural phenomena, attempts to understand what we observe, and the contemplation of natural beauty as spontaneous processes; thus, during the early phases of instruction, the teacher should merely add to the experiences the child already had by placing before the child additional objects to be examined. Because the mind was curious and felt pleasure when understanding was achieved, experience with these objects led to a desire on the part of the child to understand what was being observed. Social interests came from interacting with other human beings. A well-rounded education gave ample attention to all of these interests, whether related to the social world or the world of nature.

Interest in the natural world led to the accumulation of sense impressions, which was the first step in Herbart's instructional process. According to Herbart, the teacher's job was to build an understanding of concepts from the starting point of these experiences with the world of nature. Children should be provided with opportunities to observe living animals and to make collections of plants and animals. They should observe the workings of machines and tools. In mathematics, they should measure distances and count actual objects. As the children matured and the availability of natural objects within the immediate environment became exhausted, the teacher should extend the range of a child's experiences by describing to the child what the teacher knew and had seen. But even these descriptions by the teacher needed to take into account the previous experiences of the children. In Herbart's (1901) words:

> The effect of the teacher's narrative and description should be to make the pupil realize events and objects as vividly as if they were actually present to his eye and ear. The pupil must, therefore, have actually heard and seen much previously. This recalls to our minds the necessity . . . of first enlarging the young pupil's range of experience, when found too limited, through excursions and the exhibition of objects. (p. 108)

THEORY OF CONCEPT FORMATION.   All of these direct and indirect perceptions were of no use, however, unless they could be associated into organized generalizations or principles. This process of concept formation comprised the second part of Herbart's educational method. Perceptions of sense objects were essential, but they were not sufficient for the development of mind. Herbart's view reminds us of Kant's aphorism: "Concepts without percepts are empty, but percepts without concepts are blind." According to Herbart's theory of mind, mental development came not from disorganized and haphazard bits of knowledge but from the coherence of ideas. Each new idea found a place in relation to the already existing ideas. The previously acquired ideas formed the starting point for new conceptions, and the existing knowledge of the pupil formed the starting point for instruction.

The role of the teacher in this process of concept formation was to begin with the existing experiences and knowledge of the child. Compayre (1907) in his discussion of Herbart, said that the teacher, at the beginning of each lesson, "must prepare the ground; . . . must summon up a mental escort into the presence of the newcomer to welcome and introduce him" (p. 36). The teacher was to place before the child ideas that could easily be combined with those the child already had, thereby forming "groups of ideas associated logically and united strongly" (p. 36). It was essential that the teacher not present the child with something new that could not be linked to something already known. As Compayre said: "There is no true instruction except when a new notion is introduced exactly in its right place in the series of notions already fixed, when it forms one of the loops in the tissue, one of the rings in the chain" (pp. 59–60). Thus instruction had to be in harmony with the existing conceptual development of the child's mind.

According to Herbart (1835/1901), the best way to develop the new conceptions was inductively. It was better if the child could *discover* the relations between natural phenomena because that would produce a fuller and more meaningful understanding of the concept. The teacher's role was to provide guidance through skillful questioning, not simply to state the principles or rules as an abstract verbalization. Herbart felt that informal conversation was the best way to accomplish this inductive learning. Conversation would give the pupil an opportunity "to test and to change the accidental union of his thoughts, to multiply the links of connection, and to assimilate, after his own fashion, what he has learned" (p. 56). In addition, informal conversation would allow the student to develop this understanding in the way that was most easy and convenient to the student. "He will thus escape the inflexibility of thought that results from a purely systematic learning" (p. 56).

The third and fourth steps in Herbart's instructional method were also related to formation and strengthening of conceptual understanding. The third step involved direct instruction on the part of the teacher, whereby the teacher systematically explained to the pupil something that the teacher understood but the pupil could not discover alone. In this as well as in all other phases of instruction, Herbart expected the teacher to teach skillfully and attractively, showing enthusiasm and personal interest in the subject. The fourth step was that of application. In this phase, the teacher would ask the pupil to do something to demonstrate that the acquired knowledge was understood well enough to be applied in other contexts. The student would be asked to solve problems, to write compositions, or to perform other tasks that depended on the acquired knowledge.

These four steps of instructional method that were developed by Herbart represented one of the first attempts to systematize teaching, and they were used many times by educators in their own instructional schemes over the years. Lange and DeGarmo identified several of these adaptations in their annotated translation of Herbart's *Outlines of Educational Doctrine* (1835/1901). Most of these schemes followed a three-step classification to match the processes that the mind was thought to go through as it assimilated new knowledge. These included perception of new facts, thought, and application. According to Lange and DeGarmo: "Perception gives the *percept*, thought gives the *conception* (or rule, principle, generalization), and application gives *power*" (Herbart, 1835/1901, p. 58). In this general model, Herbart's second and third steps in instruction, namely independent discovery and direct teacher instruction, which together describe his process of concept formation, were collapsed into a single category called "thought."

ORGANIZATION OF THE CURRICULUM.   Besides laying out a theory of mind and a compatible instructional sequence, Herbart also contributed to our thinking about the organization of the curriculum. His notion that an education should be well rounded and focused on the single aim of character development led to a number of attempts to create unifying themes to relate two or more areas of the curriculum. Although associated with Herbartianism generally, the idea of unifying school subjects on the basis of some general overarching principle was not so much Herbart's idea as that of several of his followers. DeGarmo (1895) discussed a number of these schemes for the correlation of studies and weighed their relative merits. He concluded that the *coordination* of individual courses in the curriculum was a better idea than the attempt to *correlate* all knowledge with respect to some overarching principle. He said:

> Coordination allows each important subject, or group of subjects, to have its own principle of development, contenting itself with natural and easy associations in the lower grades, and not attempting to give a philosophic grasp of the highest unity of knowledge until the pupil is sufficiently mature to comprehend this phase of thought. Furthermore, coordination permits us to present one subject at a time, thus relieving us

from the need of abandoning important studies to the hazard of incidental treatment. (p. 240)

In general, it was this idea that would prevail in American education
and allow for the development of individual academic disciplines as
opposed to broadly unified areas of interdisciplinary study.

PRACTICAL AIMS FOR EDUCATION.   Another idea that has been associated with the Herbartians is that instruction should be practical
rather than overly abstract and for the masses rather than for the elite
alone. Thus the function of education was to "fit the pupil for life."
DeGarmo said:

Too many of our educational ideals are mediaeval in their origin; they
take as their model some worn-out conception of culture, or they fix
their gaze upon some special calling, forgetting that education is no
longer the prerogative of the few professional classes, but has become
the just privilege of all classes. If, then, we are in earnest about universal
education, we must abandon these one-sided ideals, and, once for all,
recognize that our education succeeds just to the extent that we make it
focus upon the real activities of life. (p. 241)

DeGarmo's defense of practical subjects included the study of science and the economic value of such study, even though defenders of
the classical curriculum found the intrusion of economic concerns
into school subjects to be abhorrent.

Is botany less noble when discovering the laws of plant organization and
investigating the conditions of healthy growth, than it is when it leads
the youth of our land into field and forest in order to gather and name
the flowers? Are not chemistry and physics quite as interesting, instructive, and educative when developed to the point of their economic application, as they are when arrested at their abstract stages out of all felt
relations to ultimate ends? (pp. 235–236)

To DeGarmo and many other educators at the end of the nineteenth
century, solving economic and other social problems was the most
important thing that education could accomplish, and it was this aim
that became the predominant focus of educational efforts from that
point onward. It is tempting to associate these aims with crass economic materialism, but that was not the intention of either Herbart
or his followers. Herbart (1901) said of technology, for example:
"Technology ought not to be considered merely from the side of the

so-called material interests. It furnishes very important connecting links between the apprehension of the facts of nature and human purposes" (p. 260).

The notion of education as a practical activity whose purpose was the preparation of a person fit for life was one that continued to gain support as universal schooling developed and as secondary education began to separate itself from the aims of higher education. Higher education, at least that which called itself "liberal," still shunned the practical aims, especially when the practical aims were associated with economic concerns. Elementary and secondary education, however, would increasingly become the place for both practical courses and utilitarian aims.

American Influences

Charles W. Eliot

A major contributor to the development of science teaching in American schools during the late nineteenth century was Charles W. Eliot, president of Harvard University from 1869 to 1895. Eliot did much to advance the teaching of science not only in American colleges but in the secondary and elementary schools as well. He was a frequent speaker at national as well as local meetings of teachers' groups and, in 1893, chaired and wrote the final report for one of the most prestigious commissions on educational reform in American educational history, the National Education Association's (NEA) Committee of Ten. He was a vigorous advocate of the laboratory method in science teaching at all levels and a champion of science teaching as a way to develop mental abilities and to empower persons for useful action in their lives.

THE NEED FOR SCIENCE IN THE CURRICULUM. In his 1869 presidential inaugural address, Eliot (1898) gave notice that what he called "the endless controversies whether language, philosophy, mathematics, or science supplies the best mental training, whether general education should be chiefly literary or chiefly scientific" (p. 1) were over at Harvard. Science teaching was there to stay, and there should be no antagonism between it and the other studies. He was deeply concerned, however, about the way that science was taught and the little time devoted to it in the curriculum. Eliot believed that science should be taught with "objects and instruments in hand—not from books merely, not through the memory chiefly, but by the seeing eye and the informing fingers" (p. 6). Science teaching in both the schools and colleges should "develop and discipline those powers of the mind by which science has been created and is daily nourished—the powers of observation, the inductive faculty, the sober imagination, the sincere and proportionate judgment" (p. 6). According to Eliot, this could not be accomplished by studying textbooks or even by attending well-delivered lectures by eminent scientists, but only through direct study of the physical world.

By 1884, however, Eliot's optimism about science teaching had faded, and he found himself lamenting the fact that the educational system as a whole was not giving adequate attention to the teaching of science. In an article he prepared for *The Century* entitled "What is a Liberal Education?" Eliot (1898) complained that we had failed to recognize the study of science as an important part of the liberal arts curriculum. Fifteenth-century educators had taken the best intellectual and moral materials of their day and made them the substance of their liberal education. When nineteenth-century educators do the same, should science be omitted—"that natural science which in its outcome supplies some of the most important forces of modern civilization?" (p. 111). Eliot's answer was that schools of his day did omit it. He said he did not know of a single preparatory school in the country that gave enough attention to the teaching of natural science. Most science in those schools was taught from a book "as if it were grammar or history" (p. 112). Eliot said that although book study may provide some information on scientific subjects, none of the mental discipline that scientific thinking offers is provided by book study.

Concerning science teaching in colleges, Eliot said that students were still getting little more than some information taught from lectures and books; they were receiving very limited training in scientific thinking. Part of the problem was that science study was begun too late in the student's college career, often not until the junior year, and by that time the student found the application of the scientific method to be too burdensome. Students had been trained in the authoritarian methods of the languages and mathematics, making the investigative approach of the sciences seem unnecessary and as so much wasted time.

QUALITY OF SCIENCE EDUCATION.   Besides the little attention that was paid to science in schools and colleges, the quality of instruction was also generally poor. As influential as Eliot was and as popular as Pestalozzian and Herbartian pedagogy had become in the educational literature and at educational conferences by the last decade of the nineteenth century, the teaching in many schools still resembled more the "school keeping" of an earlier age than the more modern child-centered approaches. In 1890 Eliot (1898) addressed the Massachusetts Teachers' Association and reported to them on observations that he had made of "an average Massachusetts grammar school" (p. 179). He had two major criticisms of the school. First was the excessive emphasis on memory studies at the expense of the development of observational skills. Eliot mentioned geography as one subject that was "admirably adapted for the training of the observational faculties," but it, too, was taught as a memory subject. "There is not a photograph or a raised map in the school. There is nothing whatever with which to teach geography as a science of observation" (p. 188). Other courses that were taught as memory subjects included history, physiology and hygiene, patriotism, morals, and manners.

He was particularly concerned about the way that science studies were treated. He recounted his observations of a class in physiology, anatomy, and hygiene.

> I imagined that there might be a skeleton in that school, or a manikin, or a model of the brain, stomach, lungs, eye, ear, head, or arm, and that the children might be shown some of these beautiful organs. But no; there was nothing of the sort in the school-house, and there never had been. Everything concerning that natural-history subject was taught out of a little book; the children had nothing but flat figures of the things described, and were required to make them stand for the various members of the human body. . . . Observational teaching of the human body is, of course, a fascinating and profitable study for children, just as observational teaching in geography makes that subject one of the most charming in the world whether for children or adults. Until we can get the means of teaching scientific subjects properly, let us not teach them at all. (p. 190)

Eliot's second concern was with the artificial difficulty of the curriculum and its oppressive drudgery. There was an excessive focus on accuracy in the children's work to the point that success became virtually impossible. Part of the argument of mental disciplinarians was that the will could be strengthened through hard work. Education that was difficult would help develop the habits of persistence and effort. Since children would not choose to work hard on their own, they had to be forced to do so by their teachers. Michael Faraday's (1867) comments on the importance of effort to strengthen the mind exemplified this idea. Faraday said: "It matters not on what subject a person's mind is occupied, he should engage in it with the conviction that it will require mental labour" (p. 214).

Influenced by the child-centered approaches that were becoming so popular by the late nineteenth century, Eliot favored a more humane approach in which the interest of the child was taken into account. After examining the textbooks that were used in the school, Eliot (1898) said:

> The main characteristic of the instruction, as developed through those books,—unless lightened by the personality of the teacher,—is dullness, a complete lack of human interest, and a consequent lack in the child of the sense of increasing power. Nothing is so fatiguing as dull, hopeless effort, with the feeling that, do one's best, one cannot succeed. That is the condition of too many children in American schools—not the condition for half an hour, but the chronic condition day after day and month after month. Make the work interesting, and give the children the sense of success, and the stress which is now felt by them will be greatly diminished. (pp. 184–185)

CONTRIBUTIONS OF SCIENCE STUDY TO MEETING THE GOALS OF EDUCATION. Although the pace of change was slow when measured against the standards set by Eliot and other advocates of science teaching, by the end of the century science was being taught, and increasingly the laboratory method was being used. In 1892, Eliot (1898) admitted that the substitution of the laboratory method for the book method in teaching natural science was "the most important improvement in educational methodology during the past twenty years; for it gives science, for the first time, a fair chance in the competition among subjects as discipline" (p. 299).

Given the power of science study to strengthen the mind in a variety of ways, it contributed nicely to what he considered to be the major goals of education. In "The Unity of Educational Reform," written in 1894, Eliot (1898) enumerated "six essential constituents of all worthy education" (p. 320):

1. Training of the sense organs, since communication with the external world is through the senses
2. Practice in grouping and comparing sense impressions and drawing inferences from those organized data
3. Training in making accurate records of these impressions, comparisons, or groupings of data either in written form or in the memory

4. Training of the memory so that the organized sense impressions could be held in the mind
5. Training in the power of expression, that is, the ability to formulate well-reasoned, clear, logical statements about the nature of things
6. Inculcation of what Eliot called the "supreme ideals through which the human race is uplifted and ennobled—the ideals of beauty, honor, duty, and love" (p. 322).

Besides presenting these six components of quality education, Eliot (1898) also suggested that they should be oriented toward what he referred to as a new development in education, the idea that education was a source of personal empowerment:

> Effective power in action is the true end of education, rather than the storing up of information, or the cultivation of faculties which are mainly receptive, discriminating, or critical. We are no longer content, in either school or college, with imparting a variety of useful and ornamental information, or with cultivating esthetic taste or critical faculty in literature or art. We are not content with simply increasing our pupils' capacity for intellectual or sentimental enjoyment. All these good things we seek, to be sure; but they are no longer our main ends. The main object of education, nowadays, is to give the pupil the power of doing himself an endless variety of things which, uneducated, he could not do. An education which does not produce in the pupil the power of applying theory, or putting acquisitions into practice, and of personally using for productive ends his disciplined faculties, is an education which has missed its main end. (pp. 323–324)

As an illustration of this emphasis on empowerment, Eliot provided the example of a student analyzing an unknown substance in chemistry. The student should be able to apply information and methods to identify the substance and prove that the identification is correct. The solution of a problem of this sort, where the answer cannot be known in advance, would demonstrate that the student had acquired more than information, that the student had acquired the power of thought.

J. M. Rice

Eliot was not alone in criticizing the American educational system, nor in recognizing what changes were needed to bring about reform. One of the most revealing accounts of educational practices in the early 1890s was provided by J. M. Rice in a series of articles that he wrote for *The Forum.* These were published as *The Public-School System of the United States* in 1893. In this set of accounts, Rice described how some schools had begun to use scientific principles in their teaching, but how many still followed the mechanical practices of the past. Rice described the mechanical school as one whose function was the "crowding into the memory of the child a certain number of cut-and-dried facts—that is, giving the child a certain amount of information" (p. 20). In contrast, the aim of the new, more modern approach "is to lead the child to observe, to reason, and to acquire manual dexterity as well as to memorize facts—in a word, to develop the child naturally in all his faculties, intellectual, moral, and physical" (p. 21).

One of the schools that Rice visited offered sense training as a significant feature of the curriculum. Practice in the use of the senses to strengthen the powers of observation was part of the new education that was developing, but somehow the teacher in this school had missed the spirit of the innovation. Rice (1893) described a lesson that taught shapes and colors at the primary level:

> Before the lesson began there was passed to each child a little flag, on which had been pasted various forms and colors, such as a square piece of green paper, a triangular piece of red paper, etc. When each child had been supplied, a signal was given by the teacher. Upon receiving the signal, the first child sprang up, gave the name of the geometrical form upon his flag, loudly and rapidly defined the form, mentioned the name of the color, and fell back into his seat to make way for the second child, thus: "A square; a square has four equal sides and four corners; green" (down). Second child (up): "A triangle; a triangle has three sides and three corners; red" (down). Third child (up): "A trapezium; a trapezium has four sides none of which are parallel, and four corners; yellow" (down). Fourth child (up): "A rhomb; a rhomb has four sides, two sharp corners and two blunt corners; blue." This process was continued until each child in the class had recited. The rate of speed maintained during the recitation was so great that seventy children passed through the process of defining in a very few minutes. The children are drilled in these definitions as soon as they enter the school, and the definitions are repeated from week to week and from year to year, until the child has finished his primary-school education. (p. 35)

Rice concluded: "In no single exercise is a child permitted to think. He is told just what to say, and he is drilled not only in what to say, but also in the manner in which he must say it" (p. 38). But some of the activities in that school at least utilized concrete physical objects in the instruction. In so much of what Rice saw, the memorization took place from books. He described two separate observations that he made of physiology lessons.

> In one class where they were having physiology, in answer to the question, "What is the effect of alcohol on the system?" I heard a ten-year-old cry out at the top of his voice, and at the rate of a hundred miles an hour, "It—dwarfs—the—body,—mind,—and—soul,—weakens—the—heart,—and—enfeebles—the—memory." "And what are the effects of tobacco?" asked the teacher. In answer to this, one boy called off, in rapid succession, more diseases than are known to most physicians. (p. 60)

In the second example, he described a performance that the teacher and children had worked up to demonstrate their knowledge of human anatomy and physiology. He observed these children recite continuously in chorus for ten minutes a performance that described the parts of the body and their functions. The performance came complete with dramatic hand demonstrations and alternate standing and sitting throughout.

Rice was appalled by the mindless, meaningless recitations, the harsh discipline, the absence of active thought on the part of the children, and the excessive use of textbooks in place of real-world experiences. These practices were common in all of the major cities of the country and only occasionally did he find pockets of an enlightened modernized approach to education. In those few places he found the schools to be warm, happy, and beautiful. He described one such primary science class in a school in Indianapolis.

> I entered one of the rooms containing the youngest children at the time of the opening exercises. The scene I encountered was a glimpse of fairyland. I was in a room full of bright and happy children, whose eyes were directed toward the teacher.... She understood them, sympathized with and loved them, and did all in her power to make them happy. The window-sills were filled with plants, and plants were scattered here and there throughout the room....
>
> After the children had sung a few little songs the first lesson of the day was in order. This was a lesson in science; its subject was a flower. It began with the recitation of a poem. The object of introducing these poems into the plant and animal lessons is to inspire the child with love for the beautiful, with love for nature, and with sympathy for all living things....
>
> Before the teacher endeavored to bring out the points to which she desired to direct the special attention of the class, the children were

urged to make their own unaided observations and to express them. As each child was anxious to tell what he had observed in relation to the plant itself, what he otherwise knew of it, how it grew, where it grew, and perhaps some little incident that the flower recalled to him, the class was full of life and enthusiasm. . . .

The teacher . . . by her careful questioning led the children to observe the particular things to which she had decided to call their attention that morning. Her questions were not put to individual children, but to the whole class, so that every question might serve to set every pupil observing and thinking. (pp. 101–104)

Summary

Rice's description of this modern school captured much of what late nineteenth-century educators such as DeGarmo and Eliot believed was good education—teaching as a process of bringing meaning to children through objects and words in a way that was pleasurable for the child. By the 1890s this had been accomplished in a number of places, and the momentum for change was increasing rapidly. Throughout the educational system, there was widespread condemnation of the formality, harshness, and mindlessness of the old traditional ways of education. The ideas that had been developed by Rousseau, Pestalozzi, and Herbart began to exert pressures that were felt throughout the educational world. When William James (1899) offered his *Talks to Teachers* in the 1890s, soon to be followed by John Dewey's exhortations, the new modern ideas became popularized to the point that they became the new educational orthodoxy. Child-centered education would dominate educational thinking without serious challenge for the next half-century.

But before that would happen, a group of progressive reformers whom we now associate with the earlier traditionalists would have one last moment of glory. Charles Eliot, influential as he was and concerned as he was with the developing secondary school curriculum and its relation to the collegiate program, became chairman of the prestigious Committee of Ten of the National Education Association. As chairman of the group he reported to the educational community a set of reforms that would bring a sense of unified organization to the entire educational enterprise. Eliot's motives were noble and his support was widespread, but he had the misfortune of making his case at the wrong time. Even as he spoke, more powerful movements were at work that would overwhelm his own, and just 20 years after his vision of educational reform was proposed it would seem that it had been written a hundred years earlier. Eliot the reformer, the champion of laboratory-based science teaching, the advocate of education for personal empowerment became the elitist representative of the collegiate establishment, the disciple of faculty psychology, the traditionalist.

Chapter 3

The Turn of the Century and the Committee of Ten

The inclusion of the sciences and other modern studies alongside the classical studies produced a curriculum so congested with offerings that a need for some kind of organization became evident by the end of the century. As colleges expanded their curriculum, admission was based not just on a knowledge of Latin, Greek, and mathematics, but on an increasingly long list of new subjects, including English literature, U.S. history, modern languages, and the physical sciences. Since different colleges required different sets of courses for admission, the high schools were forced to offer a greater variety of courses to accommodate their college-bound students. Because the number of college-bound students was small, the effect of college admission requirements on the high school curriculum was greatly out of proportion to the number of students affected. This often led to resentment on the part of school people who objected to what they called college domination of the high school curriculum.

The high school was also beginning to feel pressure from a growing non-college-bound student population that was interested in applied and practical studies as well as the traditional classical studies. Even though the number of students attending high school was small in 1892 and few of those who attended high school went on to college, the secondary school population was beginning to enter a period of explosive growth, and the system would soon be forced to accommodate a considerably wider range of student interests. In 1890, for example, only 360,000 14- to 17-year-olds attended high school, making up 6.7% of the age group. By 1920, the numbers had swelled to 2.5 million students and 32.3% of the age group (National Center for Education Statistics, 1981, p. 49). In many urban areas there were demands for commercial courses, manual-training courses, and other more applied and vocational courses in addition to the traditional academic subjects more likely to be used for college admission. The school responded to these pressures by offering long lists of subjects on an elective basis and by creating groupings of those subjects into "courses" that could be chosen by the students on the basis of their future plans. Thus in many school systems students could choose a classical course, a Latin-scientific course, or an English course, with the classical course being the most likely course of study for the college-bound student.

The Committee of Ten

In July of 1892, in response to the need to make college entrance requirements more uniform, a committee of ten college and school leaders was appointed at the annual meeting of the National Education Association in Saratoga Springs, New York. The purpose of the committee was stated in its recommendation to the approving body:

> That it is expedient to hold a conference of school and college teachers of each principal subject which enters into the programmes of secondary schools in the United States and into the requirements for admission to college—as, for example, of Latin, of geometry, or of American history—each conference to consider the proper limits of its subject, the best methods of instruction, the most desirable allotment of time for the subject, and the best methods of testing the pupils' attainments therein, and each conference to represent fairly the different parts of the country. (National Education Association, 1893, p. 3)

The motivation for establishing the committee was to create a smoother transition from high school to college that would be in the best interests of both the colleges and the secondary schools. It would especially ease the burden on secondary schools that were trying to provide adequate preparation for their college-bound students. With uniform entrance requirements, the secondary schools could offer fewer subjects. Deciding what those subjects would be, how they should be taught, and how much time should be allotted to them became the work of the Committee of Ten. It was an important task, and one that would place in the hands of the colleges an enormous amount of control over the programs of the secondary schools.

The Committee of Ten was headed by Charles Eliot, the president of Harvard University. He was joined by William T. Harris, the U.S. Commissioner of Education, the presidents of the University of

Michigan, the University of Missouri, the University of Colorado, Vassar College, a seventh member who was soon to become the president of Oberlin College, and three principals of secondary schools. The committee organized nine conferences on what they felt to be the major areas of the curriculum, including three separate conferences in science. Ten members were selected for each conference. The subject areas chosen included both the old and the new—Latin, Greek, and mathematics on the one hand, and English literature, other modern languages, history, and the sciences on the other hand. Not included were applied subjects such as stenography, mechanical drawing, or other manual arts. The subjects were selected because of their disciplinary value and for their ability to develop the intellect, not their informational value or commercial utility. The task for the representatives of the new subjects, such as the natural sciences, was to demonstrate that they were indeed worthy of their recent inclusion in the school curriculum.

The individual conferences met in December of 1892 and submitted their reports to Eliot the following spring. The Committee of Ten met again in November of 1893, and its final report was issued the following month. Eliot, as a scientist himself, had arranged for the three separate conferences on science: one on natural history, encompassing physiology, zoology, and botany; one on physics, chemistry, and astronomy; and a third on geography, including physical geography, geology, and meteorology. In addition to the separate meetings that the science groups held, they also held a joint meeting at which they discussed the amount of time that should be allotted to the total science program. At that meeting they passed a resolution that science should make up 25% of the high school curriculum.

The recommendation to devote 25% of the total program to science reflected a substantial increase over the current practice. The sciences were relative newcomers to the curriculum, and their value as disciplinary studies was still very much in doubt among many educators. Eliot, in fact, noted the greater length of the reports in the science areas and attributed it to the fact that these subjects were "more imperfectly dealt with in primary and secondary schools" than were the other subjects, so that the conferees "felt the need of setting forth in an ample way what ought to be taught, in what order, and by what method" (National Education Association, 1893, p. 13). Continuing to speak of the representatives of these groups, he said:

> They ardently desired to have their respective subjects made equal to
> Latin, Greek, and Mathematics in weight and influence in the schools;
> but they knew that educational tradition was adverse to this desire, and

that many teachers and directors of education felt no confidence in these subjects as disciplinary material. Hence the length of these reports. (National Education Association, 1893, p. 13)

Since the purpose of the committee was to make recommendations concerning college admission requirements, it was not surprising that membership on the committee, as well as on the individual subject-matter conferences, was heavily represented by the college professorate. At least half of the science conference members were professors of science, and these conference members were highly respected and influential people. Whether he was choosing people from college or school ranks, Eliot's standing in the educational community enabled him to attract persons of considerable prestige to all the conferences. Key figures in science included John Coulter, the president of Indiana University, for the Conference on Natural History and Ira Remsen, a noted chemist from Johns Hopkins University, to head the Conference on Physics, Chemistry, and Astronomy.

The Conference on Physics, Chemistry, and Astronomy

The report of the Conference on Physics, Chemistry, and Astronomy included 22 resolutions for the teaching of the physical sciences in the elementary and secondary grades. The conference members recommended that both chemistry and physics, but not astronomy, should be required for college admission. The college admission test in these subjects should be made up of both a written test and an experimental component. They felt that the study of the physical sciences should be started early in the elementary grades and be taught as much as possible by means of experiments carried out by the pupils. A full course in chemistry should precede work in physics in the high school so that the pupils would have enough time to master the mathematics needed to study physics as a quantitative science. Laboratory work in physics was to be quantitative in nature. Fully half of the work in high school science was to be laboratory work, and the laboratory activities were to be carefully recorded in a well-kept notebook. Although science instruction was to be carried out largely in the laboratory, the conference members felt that students should not be encouraged to "rediscover" the laws of science. Laboratory work was to be carried out under the direction of an intelligent teacher to aid in the interpretation of results and to show the student how to work. The conference objected to what they called "loose work" in the laboratory and said that much of the undirected activities in chemistry laboratories in colleges and high schools fell into that category.

The recommended physics laboratory exercises included two kinds of activities. The first involved measurements and calculations to determine the properties of objects and phenomena. Students would be expected to calculate the density of objects, map the lines of magnetic force for a bar-magnet, measure electrical resistance, or calculate the work done in moving bodies up an inclined plane. The second type of activity involved the verification of physical laws. Recommended activities included the following: "Study the elasticity of stretching of rubber, or brass wire, and see whether the results agree with the law." "Verifying the freezing-point and boiling-point of a thermometer." In chemistry the recommended laboratory work focused almost exclusively on the preparation of simple compounds and on an examination of their properties. Titles of experiments included "Preparation of oxygen," "Properties of oxygen (With iron)," "Preparation of hydrochloric acid," "Properties of hydrochloric acid," "Action of hydrogen sulphide upon salts," and so on (National Education Association, 1893, pp. 124–137).

The Conference on Natural History

The Conference on Natural History had responsibility for the subjects of botany, zoology, and physiology at the elementary and secondary levels. Ever since its inclusion in the school curriculum earlier in the century, physiology had typically been oriented toward health and hygiene, especially at the elementary school level. In the high school course it was sometimes part of a three-part, year-long course that also included zoology and botany. Even at the high school level, the primary purpose of the course was to teach health and hygiene and some of the basic body structures and functions. The conference's recommendations for physiology did not oppose current practice. The group felt that it was not wise to teach young children a great deal of anatomy, fearing that such knowledge would lead in some instances "to morbid if not prurient curiosity that is productive of far more evil than the instruction is likely to counterbalance with good" (National Education Association, 1893, p. 159). Instead children should be given instruction

> on the subjects of personal cleanliness; pure air, and the relation of the carriage of the body to healthy respiration; wholesome foods, and moderateness and regularity in their use; regular and sufficient sleep; regu-

larity in other bodily habits; care as to temperature, and prudence concerning exposure; and abstinence from narcotics and stimulants, and from drugs generally. (National Education Association, 1893, p. 159)

The high school course in physiology was to be a half-year course following chemistry, physics, and other biology courses. It would be primarily informational rather than disciplinary in approach and would provide a study of basic body organs and functions as well as principles of hygiene. Since it was felt that opportunities for experimental work in physiology at the high school level were limited, the course would be taught primarily from a textbook, with the teacher making the knowledge "real, by the aid of suitable practical exercises and demonstrations" (National Education Association, 1893, p. 161).

Concerning the subjects of botany and zoology, it was generally agreed that botany was the more important of the two subjects for school instruction. Botany was the subject of choice because it was felt that plant materials were easier to obtain, the study of plants was more attractive to the pupils, and many students had aversions to the handling of animals that would be difficult to overcome. However, the conference members left the decision of which of these two natural science courses would be taught to the discretion of the teachers and recommended that only one of them be a requirement for college admission.

It was also recommended that study of these subjects begin in the earliest grades and be oriented toward direct observations of the structures and functions of a wide range of plants and animals. The first purpose of nature study was to interest the children in nature. The second purpose was to develop certain mental abilities or, as the conference members put it, "to cause them to form the habit of investigating carefully and of making clear, truthful statements, and to develop in them a taste for original investigation" (National Education Association, 1893, p. 142). And the third purpose was the acquisition of knowledge—not knowledge that was disconnected and taught by authority, but knowledge that was gained by personal experience. The conference recommended that one hour per week be given over to nature study at the elementary grades and that all work be conducted *without the aid of a textbook*. In addition, every attempt should be made to correlate the science observations with work in language, drawing, and literature.

This early study of nature would lead into a more detailed study of the morphology of plants and animals in the high school. There it was recommended that either botany or zoology be studied daily for a full year so that sufficient depth could be acquired. The conference members strongly recommended that the courses be laboratory-based, with three days per week spent in direct observation of the objects of study and two days spent in discussions of those observations, organized lectures, and quizzing. Sixty percent of the time would be spent in the laboratory, and the *entire* course would be focused on the observations made in the laboratory. The conference members felt that no books should be put into the hands of the students except those laboratory guides and reference books that would aid them in their work.

At the time the Committee of Ten met, the biological sciences (with the exception of physiology) were still largely descriptive rather than experimental fields. Thus their primary use as school subjects was to train the powers of observation, discrimination, and classification. As such, one of the widely used instructional practices was to have students make careful sketches and drawings of observed specimens. It was felt that this would enhance the observations themselves and improve the development of one's observational ability.

An examination of the outlines of the courses in zoology and botany reveals what one might expect from a course in morphology. Students were expected to carefully observe a wide range of specimens from the plant and animal kingdoms, beginning with the amoeba and ending with mammals in zoology, and beginning with the green algae and ending with dicotyledons in botany. For each organism, the observations of structure were to be coupled with a study of relevant functions. Although such a course could easily lead to a focus on memorization and the acquisition of knowledge, the conference members insisted that the primary purpose of the course was not the acquisition of knowledge but the mental discipline and intellectual growth that came from careful observation of nature.

The Conference on Geography

By 1893, geography had been part of the school curriculum for nearly a century. Geography was first listed as a college entrance subject by Harvard in 1807. It was a diverse subject encompassing the physical aspects of the earth's surface and dealing broadly with the environment and social aspects of the inhabitants of the earth. Because it involved direct study of the physical world, geography was included as one of the sciences in the school curriculum. The responsibility of the Conference on Geography was to make recommendations for the study of geography, broadly conceived, for both the elementary and secondary schools. This included both the study of people and places as well as the subjects of geology and meteorology.

The conference members proposed that all students be exposed to a study of general geography in the elementary grades that would encompass "a broad treatment of the earth and its inhabitants and institutions" (National Education Association, 1893, p. 209). This would be followed by a number of specialized courses in high school that would be elective and accepted for college admission but not required. The recommended specialized courses would include physical geography, physiography, meteorology, and geology. Physical geography would be studied just before entering high school, and the other three would be studied as half-year electives in the last two years of high school, following the study of chemistry and physics.

The primary objectives for study in this area included the development of (1) powers of direct observation, (2) the ability to form clear mental images and accurate conceptions of geographical features that were beyond the range of observation, and (3) reasoning powers. Observation of the natural features of the earth's surface and the processes by which surface features are produced, as well as the observation of the artificial features that humans had created in their towns and cities, would provide the students with a base of impressions upon which to build. These impressions would "arouse a spirit of inquiry and a thirst for geographical knowledge" (National Education Association, 1893, p. 211). In all of the courses, direct observation of the immediate environment was to be of first importance. Adequate provision should be made for excursions into the surrounding areas both during and after school hours, and incidental trips made by students outside of school should be incorporated into the teaching of these subjects as much as possible. An important part of the observational work was to make a written record of what was seen in the form of sketches, maps, models, and verbal descriptions. Like the biologists, the earth scientists felt that these records would interact with the observations to make them clearer, sharper, and more definite.

Since it is difficult to study more than just a small part of the earth's surface features through direct observation, it was recognized that eventually the students would have to rely heavily on the observations and descriptions of others. Thus the conference members listed the ability to form accurate conceptions based on indirect evidence as the second major objective of teaching in this area. However, they warned against excessive reliance on these vicarious experiences, noting that teaching often becomes almost exclusively based on the words of the teacher and textbook and not enough on direct observations. They felt strongly that the observations of the students themselves should continue throughout all the courses side-by-side with the descriptions of other people. They also made it clear that teachers in this area should previously have had a wide range of direct experiences with earth phenomena and be capable of making the maps, drawings, and models expected of their pupils.

The third major objective of the courses in the earth sciences was the development of reasoning ability. Students should be led to an understanding of the reason of things. In the words of the conference members, "the pupils should be induced to observe changes and processes as well as the simple passive facts of geography" (p. 213). Rather than merely "noting and memorizing facts," students should be led to "an understanding of the origin, the development, and the future history of geographic features" (National Education Association, 1893, p. 213). In addition, "the evidence leading to the conclusions, and not simply the conclusions, should receive careful consideration" (pp. 233–234). One caution they offered was that the emphasis on cause and effect relationships should be in relation to the ability of the students to reason abstractly. Overloading the students with more than they could handle would lead to memory without understanding. "The reasonings should be such as they can follow understandingly, if not work out themselves. If they merely commit them to memory, they are as dead as other things simply memorized and lose entirely the rational element" (p. 214). The conference members admitted that it might be useful to have the students memorize certain facts that they did not understand, but they warned that teachers should not think they were increasing their students' powers of reasoning by doing this.

The conference members stated that these three objectives should be viewed not as sequential but as integrated, one with another. At all times the teachers should keep in mind that the topics they were teaching were for the purpose of exercising certain mental powers. Not only the mastery of subject matter but also improved mental power was the goal of teaching about the earth.

Unlike the Conference on Natural History, the Conference on Geography favored the use of a textbook, although they warned against its excessive use, preferring that the individual teacher, not the textbook, should lead the class. They also found that the material in most textbooks was "too condensed and often too dryly stated"

(National Education Association, 1893, p. 220), and they recommended the use of books on travel in which the personal element is more interesting to the pupil.

Overview of the Science Conference Reports

As was indicated by the individual science reports, science educators in the early 1890s believed that science education should be based on direct experience with the physical world rather than the words of teachers or textbooks. It was the direct contact with the objects and phenomena of nature that made science a unique subject in the curriculum and justified its presence as a disciplinary subject. The conference members did not expect that students would be left alone to discover generalizations independently, however. Students should make their own observations, but it was the job of a teacher to guide those observations and to lead the students to the appropriate generalizations. Thus it was the authority of the textbook more than that of the teacher that was suspect. Feelings about the textbook were a reaction to the old "book science" that had been prevalent before laboratory science began to take hold in the latter part of the century.

Science conference members were also opposed to the rote memorization of meaningless facts. This, too, was a reaction to an outmoded teaching practice that viewed the development of the memory and the will as primary goals of education. The science educators of the 1890s believed that knowledge must come with understanding, and understanding in turn must come from direct experience with the objects of study and from the vivid explanations of a competent teacher. Conference members repeatedly cautioned that poorly prepared teachers who did not understand the natural world themselves would be forced to rely on the old techniques of rote memorization and recitation.

The Committee of Ten's Report

The Committee of Ten was sympathetic to the arguments of the science conferences for more time in the curriculum, and they included significant amounts of science study in each of the proposed curriculum models. To accommodate differing interests in the curriculum, the committee listed subjects for four sample "courses" that could serve as models for school districts interested in providing for a range of student needs. In each of the four courses (classical, Latin-scientific, modern languages, and English), the sciences held an important position. Even the classical course, which was dominated by linguistic studies, included the study of physical geography, physics, and chemistry in the first, second, and fourth years, respectively. The other three courses added zoology or botany; astronomy and meteorology; geology and physiography; and anatomy, physiology, and hygiene. Overall, approximately one-fifth of a student's total time in high school would be devoted to the study of science under these sample plans.

The committee also strongly supported the use of the laboratory in teaching science courses, advocating double periods for laboratory instruction, Saturday morning laboratory exercises, and one afternoon per week to be set aside for "out-of-door instruction in geography, botany, zoology, and geology" (National Education Association, 1893, p. 50). The committee disagreed with one of the conference recommendations and supported the minority opinion that physics should precede chemistry in the curriculum. Their reason for taking this position was that physics was seen as an important prerequisite not only for chemistry but also for courses such as meteorology and physiography that would be taught in the last year of high school.

Concerning the relationship between the colleges and the schools, the committee agreed that college admission should be based on the satisfactory completion of a comprehensive course of study developed along the lines of the model courses they proposed. Since all the courses would be taught to develop intellectual ability, it would not matter whether the students chose the classical course or the Latin-scientific course. As long as the various areas of the curriculum were studied in depth and over a period of several years, they should prepare a person for college admission. In addition, all of these courses of study were viewed as appropriate preparation for life. Thus the added burden of differentiating subject matter and approaches for the college-bound and non-college-bound student would not be necessary.

The Effect of the Report

Theodore Sizer, in *Secondary Schools at the Turn of the Century* (1964b), provided an important look at the impact of the report of the Committee of Ten on educational practice over the next several decades. According to Sizer, the report was an influential document, and one that people read and used as they created programs in schools. The effects, however, rather than coming from the specific recommendations of the report, were more indirect. For example, over time there was a reduction in the number of subjects that were taught by schools. Instead of the long lists of subjects of the earlier years, a smaller number of areas of study developed, tending toward those recommended by the Committee of Ten. A study by Edwin Dexter in 1906 showed that astronomy, which was recommended as an elective in the report, showed a 50% decline over the ten-year period and that other elective courses, such as geology and meteorology, also showed declines. Dexter pointed out, however, that reports of the U.S. Commissioner of Education showed that science enrollments grew rapidly between 1890 and 1910, an effect that was certainly in keeping with the committee's recommendations.

The Committee on College-Entrance Requirements

Almost as soon as the report of the Committee of Ten was published, the National Education Association (NEA) membership began to discuss ways to implement the specific recommendations. At the 1895 meeting of the Department of Secondary Education of the NEA, a paper was read entitled "What Action Ought to Be Taken by Universities and Secondary Schools to Promote the Introduction of the Programs Recommended by the Committee of Ten?" (National Education Association, 1899). Discussions of that paper led to a proposal that a joint committee from the Department of Secondary and Higher Education be established to make recommendations concerning requirements for admission to college. By early 1896, the Committee on College-Entrance Requirements had begun its work, and it submitted its first preliminary report at the July 1896 meeting of the NEA in Buffalo. The committee also decided at that time to invite existing associations to organize subcommittees to assist in the effort of coordinating college entrance. As with the Committee of Ten's report, the newer subjects, such as science, English, modern languages, and U.S. history, were included in the discussions alongside the classical languages and mathematics, but commercial and industrial arts courses were not, even though these were becoming increasingly important in the secondary school curriculum. In science, the Science Department of the NEA was asked to organize subgroups for each science area and to submit reports to the committee.

The Final Report of the Committee

The final report of the Committee on College-Entrance Requirements was presented at the annual meeting of the NEA in Los Angeles in 1899 by Dr. A. F. Nightingale, chairman of the committee. Nightingale was pleased with the work that had been done by most of the subcommittees but disappointed with the work of the science groups. In his report he said:

> It was a matter of the most poignant regret that the committee appointed to co-operate with us by the Science Department of this association did not furnish us with as harmonious, elaborate, and satisfactory reports as those which came from other organizations on other subjects. The report on zoology came too late for our careful examination; that on physics is incomplete, by reason of a lack of harmony in the subcommittee as to matter and method. No reports were presented on geology, astronomy, or physiology, subjects which are considered worthy of a large place in secondary-school programs. (National Education Association, 1899, p. 627)

For reasons that were not clear, the Science Department of the NEA did not take their charge as seriously as they might have.

The spirit of the overall report was this: The programs of study laid down by the committee were expected to serve as norms for secondary schools, and colleges were expected to accept satisfactory completion of these programs for college admission. In addition, colleges would be expected to make provision for students once they reached college to take more work at an advanced level in the subject that was being submitted for college entrance. Under such a plan, students would not have to repeat material they had studied in high school. None of this was to be compulsory. The committee was asking schools and colleges to reach an understanding concerning the nature of courses required for high school graduation and college admission.

The committee determined that there should be free election of courses around a set of constants that would satisfy both high school graduation and college entrance requirements. The recommended constants were four units or years of study in languages, two in English, two in math, one in history, one in science, plus six electives, for a total of 16 units. This system would provide a substantial amount of freedom in the election of subjects to be used for college admission and at the same time ensure that students took some work in each of the important academic areas. The plan was essentially a refinement of the more cumbersome practice in effect at the time that was supported by the Committee of Ten. Under that plan students elected a particular course of study, such as the classical, English, or Latin-scientific course, in which the subjects were laid out in advance for the four years of high school. Under both plans, however, the principles of equivalence of subjects for the purpose of mental training and the importance of free election of courses were advanced. Finally, the expectation was that all students, whether college-bound or not, would be in the same classes together. There would be no differentiation of subjects or teaching methods on the basis of occupational intentions.

Although science had now become firmly established on the lists of important subjects for all students to study, and the principle of election made it possible for students to apply several science courses toward high school graduation and college admission, the sciences were a long way from achieving the lofty status that language study still held. Even though the Committee of Ten had created programs that increased science study to about 20% of the student's time in school, the expectation of the Committee on College-Entrance Requirements was that students would complete only one year of science for high school graduation and college admission. Additional science courses would be taken as electives. The requirement for linguistic studies, on the other hand, was six courses—four in languages and two in English.

The Science Subcommittees

The statements by the science subcommittees added little to what had been recommended earlier by the science conferences of the Committee of Ten. The subcommittee members believed that science, unlike the other subjects in the curriculum, offered direct experience with natural phenomena, and for this reason the sciences were an essential component of the secondary school program and should be accepted for college admission. To foster direct contact with the physical world, they believed the laboratory should be the central focus of the science courses, even though it was clear from their comments that the subcommittees recognized that the laboratory was not being utilized effectively in the schools. A comn.ent by the subcommittee on zoology illustrated this sentiment.

> Probably the most general method of teaching zoology in secondary schools at present is the text-book method. A large amount of information *about* animals is acquired thereby in a limited time, and the minimum of attainment and preparation is demanded of the teacher. Your Subcommittee on Zoology is unanimously opposed to this method for not only is undue emphasis laid on the larger forms of animal life, but also no course has any right to be regarded as a course in science unless

it include laboratory work. (National Education Association, 1899, p. 806)

Besides their focus on the laboratory, there were several other issues that received special mention by the science subcommittees. Two in chemistry were especially noteworthy. The first had to do with the teaching of chemical formulas and equations, and with the use of atomic theory to explain chemical phenomena. Committee members felt strongly that this material should be taught inductively and not stated as dogma. In their words:

> When symbols and formulae are first introduced, special care must be taken to show how they are derived from quantitative measurements. The pupil's own observations and other examples must be used to show how the formulae, and finally the equations, are reached as expressions of quantitative relations. The whole process of determining the proportions by weight and constructing the formulae and equations must be done or described in connection with every chemical change, until the pupil is thoroughly familiar with the formulae and the exact significance of the equation is perfectly clear. Formulae must on no account be used before this can be done, as otherwise they will inevitably appear to be the source of information instead of the receptacle for it. All "exercises in writing equations" and rules for constructing them, as if they were mathematical expressions, must be rigidly excluded as fantastic and misleading. (National Education Association, 1899, p. 796)

Another issue that was brought up by the chemistry subcommittee had to do with the introduction of commercial processes in the course to make the content more relevant to everyday experience. The concern was that most applications of chemistry to commercial processes were too complex to be understood at the elementary level. The teaching of them would, it was feared, degenerate into mere empirical knowledge that would have to be memorized without understanding. It was not that applications were not considered important as a way of deepening one's understanding of the subject and as a source of interest, but rather that those applications must be chosen carefully so that they did actually deepen the understanding of important chemical principles and did not just add to the mass of uncomprehended facts.

Science Education at the Turn of the Century

Although the statements by the science subcommittees were less than thorough, two of the chairmen of these subcommittees collaborated three years later on a book entitled *The Teaching of Chemistry and Physics in the Secondary School* (Smith & Hall, 1902) in which they elaborated on many of the ideas presented in the report and offered their insights into practices that were being used in the schools at that time. Alexander Smith, Associate Professor of Chemistry at the University of Chicago, discussed the teaching of chemistry, and Edwin H. Hall, Professor of Physics at Harvard University, discussed the teaching of physics. Both presented well-developed and coherent approaches to the teaching of their subjects and at the same time recognized points of controversy that existed in the teaching of science in general.

Alexander Smith

Smith left little doubt that in his mind science as a relative newcomer to the curriculum had a long way to go before it achieved the same quality as the older subjects. He said that "the chemistry work in the average school is not a trial worthy of the powers of the pupils" (Smith & Hall, 1902, p. 25). If you were to visit a high school chemistry class what you would see is pupils "puttering with a kind of chemistry which . . . would not have overtaxed the ability of a reasonably intelligent infant" (p. 25). According to Smith: "There is reason to fear that chemistry has gained admission before the means of using it effectively have become widely known" (p. 26).

Smith attributed the problems in chemistry instruction to insufficient science instruction in the elementary school years, a lack of agreement on the part of educators concerning the goals of chemistry instruction, and poorly prepared teachers. Many teachers responsible for teaching chemistry had not been trained specifically for that task, and the preparation of those who were trained was insufficient. According to Smith, the instruction that the teachers received was too dogmatic and based too much on the textbook.

CONTRIBUTIONS OF SCIENCE TEACHING TO EDUCATION. What could science teaching in general and chemistry teaching in particular accomplish educationally, assuming they were taught well? What justifies their place in the curriculum? Smith identified five potential contributions of science teaching to education:

1. Training in the powers of observation of the natural world
2. Training in a powerful method of generating new knowledge that is based on observation and experiment
3. Exercise of the imagination and creative impulses

4. Training to view problems objectively
5. The generation of useful information

Not only did the study of science provide mental discipline, but the *information* gained through science study was an important outcome as well. Smith cited both Herbert Spencer's (1864) essay "What Knowledge Is of Most Worth?" and Thomas Huxley's (1899) "A Liberal Education and Where to Find It" in support of the idea that the knowledge gained through science study is useful in our everyday lives. Smith believed that if science could be shown to provide both useful information and to have disciplinary value, then the subject would be "practically indispensable." As an added value, Smith argued that the information of science "assists in holding the interest of the majority of pupils who would not be so much attracted by a purely disciplinary study" (Smith & Hall, 1902, p. 14). In his discussion of the informational value of science, Smith was sensitive to the potential for the sciences to be labeled as "information studies" rather than the more prestigious "disciplinary studies," but he was unwilling to deny the importance of science knowledge itself.

APPROACH TO TEACHING CHEMISTRY.   In spite of the critics, science by this time had won its place in the curriculum, and there was no turning back from that. All that was left was to determine how it would be taught and the role it would play in the lives of the students who studied it. Smith laid out an approach to the teaching of secondary school chemistry that was laboratory-based, that utilized as much as possible the independent discovery of the pupils, that focused on the development of a meaningful understanding of the facts and principles of the subject instead of rote memorization, and that was oriented toward practical applications in everyday life. He implied throughout his discussion of chemistry teaching that there were two major reasons for teaching the subject. One was to acquire knowledge, that is, to understand the subject of chemistry as fully as possible. The second was to develop the ability to think, which to Smith meant the ability to compare, to discriminate, and to reason inductively. The methods that he felt should be employed in the teaching of chemistry were aimed at the accomplishment of those two goals.

Smith believed that the laboratory should be the central feature of the course. All other work would be supplemental to what was done in the laboratory. Although most teachers in 1902 agreed that laboratory instruction was important, few of them made adequate use of laboratory resources. Smith cited a New York State report of science teaching that said: "While the laboratory method is almost universally approved by the science teachers, the text-book method prevails in the schools, to such an extent that laboratory work is incidental, inefficient, and in many cases excluded altogether" (University of the State of New York, 1900, p. 706).

Smith argued that the laboratory could be used in at least two different ways. First, it was a place for the verification of chemical principles, and second, it was a place for independent discovery. Speaking of the verification of chemical laws, he said: "Practical illustration will be required in order to make the understanding of the law more vivid, the recollection of its content more lasting, and, above all, to show by means of a sample, admittedly rough, what the general nature of its experimental basis is" (Smith & Hall, 1902, p. 106). In Smith's view, all science teaching was to be done in a way that would make the principles and generalizations real to the students. The laboratory would help in this regard by confirming the existence of those chemical laws directly through the student's personal experience.

The most important feature of the laboratory to Smith, however, was that it could be used to place the student in the role of discoverer. In its pure form, this mode of teaching was referred to as the "heuristic method." H. E. Armstrong (1898) had developed and popularized heuristic teaching a number of years earlier in England. Under this method, no books and no directions from the teacher were employed, and, as much as possible, the questions for investigation came from the students themselves as they examined the materials that were presented to them. The major purpose of the method was to teach the pupils how to learn, how to raise interesting questions, how to investigate, and how to find answers on their own.

In support of the success of this method, Harold Picton reported in 1899 an experience with four 12-year-old boys in a British school who investigated, on their own, the rate of expansion of water from the freezing temperature upwards. They soon became involved with the problem of the expansion of the container itself as a source of error in their investigation, and they made corrections based on research that they were able to find reported in the literature. Regarding this experience, Picton said:

> The "investigation" above mentioned occupied the better part of a term, during which, no doubt, the boys might have read through some little text-book, or pottered through a course of ready-made "experiments" on "heat." It also cost the master . . . a good deal of labour. But he finds

that a very little of this sort of work goes a very long way. . . . It seems to confer a power that is not acquired in any other way. The pupil's mind gains a freedom, a power of seeing things for itself, an alertness and adaptability in turning to fresh matter, which make great gaps in methodic knowledge of comparatively little importance. (Picton, 1899, cited in Smith & Hall, 1902, p. 108)

As appealing as the method sounded, Smith believed that it took too much time and did not furnish the knowledge of chemistry that was needed at the secondary level. As a method for younger students, where the knowledge requirements were fewer, he found it to be ideal. While recognizing the difficulty of employing the method exclusively in chemistry instruction, Smith believed that as much heuristic work as possible should be incorporated into the secondary course. He said that whether our goal is one of "awakening or sustaining interest, or of fostering the scientific habit of thought, it is evident that leading the pupil to adopt the attitude of a discoverer will be most likely to accomplish the result desired" (Smith & Hall, 1902, p. 105).

His solution to the dilemma presented by the obvious strengths and weakness of the heuristic method was to carefully guide the student through the discovery process for most of the laboratory activities and to only occasionally leave the students to devise their own methods of attacking the problems. Under this guided approach, the teacher would raise the questions, provide the materials; and carefully move the students along the way. The students would be asked leading questions both orally and in the laboratory outlines, and there would be hints concerning what to look for next, when to make comparisons between two reactions, and so on. Under this modified approach, students would still be making careful observations and reasoning from those observations, although they would not be developing the sense of independence that could come only from solving their own problems.

The laboratory was expected to lead not only to the development of observational and reasoning abilities but also to an understanding of the subject matter of chemistry. When discussing this acquisition of knowledge, Smith made it clear that he was talking about a coherent understanding of the subject of chemistry, not memory of isolated facts. He felt that the rote memorization of meaningless facts should be avoided throughout, and he cautioned that even laboratory activities ran the risk of being conventionalized and mechanized such

that the student could describe what had happened without understanding any of the chemistry involved.

According to Smith, there were two ways to assist the student in
gaining a genuine understanding of the content of chemistry. One
was to have the student learn as much as possible from direct contact
with the objects of chemistry. Direct experience was considered to be
fuller and to have a greater impact on the student than any second-
hand explanation could. This would be accomplished by making the
laboratory the central feature of the course. The second way was to
relate new knowledge to other things that the student knew or had
experienced. This included correlating the subject of chemistry with
other subjects that the student was studying, building a coherent and
integrated rather than piecemeal and fragmented understanding of
chemistry by relating each concept to other concepts already learned,
and demonstrating the applications of chemistry to the everyday lives
of the students.

The way to give flexibility to the student's knowledge and at the
same time to make the content of chemistry interesting and real was
to continuously point out the applications of chemistry to real-world
phenomena within the experience of the student. Smith felt that numerous applications of chemistry were present in the student's immediate environment, and, when appropriate, field trips should be
taken to sites where direct observations of natural phenomena could
be made. Applications of chemistry would include ones in agriculture, industry, and the home. For example, oxidation could be shown
in the natural processes of rusting and organic decay; reduction, in
photographic processes and dyeing; osmotic pressure, in the root
pressure of plants; and the synthesis of industrial products, at the
industrial plant itself.

Smith was quick to caution, however, that the applications themselves should not become the end toward which the chemistry was
taught. He warned against "so-called chemical instruction in the
schools which is perverted into the teaching of odds and ends about
various domestic and industrial applications" (Smith & Hall, 1902, p.
142). The important thing was that students become aware that
chemistry existed outside the classroom and that the chemistry of the
classroom and the chemistry of the everyday world were one and the
same. The ultimate purpose for teaching chemistry was to develop an
understanding of the science in its fullest sense, including its applications, and to develop the student's mental abilities through the
study of the subject.

Edwin H. Hall

Edwin H. Hall was Professor of Physics at Harvard University and chairman of the NEA's physics subcommittee. Like Smith, his discussion of physics teaching was a discussion of the new science teaching—of science teaching organized around the laboratory. Hall pointed out that only 20 years earlier laboratory work had been virtually nonexistent in science instruction. Textbooks were used to give information in an encyclopedic way, with little concern about training the senses or the powers of observation. Teachers themselves had not had laboratory experiences in their own science training and were not inclined to arrange such experiences for their own students. Hall credited A. P. Gage of the Boston English High School for writing the first physics textbook that made use of the laboratory. The book appeared in 1882 and became a widely used text in secondary schools. The book carried on its cover the statement: "Read Nature in the Language of Experiment" and the preface contained the justification for laboratory instruction: "It is a cardinal principle in modern pedagogy that the mind gains a real and adequate knowledge of things only in the presence of the things themselves. Hence, the first step in all good teaching is an appeal to the observing powers" (cited in Smith & Hall, 1902, p. 270).

THE HARVARD DESCRIPTIVE LIST.   Another factor in the movement toward laboratory-based courses was the decision by Harvard University in 1886 to allow a course of experiments in physics to be used for admission to the college. The student applicant would be required to have completed 40 experiments taken from several approved laboratory manuals and to pass a written examination testing the student's knowledge of the experiments and the principles of physics. The original notebook in which the results of the experiments were recorded would also be submitted at the time of the examination. In 1887, the college published a descriptive list of 46 experiments in physics acceptable for college entrance. In 1897, Harvard's admission statement was changed to place more emphasis on learning the facts and principles of physics and on the teacher's role in the lecture room, but the laboratory was still retained at the center of the requirement. Although the Harvard requirements had an important impact on the kind of teaching that went on in many schools, and a number of publishers offered textbooks based on Harvard's list of physics experiments, most teachers were slow to switch to a laboratory-based course. Hall noted, for example, that the most successful textbooks from the point of view of sales were those that made little use of laboratory work (Smith & Hall, 1902).

APPROACHES TO LABORATORY INSTRUCTION. As laboratory instruction began to emerge as an important issue in science teaching, a number of differing orientations and approaches toward the laboratory were developed. Hall identified three separate theories of laboratory instruction. The first was the discovery, or heuristic, approach; the second was the verification approach; and the third was the inquiry approach. As we saw earlier, the discovery, or heuristic, approach was an inductive strategy in which students were expected to discover the important facts and principles of science largely on their own. As with so many formulas for good teaching, the approach had a tendency to become mechanized and used in an unthinking way. For example, laboratory manuals that were organized around student discovery might ask students to make observations of some object or phenomenon and then to record their "inference." Hall cited two examples of the misuse of this approach. In the first, the students were expected to observe a block of wood at rest and then in motion. The "inferences" they were to record were that "*Matter cannot set itself in motion*" and "*Matter can be set in motion by force*" (Smith & Hall, 1902, p. 275). In the second example, the students were given several solid objects to handle and then, in an apparent non sequitur, asked to make an inference about whether sunlight was "matter" or not.

There were other problems with the discovery approach besides its tendency to become mechanized in the hands of an unthinking teacher. For one, the general laws or relations in physics tended to be too difficult for the pupils to discover independently, and the attempt often led to frustration. Hall believed that in the hands of a very competent teacher who was responsible for only a small group of students, the discovery method might have some potential. This teacher would be one who "knows the ground thoroughly, and will not delude himself or his pupils with exaggerated notions of their independence and originality in science" (Smith & Hall, 1902, p. 276).

But the discovery method was not the only approach that was fraught with difficulties. The method of verification that asked students to confirm some scientific fact or principle in the laboratory was equally deficient because it developed an unscientific attitude. Hall (Smith & Hall, 1902) said:

> It is hard to imagine any disposition of mind less scientific than that of one who undertakes an experiment knowing the result to be expected from it and prepared to look so long, and only so long, as may be necessary to attain this result. Better by far to take a statement on faith than to cultivate the habit of hunting for evidence in its favour and shutting one's eyes to inconvenient evidence against it. (p. 277)

Besides developing an attitude that was inconsistent with the actual practice of science, there was also a tendency on the part of students to distort the evidence that they gathered in support of the scientific law. Often this was unintended, and even when intentional it was usually not malicious. Hall said students would often say in all sincerity: "Why should I put down an observation which I know can't be right?"

Just as Smith had settled on guided discovery in the laboratory as a middle ground between the extremes of verification and independent discovery, Hall suggested that the appropriate way to approach the laboratory was as a place for what he called "inquiry." Using an inquiry approach did not mean that students had to discover everything on their own, but that they should seek answers to questions for which they did not have the answers. He said the method of inquiry was one that kept the pupil "just enough in the dark as to the probable outcome of his experiment, just enough in the attitude of discovery, to leave him unprejudiced in his observations" (Smith & Hall, 1902, p. 278). Hall was particularly fond of pooling data that the students generated in the laboratory for post-laboratory discussions in which the teacher developed the generalizations with the class as a whole. In this approach, all the student data were averaged except for those that were obviously recorded improperly. The pooling of data usually provided results from which the intended relationships could be derived. As long as students were unaware in advance of the relationships being studied, they could assume the posture of genuine investigators in the laboratory.

OTHER INSTRUCTIONAL APPROACHES.   Unlike a number of other science educators of the day, Hall did not believe that the laboratory should constitute the entire course. According to Hall, students usually enjoyed laboratory activities, but there was too great a tendency for them to ignore the hard mental effort that had to accompany the mechanical operations if their understanding of the science was to be increased. Hall also felt that learning by experience was too slow. He said: "Learning by experience is a plodding method, and the student who aspires to any great height or breadth of intellectual reach must not confine himself to it" (Smith & Hall, 1902, p. 305). For this reason, the teacher needed to organize lecture and recitation sessions in which the laboratory experiences could be related to the facts and principles of physics. The teacher would also provide demonstrations of phenomena that the students could not experiment with themselves and would give the students practice in solving numerical problems. Most important, the teacher would arrange for students to see firsthand the applications of physics in their everyday lives.

According to Hall, the immediate aim of physics instruction was "to give the power and the habit of using physical knowledge" (Smith & Hall, 1902, p. 314). The student was to see and think about physical phenomena outside of the classroom. He said that students "should acquire a good general understanding of ordinary domestic scientific appliances, and, in their simpler forms, of the steam-engine, telegraph, telephone, dynamo, and motor" (p. 314). Like Smith, however, Hall was suspicious of courses that were too practical.

> The word of caution which I would give to those who aim especially to make their teaching "practical" is, that they should beware of encouraging the idea, which many of their pupils are only too much inclined to hold, that the object of schooling is to give a certain final and sufficient store of knowledge and not, rather, so to fit the pupil that he may, after his school days are over, go on increasing in knowledge, finding constantly new uses for that stock of elementary fundamental ideas which a well devised school course should inculcate. (p. 340)

Summary

As the nineteenth century came to an end, science as a course of study had become firmly established in the school curriculum. Reports by the Committee of Ten and later by the Committee on College-Entrance Requirements showed that educators had made a very substantial commitment to science as a body of useful knowledge, as a way of thinking, and as a tool for disciplining the mind.

The discussions by Smith and Hall provide insight into some of the more enlightened attitudes toward the teaching of science at the turn of the century. We see the continuing emergence of the laboratory approach as the favored pedagogy of educational theorists, the variety of ways that the laboratory could be used and abused, and the resistance to its use by school people themselves. We also see the movement away from memory culture and toward meaningful understanding firmly take hold in the minds of science educators. Smith and Hall were both strong supporters of laboratory-based instruction but not of the discovery, or heuristic, approaches advocated by some. Both were advocates of genuine inquiry in the laboratory aimed at meaningful understanding of the facts and principles of their respective disciplines. We also see the beginnings of the movement to make science courses more applied and relevant to the everyday lives of the students, a force that would continue to grow in the years ahead.

Chapter 4

The Reorganization of Science Education

During the decade following the Committee of Ten Report there were numerous attempts to coordinate the programs of the schools and colleges to make it easier to plan for college admission and to make the experience of college preparation more satisfactory to the high schools and the individual student. The College Entrance Examination Board was formed in 1900, and admission exams created jointly by college professors and high school teachers were administered in 1901. In the Midwest, the practice continued of having colleges certify secondary schools and admitting those students who satisfactorily completed the college preparatory program at the certified high school. In general, the efforts at coordination between schools and colleges paid off during the 1890s and early 1900s, and college entrance requirements became more flexible. It became increasingly difficult, however, during the subsequent decades for secondary school people to accept as appropriate for life preparation the plans that had been recommended by the Committee on College-Entrance Requirements or the Committee of Ten. Pressures mounted for an increasingly more practical curriculum and for more opportunities to select commercial and industrial arts courses in addition to the traditional courses identified by those standardizing bodies.

High school enrollments had grown rapidly during the 1890s and the early 1900s, but high schools still attracted only a small percentage of the eligible students. Only 10.2% of 14- to 17-year-olds were enrolled in public and private secondary schools in 1900 (National Center for Educational Statistics, 1981), and most of those attending high school did not graduate. The high dropout rate was due to a number of factors, including the economic difficulty of having a

64

potential wage earner lost to an enterprise of questionable practical utility and a general disinterest in what went on in schools. The dropout rate was a major concern for school people, who hoped to increase enrollments by making the high school program more useful to the students.

The practical utility of education was an issue that American educators had debated since the time of the first academies. As we saw in Chapter 1, one of the most outspoken nineteenth-century advocates of practical education was Herbert Spencer, who justified the teaching of science on the basis of its application to the major activities of everyday living. Spencer's utility, however, was aimed at the individual person—parenting skills, self-preservation, and the use of leisure time. The practical education that was developing at the beginning of the twentieth century was education for social utility. The development of a stable economic system, maintenance of the public health, and the socialization of youth for life in a democratic society began to take on ever greater importance. In fact, these social aims were pressed with such vigor that they began to eclipse those aims that were personally satisfying. In an age of reform aimed at curbing such social ills as the misuse of alcohol, the spread of infectious diseases caused by poor sanitation and promiscuous sex, and the increase of urban poverty and crime, education came more and more to be viewed as a way to produce socially effective and productive citizens. In an age of new arrivals from foreign lands and the new lifestyles and values the immigrants brought with them, education was seen as a way to socialize the newcomers into the ways of their adopted home. Education for social control and for social efficiency became the dominant themes of educational debate by the second decade of the twentieth century. Schooling would teach the values of the New World so as to control antisocial tendencies, and it would produce citizens who would fit into the American system and make them useful contributors to American society.

To this end, the curriculum needed to be reorganized to prepare people for potential employment, to teach the dominant values of the society, and to provide knowledge that would transform individuals into valuable members of the society. If this meant differentiating courses according to the probable destinies of the students, then that was what should be done. If this meant focusing on the masses of students who would not be going to college and offering them a program of studies appropriate to their anticipated life work, then that was what educators should do. The academic program of the high school that had been worked out jointly between school and college representatives might still be appropriate for college-bound students, but it was no longer considered appropriate for the large number of students who might not even graduate from high school. The desire of the members of the Committee of Ten and of the Committee on College-Entrance Requirements to offer a curriculum that would be suitable for all regardless of their future plans met with general acceptance for only a short time. By 1910, the call for practical studies for non-college-bound students was loud and clear.

Educators who advocated practical courses for social utility found little of value in the current academic curriculum. History was thought to be useless for producing effective members of society. Social studies as a generic study of good citizenship and social betterment through subjects such as geography, economics, and civics would need to replace it. Latin and mathematics were condemned for their bookishness and irrelevance. English could be saved if it was geared toward everyday communication skills and an awareness through literature of social activities and needs. Science could be salvaged if made more practical. Its relationship to technology, industrial processes, sanitation, and economic development made science courses potentially of great social value.

The Committee on the Articulation of High School and College was formed by the Department of Secondary Education of the NEA in 1911 as social utility arguments were growing in intensity (National Education Association, 1911). The thrust of the committee's recommendations was to reduce the current graduation requirement in foreign language from four units to two, to allow students to choose up to four electives from either the regular academic offerings or from the vocational offerings, and to make it possible for students to avoid foreign language or mathematics altogether if an extra course in science and social studies was used as a substitute. By providing this additional flexibility in graduation and college admission requirements, it was felt that more students would complete high school and enter college and that their education would be more broadly useful.

The significance of the Committee on the Articulation of High School and College was not in these recommendations for liberalized graduation and college admission requirements, however, even though a number of prestigious colleges did alter their entrance requirements in keeping with the committee's suggestions. It was, rather, in the establishment of individual subject-matter committees and the continuation of the parent committee as the Commission on the Reorganization of Secondary Education (CRSE). In 1913, Clarence Kingsley became chairman of this major effort to examine secondary education and make recommendations for its reorganization.

Five years later, the commission issued its report, entitled *Cardinal Principles of Secondary Education* (National Education Association, 1918), and in 1920, the science committee submitted a report entitled *Reorganization of Science in Secondary Schools* (National Education Association, 1920).

Commission on the Reorganization of Secondary Education

According to the CRSE, the reason that secondary education needed to be reorganized was because society had changed and education was not keeping pace with those changes. The argument was the same as that offered during the nineteenth century as the sciences and other modern subjects fought for a place alongside the classical studies. In 1918 this argument became a call for social relevance in the entire curriculum, a curriculum that needed to meet the practical demands of the great masses of people, not just those seeking education for personal enrichment. Kingsley cited urbanization, industrialization, increased leisure time, the decline in the educational effectiveness of the family, and changes in the secondary school population as factors that demanded a change in secondary education. He also noted that educational psychologists had begun to seriously question the educational value of "general discipline," that is, the value of school studies in developing the general intellect, the principle that had so dominated educational discussions just 20 years earlier. Kingsley also said that educators were beginning to recognize the importance of differences in the mental capacities of individual students and the importance of determining the value of educational materials and methods in terms of "the application of knowledge to the activities of life, rather than primarily in terms of the demands of any subject as a logically organized science" (National Education Association, 1918, p. 8).

The commission argued that education should be aimed toward a democratic life for all, with neither the individual nor the society being subordinated to the other. The role of education was to develop the individual for effectiveness in a social world. The main objectives of an educational program could be determined by an analysis of the activities of individuals in society. Kingsley identified seven types of activities in which individuals were involved in much the same way that Spencer had in his analysis of "What Knowledge Is of Most Worth?" Since an individual was usually a member of a family, a vocational group, and various civic groups, education must pay attention to worthy home membership, vocation, and citizenship as important goals. With a shortened work day, it was important that a person use leisure time productively and not fall into patterns of antisocial behavior. Good health was essential for all of these activities and was a fifth objective of education. Certain fundamental processes, such as reading, writing, arithmetical computations, and oral and written expression, were also necessary tools for conducting the affairs of life. Finally, the importance of ethical behavior in all of one's life activities made this an essential goal of education. Thus the seven categories of goals were (1) health, (2) command of fundamental processes, (3) worthy home-membership, (4) vocation, (5) citizenship, (6) worthy use of leisure, and (7) ethical character.

The emphasis on vocation as a separate goal was remarkable in comparison to the complete absence of any discussion of vocational education in the Committee of Ten report. It is particularly interesting to note in this regard the CRSE's comments about college admission and about differentiated curricula in the secondary schools.

> The tradition that a particular type of education, and that exclusively nonvocational in character, is the only acceptable preparation for advanced education, either liberal or vocational, must therefore give way to a scientific evaluation of all types of secondary education as preparation for continued study. . . . Pupils who, during the secondary period, devote a considerable time to courses having vocational content should be permitted to pursue whatever form of higher education, either liberal or vocational, they are able to undertake with profit to themselves and to society. (National Education Association, 1918, p. 20)

With respect to vocational courses in the secondary schools, the commission said:

> The work of the senior high school should be organized into differentiated curriculums. The range of such curriculums should be as wide as the school can offer effectively. The basis of differentiation should be, in the broad sense of the term, vocational, thus justifying the names commonly given such as agricultural, business, clerical, industrial, fine-arts, and household-arts curriculums. Provision should be made also for those having distinctively academic interests and needs. (National Education Association, 1918, p. 22)

Thus academic training, which had been the main focus of the Committee of Ten Report, seemed to be presented in this report almost as an afterthought.

To the Commission on the Reorganization of Secondary Education, all school subjects, whether of the traditional academic type or of the commercial and vocational type, had to defend themselves in relation to the seven objectives, or Cardinal Principles, of education. The ultimate goal was "complete and worthy living for all youth" (National Education Association, 1918, p. 32). It was not that all courses taught in the schools had to contribute to each one of these objectives, but that the case for their presence in the curriculum should be made in reference to these objectives. Kingsley cited examples of how this might be done. Science, he said, could be used to develop an appreciation of the natural world and thereby aid in the worthy use of leisure. Science courses could also assist in the maintenance of the health of all people.

Fourteen individual reports on separate areas of the curriculum appeared in the years just prior to and following the publication of the Cardinal Principles in 1918. In addition to committees on the traditional academic subjects, committees were also formed on agriculture, art, business education, home economics, industrial arts, and physical education.

Science Committee

The Committee on Science was headed by Otis W. Caldwell, Professor of Education at Columbia University Teachers College and director of the Lincoln School. The committee was made up of 47 members who represented college and school faculties in approximately equal numbers, although most college people were from education rather than science faculties. The members divided themselves into four subcommittees. The subcommittee on general science was chaired by J. F. Woodhull of Columbia University Teachers College; physics, by G. R. Twiss of Ohio State University; chemistry, by R. W. Osborne of the Francis W. Parker School in Chicago; and biology, by James E. Peabody of the Morris High School in New York City. A separate report was submitted by the chairman of each of these groups (National Education Association, 1920).

The science committee justified the presence of the sciences in the curriculum on the basis of six of the seven cardinal principles. Only "command of fundamental processes" (the basic skills of reading, writing, and calculating) was omitted. Their rationale went as follows:

1. Science is valuable in the realization of "good health" because knowledge of public sanitation and personal hygiene can protect people from illness and help to control disease.
2. Almost all sciences can be oriented toward "worthy home membership" by teaching about the functioning of electrical appliances, repairs of heating and ventilating systems, and the operation of a host of other conveniences found in the home.
3. Science courses are valuable preparation for specific "vocations" and for vocational life in general. In the committee's words: "In the field of vocational preparation, courses in shop physics, applied electricity, physics of the home, industrial and household chemistry, applied biological sciences, physiology, and hygiene will be of value to many students if properly adapted to their needs" (National Education Association, 1920, p. 13).
4. With regard to the goal of "citizenship," science courses will give individuals a greater appreciation of the work and contributions of the scientist and give the citizen the ability to select experts wisely for specialized positions in society.
5. Science's contribution to the enhancement of "leisure" is through the many enjoyable avocations that science courses offer. These include such things as understanding the optical and chemical principles behind photography and making intelligent observations of nature while walking in the country or along the seashore.
6. Finally, science study can contribute to the development of ethical character "by establishing a more adequate conception of truth and a confidence in the laws of cause and effect" (National Education Association, 1920, p. 14).

In the relatively short time between 1893 and 1920, the justification for science in the curriculum had shifted from an argument based almost exclusively on science's ability to develop one's intellectual skills, especially the ability to observe accurately and reason inductively on the basis of evidence, to one based on science's ability to develop an individual who would be a happy and contributing member of society. The discrediting of faculty psychology in the early 1900s brought with it a belief that general mental abilities could not be developed indirectly. To be useful, knowledge must be specifically related to the object of interest. The fundamental difference between the two positions was that under the one argument education was viewed as indirectly useful; under the other, it was useful only as it had direct consequences for everyday life. Under the first rationale, difficult science and mathematics courses did not have to have immediate relevance as long as it could be said that they developed the ability to think; under the second rationale, the immediate relevance was essential.

These differing positions had a number of important implications for science education. First, under the 1920s justification of science, the specific applications of science became the most important component of the program. In 1893, thoughtful critics of traditional education viewed everyday applications as important stimulators of student interest and an important part of a full conceptual understanding of the subject, but these applications were not the justification for science teaching. Second, under the 1893 argument, ideas about teaching and learning leaned more toward inductive approaches as a way to develop generalized observational and reasoning skills. This put the laboratory at the center of 1893 pedagogy in science. By 1920 the everyday world of the student had become the science laboratory. The student had to experience socially useful science in the real world.

Perhaps somewhat more than the 1893 reformers, the revisionists of 1920 insisted that the subject matter of science be organized in such a way that students could comprehend it on their own terms and in relation to their own experiences rather than on the basis of the expert's understanding of the structure of the discipline. In the language of the day, educators in 1920 preferred a psychological rather than a logical approach to course organization. The following statement from the 1920 science committee's report expresses their feelings about the importance of this psychological approach.

> Science for high-school students has been too largely organized for the purpose of giving information and training in each of the sciences, the material being arranged in accordance with the logical sequence recognized by special students of that science. . . . Not only is science organized and tested knowledge which in the process of testing has become highly classified, but true science includes the *process* of organizing, testing, and determining the effectiveness of knowledge. The common method of science teaching too often has been that of presenting the so-called essentials with their definitions and classifications and of subordinating or omitting the common-place manifestations of science in home, community, civic, and industrial situations which make it most easily possible for the learner to practice science. (National Education Association, 1920, p. 16)

Although the two positions contained significant differences, it is important to see that they shared common values as well. Both groups of educators recognized that science was different from other school subjects because it dealt with the physical world, and for this reason direct interaction with natural phenomena was important. In addition, both groups were sufficiently influenced by child-centered approaches to teaching that they were generally in agreement about the importance of using instructional materials that were interesting to the student.

Goals of Science Education

The reports from the individual science subcommittees provide a clear idea of what science education leaders in 1920 felt science teaching should try to accomplish and the strategies that should be implemented in order to achieve those goals. There were four subcommittee reports, one for each of the subject areas of physics, chemistry, and biology, and a fourth for general science. In 1893, a number of subjects were vying for a place in the secondary school curriculum. By 1920, most schools had settled on biology, chemistry, and physics as the three dominant courses. These were usually preceded by a general science course that was intended as an introduction to the three specific subject areas. Specialized courses in zoology, botany, astronomy, physical geography, and physiology still existed as electives in some places, but they had clearly lost ground to the three subjects for which reports were submitted in 1920.

Five major goals of science education were evident in the statements of the subcommittee members. First, there was the ever present interest in improving the general welfare of society through education. This involved dispensing information that would be of service in one's daily life. It included knowledge related to personal and public health, such as sex education and knowledge of sanitation, as well as knowledge that helped one get along with modern technology in the home and in other everyday settings. It also included the development of a greater appreciation on the part of the citizenry for the role of science in society. These things could be accomplished through the selection of specific content that addressed each socially relevant issue—public health, heating and ventilating systems, electrical appliances, and so on.

A second goal of science teaching was to develop science-related avocational interests and an enjoyment of nature, and a third was to interest students in further study of science in anticipation that they might choose to pursue science as a career and contribute to advancing the frontiers of scientific knowledge. The second and third goals were approached by making sure the content was related to the experience of the students; by making the subjects interesting, relevant, and meaningful; and by using discussions of the lives and accomplishments of great scientists to inspire and motivate the effort of students.

A fourth goal, and one that received somewhat less attention than the others in the subcommittee reports, was that science teaching should develop the students' abilities to observe, to make careful measurements of phenomena, to classify observations, and to reason clearly from what they observed. Science educators did not make as much of this goal as they had 25 years earlier, and they were careful not to make claims about the generalizability of these skills to other contexts. Mental discipline, which characterized the nineteenth-century justification of science teaching, was no longer believed to be possible. But, in spite of changes in thinking about the general transferability of learning, there were clear and repeated references to the development of mental abilities, if only in relation to the specific subject at hand. The chemistry subcommittee, for example, said that one of the principal aims of chemistry teaching was "to develop those specific interests, habits, and abilities to which all science study should contribute" (National Education Association, 1920, p. 36). And the physics group said: "Education must develop certain specific interests, ideals, habits, and powers, as well as an essential body of knowledge" (p. 50). This statement by the physics group was followed by a list of abilities that physics teaching could develop, including skill in careful observation and the interpretation and classification of those observations. No claims were made, however, that science study could develop the mind for use in other settings.

This fourth goal, which involved developing the mental abilities of observation and reasoning, was addressed by placing students in the role of scientists, that is, making students investigators of genuine problems. The "project" or "problems" approach was used to orient a student's efforts toward the solution of problems that were real to the student. Students would utilize the laboratory, the library, reference books in the classroom, and out-of-school excursions to seek answers to their questions.

Finally, and somewhat ironically given the clear focus of the CRSE on applied science, one of the most strongly emphasized goals of the subcommittees was the fifth one—the full understanding of the principles of each separate science field. Throughout their discussions there were countless references to students' gaining a coherent and organized knowledge of scientific principles. Chemistry, biology, and physics had an organized content developed by chemists, biologists, and physicists, and it was that content that was to be taught. Chemistry was to include an understanding of Avogadro's hypothesis, laws of combining weights, and atomic theory; biology was to include Darwinian theory and the relation between structure and function in organisms; and physics was to include the laws of motion and conservation of energy.

It was this fifth goal that, more than the others, determined the teaching strategies that would be used. It had its impact because of the particular way in which a "full understanding of the principles of science" was interpreted. There were two key aspects of this goal that members of the science subcommittees emphasized and that determined their recommended strategies for science instruction. The first was that the theories, laws, and generalizations of the science fields must not be taught in isolation as meaningless abstractions to be memorized. Principles of science must be organized in such a way that students would understand and remember them. It was felt that one way to do this was by creating large, coherent units of instruction in which relationships could be drawn between related principles, but it also involved relating the principles of the sciences to the life experiences of the students. The second aspect of the full understanding of science that these science educators emphasized was that science principles must be understood in relation to their applications, both the logical scientific applications and their socially relevant applications.

Recommendations for Science Instruction

In support of the first aspect of "understanding science," a major part of the reorganization of science teaching in 1920 included identifying unifying themes or topics that could act as umbrellas for large amounts of content and relating the various facts and principles to those unifying themes. If the themes or topics were broad and interesting to the student, it was anticipated that learning would be enhanced. In chemistry, for example, the predominant way of teaching about the elements had been to focus on each element's occurrence, its physical and chemical properties, methods of obtaining the element, its uses, and its important compounds. These facts were taught as isolated information to be memorized. It was argued that this approach should be replaced by a system in which information about the elements was gained through thematic study. For example, the study of fertilizers was cited as a possible unifying topic. Other broad topics included a thorough study of the chemistry of the atmosphere or the chemistry of water. It was also recommended that chemistry principles that had relevance in many contexts be applied throughout the course, not just in a single unit. Principles of oxidation and reduction, acids and bases, and hydrolysis should be returned to frequently throughout the course. The physics subgroup referred to this strategy of coming back to certain principles in different contexts throughout the course as a "spiral" method of treatment (National Education Association, 1920, p. 58).

Closely tied to the use of unifying themes to organize content was the use of projects or problems as a mode of organization. It was felt that content organized around a question or problem that was real to the student would produce greater understanding of the principles of science. Thus the physics group said:

> The teaching of the past has too frequently assumed that a principle may be readily grasped if only it be once stated in clear language and illustrated by a few examples, and that it may then be generally applied with comprehension and completeness. It is now recognized that principles may be best arrived at and comprehended through solving problems. From such experiences the teacher should guide and stimulate the pupils to recognize that they must arrive at the generalizations by their own mental processes. (National Education Association, 1920, p. 49)

Speaking more specifically of the use of problem solving as an instructional strategy, the physics group said:

> The unit of instruction, instead of consisting of certain sections or pages from the textbook, or of a formal laboratory exercise, should consist of a definite question, proposition, problem, or project, set up by the class or by the teacher. Such a problem demands for its solution recalling facts already known, acquiring new information, formulating and testing hypotheses, and reasoning, both inductive and deductive, in order to arrive at correct generalizations and conclusions. This method calls for an organization in which information, experimental work, and methods of attack, all are organized with reference to their bearings on the solution of the problem. (National Education Association, 1920, p. 52)

The project, or problem, method would then serve both to organize content and to develop skills of independent inquiry. As such, it became an important part of reorganized science instruction in 1920.

The second part of "understanding science" was understanding science in relation to its applications, especially those that were encountered in the everyday world. Science principles were considered to be thoroughly understood only when they could be used to explain common experience. If the knowledge went no further than the classroom and the laboratory, then it was incomplete knowledge. It was important for students to know that the same principles studied in school applied in the out-of-school world as well. Knowledge that could not be applied to natural, real-world events was considered isolated, bookish, and useless. To understand chemistry or physics or biology was to understand the principles of those subjects in their relation to the industrial and technological world of 1920. The point was to understand biology in its relation to health and hygiene and agricultural production, physics in relation to pumps and pulleys and household appliances, and chemistry in relation to industrial manufacturing, photography, and cooking.

Given this emphasis on applied knowledge, it is easy to see how teachers might have focused on the second aspect of understanding science at the expense of the first, that is, on the coherence of the principles of the sciences themselves. Even though the writers of this report never had such a completely applied focus as their intention, their enthusiasm for social relevance made the overemphasis on applications a problem that was difficult to avoid. Consider the impact that the following statement by the chemistry subcommittee might have had on classroom teachers.

> In the past, chemical laws, theories, and generalizations have usually been taught as such, and their applications in industry and daily life have been presented largely as illustrative material. In the reorganized course, this order should be reversed. Laws and theories should be approached through experimental data obtained in the laboratory and through applications with which the pupil is already familiar and in which he has a real interest. (National Education Association, 1920, p. 36)

By placing the applications first, the basic principles of the disciplines could, and often did, become lost.

Besides this general applied approach to teaching science, the reports of the science subcommittees also discussed a number of specific practices they believed should be used in science teaching and others they considered inappropriate. One of the most thoroughly discussed instructional practices was the use of the laboratory. Even though the laboratory had become just one in a list of acceptable modes of science instruction by 1920, it was still considered to be an essential part of the experience of learning science. Following the early fascination with the laboratory as the primary form of instruction in the late nineteenth century, other strategies took their place alongside laboratory instruction in the early twentieth century. The teacher demonstration, the lecture, the recitation, field trips, and individual and group projects all joined the laboratory as important components of well-rounded science instruction. But, despite its recognized value, there were problems with laboratory instruction, and each of the science subcommittees commented on the misuse of the laboratory and ways to correct that misuse.

THE LABORATORY.   The biology subcommittee was concerned that too much time was wasted in the laboratory on useless activities and not enough on the development of important ideas. They mentioned the time spent "in detailed microscopic work, in experiments which can not be understood, and in elaborate drawings to keep the children occupied until the end of the period" (National Education Association, 1920, p. 34). They felt that the laboratory should be viewed as a means to an end, namely to "develop a consistent chain of significant ideas . . . [through] concrete experience and instruction. The primary question is not what plant or animal types may be taken up in the laboratory, but what ideas may best be developed in the laboratory" (p. 35). Most important, they felt that the biology laboratory was only a substitute for the out-of-doors. "Living things, to be appreciated and interpreted correctly, must be seen and studied alive, if possible in the open, where they will be encountered in life" (p. 35).

The chemists were equally concerned about wasted efforts in the laboratory. In their words: "Too many experiments involve repetition of work described in the text or have no outcome beyond the mere doing and writing in the note book" (National Education Association, 1920, p. 39). Concerning the notebook they said that it

> has often been a fetish with chemistry teachers, and time has been demanded for making a record which, while beautiful in appearance and completeness, is yet full of needless repetition and useless detail. The notebook should not destroy the interest attached to an experiment, for the experiment is not for the notebook but for the pupils' clearer understanding of important chemical facts. (National Education Association, 1920, p. 39)

The real purpose of the laboratory should be to pose problems or questions that the students would seek to answer because they were interested in doing so.

The physics group found most of the current uses of the laboratory to be unsatisfactory and proposed that the project or problem be the central focus of laboratory work. They were particularly critical of the lists of approved laboratory exercises used for college admission, exercises that had become a central feature of most courses in high school physics. They said:

> The high-school physics laboratory is too often thought of as place in which to "verify laws," to "fix principles in mind," to "acquire skills in making measurements," or to "learn to be accurate observers." With a project or a problem as the unit of instruction and its solution as the motive for work, the pupil should go to the laboratory to find out by experiment some facts that are essential to the solution of his problem, and that can not be obtained at first hand by other means. With such a motive he is more nearly in the situation of the real scientist who is working on a problem of original investigation. He is getting real practice in the use of the scientific method. (National Education Association, 1920, p. 53)

The appropriate use of the laboratory was to apply the scientific method to problems that were of interest to the student. As an example, the group cited the difference in interest aroused by an exercise to determine the specific gravity of a particular liquid in the laboratory and one in which the specific gravity of milk delivered to students' homes was calculated to find out if any of it had been watered before delivery.

All of the science subcommittees felt that the main purposes of the laboratory were to solve problems that were of interest to the student and to develop an understanding of science principles through direct observation of natural phenomena. The science subcommittees also talked about developing such mental abilities as inductive reasoning and observation, but this goal did not have the prominence that it had when the Committee of Ten touted the benefits of laboratory instruction in 1893. In addition, when observational accuracy, skill in manipulating scientific equipment, and ability to draw conclusions from data were discussed, it was not in the context of general intellectual training, but as part of the process of solving problems that had both social and personal relevance.

THE IMPORTANCE OF STUDENT INTEREST.   Besides their concern about the proper use of the laboratory, another issue that ran through the reports of the subcommittees was the importance of student interest and the student's involvement in learning. The chemistry group said:

> Some motive, some compelling desire to know, must actuate the pupil in any study which is really educative. Progress in chemistry, therefore, is dependent upon a specific purpose, a conscious need to learn the facts and their underlying causes of explanation. The educational value of any problem depends upon the degree to which the pupil makes it his own and identifies himself with it. (National Education Association, 1920, p. 38)

The biology subcommittee gave an example of how student interest could be utilized in teaching the principles of the interdependence of organisms in the environment. Rather than teaching the principles in an abstract and factual way, the teacher and students could investigate "the war between organisms" (National Education Association, 1920, p. 31) that was being waged in a nearby vacant lot. Information could be gathered about the number of species of plants found in the lot, which ones occupied the greater area, and the relation between those organisms and ones in adjacent lots. Students could try to determine how the various plants got their foothold, and they could predict whether they would be able to keep it. They could study the leaf, stem, and root systems of the plants, as well as their reproductive capacities, in order to explain the status of the plants in this vacant lot.

In all of the science subcommittees there was a firm belief in the value of student interest. It was considered of utmost importance that the content of the individual sciences be related to things that students were already familiar with from both in-school and out-of-school experiences. Interest was an educational doctrine that had been elaborated by Herbart, William James, Charles Eliot, and John Dewey. In 1920, it was firmly entrenched in the thinking of American educators. If the student was not motivated to know, teaching would almost certainly fall on deaf ears. Part of the motivation to know came when new knowledge was connected to old. If new material was isolated and not connected with what was already known, the motivation to learn was limited. Finally, to be socially useful as it related to the interests of students, the knowledge should be relevant to the real-world experiences of the students for both the present and the future.

DIFFERENTIATED COURSES FOR THE COLLEGE-BOUND?   Most of what was written in the subcommittee reports was consistent with the goals laid down in the Cardinal Principles of 1918. But there were some areas in which the science subcommittees took a somewhat different tack than the larger group. The issue of college entrance requirements and differentiated courses for different groups of students was essentially ignored by the science groups. Only the chemistry group said anything at all about differentiation. After briefly describing a possible differentiated chemistry course for domestic use and several courses that might be part of a technical curriculum, they said that it still remained to be seen whether such differentiation would be successful. Concerning college admission, the specific courses in biology, chemistry, and physics that were elaborated in the report were intended for general use as well as for those planning to go to college. The chemistry group noted that a problem with the old courses in chemistry was that they were oriented too much toward those students who would pursue additional, advanced courses in science. Their solution, however, was not to create separate courses for separate needs but to modify the chemistry course so that it would appeal to the practical interests of all students. The biology and physics subcommittees made no mention at all of differentiated courses for college admission or for any other purpose. The courses they described in their report were meant to be general-purpose courses that would be taken by all students regardless of their probable life work. The main interest of the science subcommittees was focused on how to make science courses more interesting, more useful, and more relevant to the everyday lives of all students.

Reactions to Reorganized Science

Not everyone was convinced of the wisdom of the new approach. First there were those who wanted to retain the "fundamentals" and a continued emphasis on traditional approaches to education. In 1915, as the practical science movement was gaining momentum, John M. Coulter, who was at that time a professor at the University of Chicago and had been a member of the Conference on Natural History of the Committee of Ten, talked about the problems of focusing on only those things within the experience of the students: "That our science teaching should consist only in explaining to a student what he encounters in his own experience, is to limit his life, rather than to enrich it by extending his horizon" (Coulter, 1915, p. 99). Also critical of the practical sciences was Hanor Webb of the West Tennessee State Normal School in Memphis, Tennessee. According to Webb (1915):

> We cannot expect *every* fact we teach to have a visible and immediate relation to life. It may be an evil, but it seems to be a necessary one, that the student must early learn some *terms,* that the language of science may be intelligent to him. Some *rules* must be formulated for him in thoroughly scientific language—some things must be learned by heart. A few topics seem to require a certain amount of old fashioned drill, for I have conscientiously tried to teach them successfully without it. . . . I am sure that the great body of the science teachers of our Nation will have little patience with those who hold the "fundamentals" up to ridicule. Well balanced people recognize the necessity of a foundation for every structure. We must first build our wall before we spread our "practical" paint upon it. (pp. 681–682)

Even more vigorous in his condemnation of the excesses of applied science was Robert Bradbury (1915), head of the Department of Science in the Southern High School in Philadelphia. He took issue with a number of suggestions that had been made for the improvement of chemistry teaching, specifically "that the 'theory' be cut out of the courses, that the work be made more 'practical,' [and] that the subject be 'brought closer to the lives of the pupils'" (p. 783). The first problem he observed was that the textbooks that had been created to accommodate the new approach produced an unsuitable marriage of theory and applications:

> They begin with a hundred pages of formal chemistry given in a purely didactic way. This portion is a kind of highly condensed and abstract grammar of chemical science and is apparently offered in the hope that the student will be able to apply the principles in the work that follows. The remaining pages are devoted to such subjects as lime, cement, pottery, inks, electric furnaces, pigments, etc. In fact, the books are, to all intents and purposes, elementary chemical technologies. . . .
> We should firmly grasp the fact that in changing from chemistry to technology, we are deserting knowledge of proved permanent worth to deal in information whose chief characteristic is the evanescence of its value. The technology we teach now will merely mislead our students ten years hence, unless they have been able to keep up with the progress of the subject. . . .
> It seems to me little short of robbery to waste [a student's] course with chickenfeed of the fruit-spot, ink-spot, grease-spot, garbage-can type—a proceeding which leaves him, at the end, ignorant of chemistry, but the fortunate possessor of a few bits of household information. (Bradbury, 1915, pp. 785–786)

Bradbury was not criticizing the kind of science teaching that was proposed by the science committee of the CRSE or other thoughtful science educators of the day, but rather the misinterpretation and the misapplication of those ideas. Ever since the notion of practical and applied science courses had been discussed, it had been with the understanding that the applications would enrich the theory of the sciences. Even those who suggested that the applications be used as the starting point of science teaching believed the applications would always refer back to the science theory to which they applied. It was the excesses of the approach that Bradbury opposed, not the use of technology itself. Technology had its place, but that place was subordinate to the teaching of chemical theory. As Bradbury (1915) said:

> The wise teacher will vitalize his work by constant brief references to the applications. He will keep the tremendous industrial importance of chemistry continually before his students, but he will do this without discarding the main object. The proposition to omit chemistry from the high school curriculum and to substitute elementary technology for it is merely another instance of that muddle-headed worship of the word "practical" which is the bane of Anglo-Saxon thinking. (p. 787)

Muddle-headed or not, "practical" science was "good" science to teachers in the early years of the twentieth century. A study reported by Otis Caldwell (1909) in *School Science and Mathematics* showed that 25% of surveyed teachers stressed the practical aim. The following year, Hunter (1910) found that 43% of teachers whom he surveyed identified the practical aim as important. And five years later, Downing (1915) found that over 50% of the teachers responding to his survey listed the practical aim among the most important aims of science teaching.

Most educators were convinced that science concepts should be related to the everyday lives of students through a variety of home and industrial applications. The use of familiar materials would make the courses more interesting, learning would proceed more smoothly, and an important obligation to the welfare of society would be met. But relevance was a more subtle idea than the easy terms *practical science* and *applied science* implied. And it carried with it the potential for misinterpretation by those whose own education in science did not provide a thorough grasp of the relationship between theory and the applications of that theory. Without a full understanding of those important relationships, applications as well as theory were often taught in isolation and without meaning by unprepared teachers.

For those committed to the ideas proposed by the science committee of the CRSE, progress seemed slow indeed. In 1920, the year the science report was issued, George R. Twiss, chairman of the CRSE subcommittee on physics, showed his unhappiness with the failure of teachers to adjust their teaching to the new methods. He said it was

> discouraging to those of us who are . . . in touch with educational work through field observation, that this leavening process has been so slow in modifying the actual practice of the great majority of science teachers. Those who . . . keep up with the new books and papers on science teaching which are coming out from time to time would be surprised . . . how few science teachers have caught the new spirit, and how few the schools are in which science is really being reorganized or changed in any way from the subject matter and methods of twenty years ago. (Twiss, 1920, p. 2)

Science teaching was being reorganized, but the process was slow, and many teachers preferred to hold onto the traditional methods by which they themselves had been taught.

Summary

For the next 30 years or more, discussions in science education would focus on many of the same themes as they had in the early years of the twentieth century. The agenda for change was laid out clearly by the science committee of the Commission on the Reorganization of Secondary Education, and with few exceptions the decades that followed echoed the ideas found in that report. It was widely believed that science education should be related to the real-world experience of students, especially to those things that interested the students. This approach was expected to shore up sagging enrollments in the sciences, to produce a more thorough and long-lasting understanding of the sciences, and to give science teaching a usefulness in twentieth-century industrial society. Ideas such as the creation of an introductory general science course to precede the specialized science courses and the development of the project method of teaching would continue to be refined and developed for use in the classroom.

One significant change that was to occur in the years ahead was the creation of standardized achievement tests in each subject area. This would have an impact in several ways. For one, the knowledge gained and information acquired in science courses would take on new importance because factual knowledge was the thing most easily measured by the standardized tests. In addition, it would become increasingly easy to differentiate students on the basis of these tests and place them into science courses on the basis of their performance. With these exceptions, however, the next several decades would be a reaffirmation of the ideas developed during the first 20 years of the century and forcefully stated in the reports of the science committee of the CRSE.

Chapter 5

Social Relevance
and the Organized Disciplines

The years from approximately 1917 to 1957 represent a period often referred to as the "progressive era" in American education (Cremin, 1964). Although progressivism had its beginnings in American education in the nineteenth century and was well established in many quarters by the early twentieth century, a number of events served to define this 40-year period as the progressive era. The Cardinal Principles were published in 1918. The Association for the Advancement of Progressive Education, which was later renamed the Progressive Education Association, was organized in 1919 by Stanwood Cobb and held its final meeting in 1955. The journal of the organization, *Progressive Education*, appeared in 1924 and published its last issue in 1957. For a great number of educators this was a period of reaffirmation of many of the ideas that had been developed during the years preceding the publication of the Cardinal Principles and elaborated in the report itself. It was a period of confirmation of child-centered education, the importance of real-world applications, the social importance of knowledge, and the need to make school learning enjoyable and meaningful to the student.

As was the case in the first two decades of the twentieth century, much of the writing in science education during this 40-year period argued against traditional methods and content in favor of content that had greater social relevance and methods that would give students the tools to solve problems in their everyday worlds. Too many teachers were clinging to the old methods of instruction wherein memorization of facts and meaningless tasks dominated teaching and learning. Frustration was often expressed over the limited progress that had been made in moving toward the goals laid out in the Cardinal Principles. These criticisms were repeated over and over again, along with calls for an end to traditional education and suggestions for an improved approach to education.

A major accomplishment of this period was the establishment of a definite sequence of courses that included general science in the first year of high school followed by the specialized courses of biology, physics, and chemistry in the last three years. When the Committee of Ten issued its report, a large number of courses were competing for a place in the high school curriculum. Zoology, botany, chemistry, physics, physical geography, geology, astronomy, agriculture, physiology, and hygiene were just some of the high school science offerings. In part because of the recommendations of the Committee of Ten that only some of these courses be considered college entrance requirements and the others be considered electives, enrollments in subjects such as geology and astronomy had dwindled to almost zero by 1910, while chemistry and physics had become firmly entrenched in the system. On the other hand, the establishment of biology as a single course encompassing zoology, botany, physiology, and hygiene had made slow but steady progress through the early years of the twentieth century despite the Committee of Ten's recommendation that separate courses in either zoology or botany would provide better disciplinary training.

General Science

From the time of the 1893 report, science educators had recognized the need for a general introductory course in science. Largely because of its historic place in the school curriculum and because of its general nature, physical geography was suggested as that course by the Committee of Ten. The course would provide an overview of the earth and its processes and offer a point of departure for the other sciences. In addition, it would train the powers of observation, the powers of imagination, and the ability to reason. Between 1895 and 1910, however, physical geography enrollments experienced a steady decline from 30% of the high school population at the beginning of this period to only 19% by the end of the period. Writing of this decline, W. R. McConnell (1920) of Miami University said that geography had "not responded to educational demands. . . . Students are still memorizing facts and principles, isolated from all significance and from all relationship and where laboratory work is offered in the subject it has, in too many cases, become a mere liturgy" (p. 119).

At the same time that enrollments were declining in physical geography, a number of attempts were being made to establish a more suitable introductory course in science. For the most part, such courses took the name "general science," although individual courses differed considerably in content. Most science education researchers date the beginning of the general science movement to around 1900, but the course did not become well enough established for the Bureau of Education to collect enrollment statistics on it until 1922. So rapid was the growth in these courses that by 1922, 18.3% of all high school students were taking general science courses at any one time, compared with only 4.3% who were taking physical geography (Monahan, 1930), and in a 1925 article, W. R. Leker was able to identify approximately 40 books that identified themselves as general science texts.

Reasons for Development

There were a number of reasons for the creation of the general science courses. One was the realization that most of the high school students who were entering the system in the early twentieth century would not stay in school for more than a year or two and would have no other experience with science than this one course. Given this reality, it was important that these students have a general course that would provide an overview of the field of science, which for many would be their only exposure to the subject. The elementary school could not be counted on to accomplish this task, since science teaching at that level was limited to only occasional nature study experiences—if science was taught at all.

A second factor influencing the development of general science courses was the need to shore up declining enrollments in science generally and to make science courses more appealing to students. The specialized courses such as physics and chemistry had experienced steady declines in their enrollments relative to other school subjects since 1890. In that year, 22% of all high school students in grades 9–12 were enrolled in physics. Since less than 25% of high school students were enrolled in each of the grades, where physics was taught, this meant that virtually all students who remained in school for more than a year or two took physics. Physics was an entrance requirement in many colleges, a graduation requirement in a number of high school programs, and it held considerable historical prestige as part of an academic curriculum. By 1910, with the spirit of elective courses in full force, physics enrollments had dropped to

14% of total enrolled students and were headed even lower. Chemistry experienced similar declines, although they were not quite as dramatic as those in physics, largely because chemistry had never experienced the very high enrollments that physics had. In 1890, about 10% of all students were enrolled in chemistry, and by 1910 that number had dropped to just below 8%. In comparison, election of courses did not have this negative effect on enrollments in such traditional subjects as Latin and algebra, which rose quickly from 35% to 49% and from 46% to 56% respectively during the same period before stabilizing at those higher figures. Other of the newer courses, such as foreign languages, history, and English literature, also showed substantial gains during this period (U.S. Bureau of Education, 1911, vol. II).

Clearly, science had a problem and something had to be done about it. In his 1911 report reviewing educational progress during the previous decade, the U.S. Commissioner of Education, Elmer Ellsworth Brown, said: "Latin is holding its ground; French and German are gaining; algebra occupies a large share of time and is steady; geometry is gaining; English and history have gained materially; all the older sciences, rather strangely, are relatively falling off" (U.S. Bureau of Education, 1912, vol. I, p. 10). In his article entitled "The Present Status and Real Meaning of General Science," written in response to the commissioner's comments, Fred Barber (1915) pointed the finger at what he called "overspecialization" in the science courses. He argued that at the college level, the needs of the research specialist were determining the nature of the courses in science, and this in turn was affecting the nature of the high school courses. Although the needs of the research community could not be ignored, neither could the needs of those who would never again study science, let alone become research workers. It was essential, then, that the educational program develop science courses for those who would not specialize in science.

The answer was a general science course that would take into account the special interest and intellectual development of the young adolescent and that would be oriented toward the interpretation of the sciences in the context of everyday life. Speaking of the adolescent, Barber said:

> If he enters the high school at all it is generally for the purpose of spending one or two years, possibly three or four years, in better preparing himself for life's work—for the struggle of earning a living. The boys and girls from the laboring classes, indeed, from the masses of the common people everywhere, as well as their parents, have a right to demand

that they be shown the worth-whileness of the tasks set before them. (p. 222)

General science was the course that would provide such a practical orientation to science.

A third factor influencing the development of general science courses was the need to establish a course that would be appropriate for the newly emerging junior high school. The Committee of Ten had suggested that one way to provide a place for all of the subjects that were competing for space in the secondary school curriculum was to expand the secondary school downward to the seventh grade and to end elementary education in the sixth instead of the eighth grade. In the years following, a number of experiments with 6–6 plans and 6–3–3 plans joined the traditional 8–4 arrangement. Attempts to provide a suitable science experience for the first year of high school often merged with attempts to offer a course or courses for the last year of junior high school or for the entire grade-seven-to-nine program. By the 1930s, general science and science for grades seven to nine were one and the same.

Recommended Approaches

At the same time that general science was appearing as a course in the secondary school curriculum, there was considerable pressure to adjust the entire science curriculum to make it more relevant to the everyday lives of the students and to their future needs as citizens in a democratic society. The specialized courses such as biology, chemistry, and physics, however, tended to resist these pressures and continued to focus on the principles of each organized subject rather than on applications, integrated themes, and projects. To some extent this was because of a perceived need to use these specialized courses to prepare students for college. Thus it was the general science courses that provided a place for experimentation in the practical, applied, humanistic spirit of the Cardinal Principles. This fact led a number of writers to lament that the best experiments in science teaching were occurring not in physics or biology or chemistry, but in general science.

The statement on general science by the science committee of the Commission on the Reorganization of Secondary Education in 1920 described the role that general science was expected to play under the new arrangement of science courses. First, they said that the course was not to be a substitute for any one of the other specialized courses. It was intended to interest students in the other science courses and to provide them with information about vocational opportunities. But the course would also be useful for those students who would take only one science course. It would be the "science of common things" and the "science of common use" (National Education Association, 1920, p. 25). It would deal with problems from everyday experience. Instruction would include individual laboratory work using simple materials, teacher demonstrations, textbook reading, and extensive use of magazine articles that dealt with the current uses of science. In addition, well-planned field trips, or "excursions," were to be a regular part of the course and taken seriously as such by teachers and students.

In addition, the CRSE's science committee took the position that subject matter in this introductory course should be organized around problems to be solved and projects to be completed. Projects could focus on electric motors, ways to rid a community of mosquitoes or houseflies, how previous generations had tried to deal with problems of health and disease, or the planning involved in preparing meals for guests who would have to be fed for an extended period of time.

Concerning the content of the general science course, the National Society for the Study of Education's (NSSE) Thirty-First Yearbook Committee felt that topics should be chosen from "aspects of the environment which, from the point of view of science, are most significant in the everyday life of individuals and of society" (National Society for the Study of Education, 1932, p. 203). Topics would include: "food, water, air, clothing materials, materials of construction, fuels, plant life, animal life, heat, light, electricity, sound, machines, the weather, the climate, the sky, the crust of the earth, and the soil" (p. 198). Regardless of what was taught, the Yearbook Committee felt strongly that the scientific ideas as well as the applications of these ideas to society should be taught together.

The Yearbook Committee also believed that the students should learn about and practice the methods of science in a general science course. What was inappropriate was the memorization of facts and textbook study apart from the real objects of nature. According to the committee:

> The very nature of science and the objectives of science education in the seventh, eighth, and ninth grades prompt . . . the statement that mere lesson-assigning and lesson-hearing is a technique of instruction in science that the Committee highly disapproves. The present practice in

some schools of limiting the science work in the seventh, eighth, and ninth grades to mere textbook study and recitation cannot be too strongly condemned as a harmful procedure. Science is essentially an experimental study of materials and phenomena and requires, therefore, learning activities that are designed to solve problems relating to concrete and objective instructional materials, whether in pure science or in its applied aspects. (National Society for the Study of Education, 1932, p. 213)

Reactions to General Science

By way of these statements, the NSSE Yearbook Committee and, earlier, the science committee of the Commission for the Reorganization of Secondary Education strongly encouraged the development of general science as an integral part of the science curriculum of the secondary school. Not everyone was happy with the establishment of the general science course, however, especially when it appeared to be taking students away from the specialized courses. After presenting statistics from the U.S. Bureau of Education for 1921–1922 that showed general science enrollments to be growing and physics enrollments declining, W. R. Leker (1925) said: "General science has made rapid progress and it is interesting to know why general science is occupying first rank as a science course. It is crowding out many other sciences that were once considered important" (p. 724).

Also in response to the issue of increasing enrollments in general science and decreasing enrollments in the other science courses, Robert Millikan (1925) showed that the decline in enrollments in the specialized courses was essentially matched by the increase in general science enrollments and that the creation of the new general science course had not had the expected positive effect on overall science enrollments.

Millikan suggested that if general science was to remain in the curriculum it should be designed almost exclusively as a course for those who would not finish high school. He also proposed that students take each of the individual courses of biology, chemistry, and physics at the same time for three years during high school, a practice he had observed in a number of European schools during the war. In this way students would get a thorough and continuous exposure to the principles of all of the specialized sciences during their high school years. Neither proposal met with much support. The three-year plan for biology, chemistry, and physics was difficult to arrange administratively, and at least as late as 1948, general science was still a course taken by both college-bound students and students who would spend only a year or two in high school. In 1950, for example, Charles Sanford reported that 80 percent of the students entering the University of Illinois in 1948 had completed a course in general science.

Although general science quickly found a place in the secondary school science curriculum, progress was slow in organizing instruction in the spirit of the recommendations of the science committee of the CRSE or the NSSE Yearbook Committee. In an article written in 1945, J. S. Richardson talked about the challenges that general science still faced in the years ahead. On the positive side, he noted that textbooks seemed more likely to take into account student interest in the selection of topics and to provide students with more interesting activities to perform. He noted especially an improvement in the activities found in the laboratory manuals. He was concerned, however, with the lack of commitment in teacher education programs to train teachers specifically to teach general science and with the lack of interest on the part of teachers in teaching the course. He was particularly disappointed with the lack of progress in giving students practice in using the experimental method in general science classrooms.

In its successes and in its failures, the general science course was an excellent place to find the spirit of progressive education applied to science teaching. Child-centered education, social applications, and science as a method of problem solving were just some of the themes that characterized that approach. The Thirty-First NSSE Yearbook Committee summarized the philosophy of the era in relation to general science succinctly when it said:

> The demand for self-activity in our schools, the view that the child and not the subject should be the center of educational effort, the emphasis on the social values of education, the conception of education as gradual growth in the direction of habits and behaviors that make for a happy and productive life, and the growing view that subject matter is but a means to education are but a few education postulates which had direct influence upon the selection and organization of the general-science course. (National Society for the Study of Education, 1932, p. 208)

Biology

From the early part of the twentieth century until the late 1950s, courses in the biological sciences occupied a transitional place in the curriculum between the emerging general science courses on the one hand and physics and chemistry on the other. This was true both in terms of biology's position in the sequence of courses and in terms of the extent to which the focus in the course was on the needs of the student versus the structure of the discipline itself. During this time, biology was taught almost exclusively as a tenth-grade subject, following general science and preceding chemistry and physics, and it had the responsiblity of dealing with a variety of important practical issues that touched the lives of students, such as human anatomy and physiology, health and hygiene, and sex education.

Biology emerged in the early part of the twentieth century as a synthesis of three areas of the curriculum that had previously been dealt with as separate courses. Zoology, botany, and physiology were merged into a one-year course sometime around 1920. Statistics from the U.S. Bureau of Education (1911) showed that in 1910, 15.32% of all high school students in grades 9–12 were enrolled in physiology, 16.83% in botany, and 8.02% in zoology. Neither general science nor biology was listed at that time as a separate course in the official statistics. The comparatively high physiology enrollments were due to the fact that many states required students to take the course with the understanding that it would deal largely with personal health and hygiene. The enrollments in botany were in keeping with the recommendation of the Committee of Ten that if students had to select between botany and zoology, botany would be the subject of choice. By 1922, physiology enrollments had dropped to 5.08%, botany to 3.82%, and zoology to 1.53%. Biology as a separate course was now up to 8.78%, and general science to 18.27% of total four-year high school enrollments (U.S. Bureau of Education, 1924).

Uncertainty Concerning Methods and Content

This trend toward a single unified biology course continued in the years ahead. It was not clear, however, what the focus of that course would be. During the nineteenth century, the disciplinary value of the individual biological subjects had been emphasized. Students were expected to make observations of numerous plants and animals, memorize detailed descriptions of their features, and make dissections and careful drawings of those specimens. Morphological study was considered to have disciplinary value. By 1910, the agitation for more applied and practical courses had become intense, and biology as a new course was forced to consider the new social relevancy arguments in the context of these older morphological and natural history approaches.

The result of these competing pressures was that during the period from 1920 to the 1950s a great deal of uncertainty existed in the field of biology teaching concerning appropriate content and methods. In a 1930 article, Alfred Kinsey identified the variety of approaches to biology teaching that were being used:

> Inquiry among high school teachers indicates that we are drilling our students in the details of certain morphological types, or that we are trying to give them a general introduction to all the plants and animals with which they may come in contact; that we are teaching textbook facts as so much Latin grammar and sentences to be memorized and dissected; or that we are emphasizing and using demonstrations, laboratory, independent projects, or field work according to our varying dispositions and indispositions, or, incidentally, our conception of the importance of the so-called inductive method of education; that we are, in short, not quite clear whether Mendelian heredity or the physiologic effects of cigarettes and coffee, whether crayfish endopodites, exopodites, and baasipodites, or artificial resuscitation, the concept of evolution, or the daily use of the tooth brush are the more important materials to present the average future citizen who is in our classrooms. (p. 374)

Twenty years later a similar complaint was heard from Paul Klinge (1950). He said that some biology courses were courses in nature study. Others dealt with cookbook-style workbooks, lab manuals, and "standard recipes" called experiments. Some teachers focused on the theme of conservation throughout their course. Others made extensive use of the science library, and still others tried to fit everything into the "mold of human biology" (p. 380).

The Student or the Subject?

What was certain was a lack of agreement and an absence of strong commitment to any particular approach to biology teaching. The major themes of this period had to do with the old and the new, with trying to decide exactly what was meant by the new and what was wrong with the old. It had to do with the organized subject matter on the one hand and the applications of that subject matter to the lives of students on the other. How far could one go in the direction of social applications and still maintain the integrity of the science? How far could one go in the direction of the structure of the science and still maintain an experience that was meaningful to the student? These were the question with which biology educators wrestled during the 1920s, 1930s, 1940s, and beyond.

The nature of the debate is evident in some of the statements of the science committee of the Commission on the Reorganization of Secondary Education. Although the committee strongly advocated the teaching of applied, practical science that was relevant to the lives of students, in their reports they were equally firm in their conviction that the organized study of the science came first. In their preliminary report, issued in 1915, they said:

> The committee maintains that *unity of subject matter in any course in science is of first importance*, by which is meant that the subject matter should be so organized that appreciation of *underlying principles* shall form the foundation of the student's knowledge, thus giving him a scientific basis for the organization of his knowledge. (Peabody, 1915, p. 44; emphasis in the original)

In their final report of 1920, the committee reiterated its belief in the role of organized science. The committee believed that "coherence and unity of subject matter" were important in science courses at all levels. "Only through such sequence and unity does a child or adult gain a clear vision of the significant principles of a science" (National Education Association, 1920, p. 31).

Most writing of the period, however, was aimed at moving biology teaching in the direction of the progressive principles that were promoted by the science committee of the CRSE, since much of the classroom practice was too much in keeping with the traditional biology courses of the nineteenth century, which had emphasized organized principles at the expense of applications. In 1940, Thomas Smyth found it necessary to reiterate the principles of applied, socially relevant, child-centered science and to criticize a biology curriculum endorsed by the National Association for Research in Science Teaching because it succumbed to college preparatory pressures. To make his point, Smyth examined the proposed unit on protoplasm and the cell.

> Just how important is it for the high school student to go into details concerning the nature and properties of protoplasm, or how worthwhile is it to delve into cytology and know the morphology and physiology of the parts of a cell? Why burden the high school group with the intricacies of mitosis? Is there nothing more worth bringing to this group?
>
> If we are teaching for the enrichment of human life the time is here now when we must pack our high school science courses with life values and not fill them with a lot of stuff that few will ever use or even think of again the rest of their days. We must teach our science for the sake of the student and not for the sake of the subject. We must teach to arouse

a greater genuine interest in science because we make it real and believe in it powerfully ourselves. (pp. 258–259)

The student or the subject, which was more important? Could both be accommodated in the same course? Could the principles of biology be taught in a way that was meaningful and interesting to the student? Could the goal of social relevance be accepted as important and not trivialized to the point of calling it "toothbrush biology"? One of the most comprehensive attempts to do so was made by Elliot Downing, a member of the Thirty-First Yearbook Committee of the NSSE and author of the yearbook's chapter on biology.

Downing took the position that although there were many issues that individuals faced in their daily lives that involved biology, there were a relatively small number of fundamental biological principles that pertained to these issues. What we should do in our biology courses, therefore, was to teach the most important biological principles and not a long list of facts. But teaching the principles alone was not enough. Students also had to be given specific practice in applying those principles to typical life problems. Downing, along with many other educators who had been influenced by the research of Thorndike and Woodworth (1901) on transfer of learning, were convinced that skills learned in school did not automatically transfer to other contexts. In other words, the mind was not strengthened by school learning experiences in such a way as to increase one's ability to solve out-of-school problems. The applications, or at least types or classes of applications, needed to be taught directly and practiced if they were to become part of the student's problem-solving repertoire.

Downing also took the position that in order to understand biological principles, students needed prior sensory experiences with the objects of study. These experiences had to be either recalled for the student or provided at the time the biological principle was being taught. Downing provided an illustration of this idea in the context of a unit on the germ theory of disease. He said that most students were unfamiliar with the kinds of things that could be seen under a microscope and that to understand the germ theory of disease, experience with this microscopic world was essential. Students should be shown these microorganisms moving about and feeding and reproducing. They should see that bacteria reproduce to form colonies of their own kind and that the dust of the air contains microorganisms that will grow and multiply under favorable conditions. They need to see for themselves that microorganisms are present on their fingers and on their teeth and on the feet of insects. The student needs to see that bacteria can be killed by heat and germicides. In all of this, the most important thing is that the student come to see these things directly and not just be told them by the teacher. And the teacher needs to remember how long it took him or her to build up an understanding of the germ theory of disease and to realize that many of the words that mean something to the teacher are meaningless to the student. According to Downing, the students may glibly use these words, but to them "it is so much parrot talk." Finally, this material needs to be related to the life experience of the students. "Why wash the hands before meals? Why clean the teeth? Why should we use covered garbage cans? Why do we have isolation hospitals for smallpox and diphtheria?" (National Society for the Study of Education, 1932, p. 231).

Development of Scientific Thinking

But an understanding of the major principles of biology and their relation to real-world problems was only one of the goals of biology teaching listed by the NSSE Yearbook Committee. Another was the development of skill in scientific thinking. Downing's approach to the development of scientific thinking had three parts. To think scientifically one needed to know what the elements of scientific thinking were and what errors one was likely to make when applying scientific thinking, and one needed to practice the skills involved.

One way to make the elements of scientific thought known to students was through illustration. Downing suggested that Robert Koch's work on tuberculosis could be used as an example of the process of inductive thinking in action. Downing pointed out how Koch searched for regularities in the bodies of patients who had died of tuberculosis, and how he isolated the suspected disease-causing organism. Koch then hypothesized that if the isolated organism were the cause of tuberculosis, injecting it into laboratory animals would produce tuberculosis in them. Based on his observations and the logic of his experiment, he concluded that tuberculosis was indeed caused by the bacterium that he had originally found in tuberculosis victims. Through examples such as this, students would see the care required to make accurate observations, the need to eliminate possible alternative explanations for the phenomenon in question, and the role that hypothesis formation and testing played in scientific work.

In addition to making students conscious of the processes involved in scientific thinking, Downing recommended a number of classroom activities that could be used so that clear thinking would become an outcome of biology teaching.

> Let pupils be on the lookout for good examples of scientific thinking in the textbook they are using. Instruction should be given in setting up controlled experiments and in evaluating controls of various sorts. . . . After having had considerable contact with examples of good reflective thinking, they might collect magazine advertisements that do violence to the elements and safeguards. Many of them are biological in character. . . . Is there any assurance in the advertisement that the facts stated have been accumulated by accurate, extensive observations made under a variety of conditions? Is there any evidence that the statements made have been experimentally verified? Are they capable of such verification? Do the conclusions reached on the basis of the so-called facts seem to you impartial and unprejudiced? Might the facts be accounted for in some other way? In other words, have all possible hypotheses been considered? (National Society for the Study of Education, 1932, pp. 237–238)

To the NSSE Yearbook Committee, developing the scientific way of thinking was clearly an essential goal of the biology program.

A thorough understanding of the principles of biology in relation to sensory experiences and to everyday applications, knowledge of and practice in clear scientific thinking, and the need for social relevance were some of the themes of biology teaching during the first half of the twentieth century. How to balance these goals with one another in the context of historical precedents that emphasized memory of facts was the major problem with which biology educators struggled. Modern educational theory called for one approach, but teaching practices and textbook design often led students in another direction. The lack of a resolution of this issue and the failure to provide the majority of students with a learning experience of obvious value led some to say that biology did not even belong as a science course in the high school curriculum. Coming to the defense of biology in response to these critics, Paul Klinge (1950) wrote:

> Biology deserves to return to the fold of the sciences. Its importance is indisputable, but to stay with the sciences it must be taught as such, and to be taught as a science, its teacher must retain that unswerving love of the truth which shall be communicated to his students as curiosity, rather than the willing acceptance of Olympian pronouncements on the authority of that terrible trinity—text, teacher, and tests. (p. 383)

Physics

In the early part of the century, physics teachers experienced the same pressures as did those in the other sciences to make the course more practical, applied, and related to the life experiences of students. In fact, the pressures on the physics curriculum were more intense than on the other subjects because physics was the course that showed the most dramatic declines in student enrollments. In 1900, 19% of all ninth- to twelfth-grade high school students were enrolled in physics courses, but by 1915 that number had dropped to 14.2% and by 1928 to 6.8% (U.S. Bureau of the Census, 1975). The blame was laid squarely on the shoulders of the traditional, discipline-based, college preparatory physics courses that, it was claimed, had little if any relevance to the lives of most students. With declining enrollments and a rapidly increasing population of high school students who would most likely never finish high school let alone go on to college, the pressures to make the curriculum more useful to the majority of students were considerable.

Ways to Attract Students

In 1930, A. C. Monahan, formerly of the U.S. Bureau of Education, reported on a survey of opinions of science teachers, principals, and superintendents concerning why more students were not taking chemistry and physics in high school. First, many respondents said that physics and chemistry had the reputation of being difficult courses. This was especially true of physics because of the large amount of mathematics that was involved. Second, superintendents and principals felt that teachers were spending too much time on lecture and demonstration activities rather than on laboratory activities that were more in keeping with the active nature of the adolescent. Third, girls were not as interested in the physical sciences as they were in the biological sciences, and that explained some of the decrease. Fourth, science teachers said that superintendents and principals often discouraged enrollments in science courses because they were more expensive to teach than other courses.

Monahan (1930) suggested that teachers could solve the enrollment problem by making their courses "vital, practical and interesting to compensate for this 'hardness'" (p. 879). He said that much of the mathematics in chemistry and physics could be eliminated except for college-bound students. He also felt that individual laboratory experiments would "please the students" and for that reason they should be provided "even though it makes more and harder work for the instructor and takes time now given to classroom discussions on theories involved" (p. 879).

A similar theme was echoed by A. W. Hurd of Columbia University Teachers College in 1930. Hurd focused on the fact that the school population was changing and required a new educational approach. In the past, only those students who wanted to attend school did so, but now, with the new compulsory attendance laws and what he called "educational propaganda" (p. 539), many more students were in school. Based on a survey of the literature that he conducted, Hurd claimed that the most important concern to physics teachers was how to select subject matter to meet the needs of this new population of students.

Hurd's solution to the problem was to create courses that related physics to the life activities of the students. One course that he developed was based specifically on the principles elaborated by the science committee of the CRSE. Units covered such topics as hydrometers, machines, fluid pressure, heating systems, ventilating systems, humidifying systems, refrigeration, electric lighting systems, light projectors, telescopes and microscopes, color and some of its phenomena, musical instruments, X-rays and other radiations, and the automobile.

But for the most part, the physics teaching that occurred in schools was not related to the life interests of the students in the class. The Thirty-First Yearbook Committee's appraisal of the state of physics teaching showed how little progress had been made by 1932 in adapting instruction to the interests or learning styles of the students. Speaking of the physical sciences, the committee said:

> Two general ideas have governed the thinking of teachers of both physics and chemistry in the past. These ideas are the mastery of the subject matter of the field as such and the disciplinary value of the subject expressed in terms of training in scientific method. The typical reaction of the teachers of physics to the problem of what might be accomplished with boys and girls in the course as it is offered in the high school seems to be, "the purpose of teaching physics is to teach physics—what more?". . .
>
> The workers in the field of physics have been especially in need of some stimulus which would center attention upon the needs of the learner rather than upon the mere structure of the subject matter involved in the instruction. (National Society for the Study of Education 1932, pp. 246–248)

More than ten years after the science committee of the CRSE had issued its final report in 1920 and more than 20 years after the pressures to adjust the science curriculum had begun to mount, physics was still oriented toward the memorizing of facts and principles, with little attention paid to the everyday world of the learner.

The Learner Versus the Content

The Thirty-First Yearbook Committee tried to take a balanced position on the issue of the learner versus the content. In the first of three major objectives for physics teaching, the committee emphasized both the understanding of the subject matter of physics and the ability to use it to solve real problems. They felt strongly enough about the need for a balance between the learner and the content to say:

> The first of these [objectives] does not indicate that the Committee believes in the formulation of objectives in terms of subject matter as such rather than in terms of the effects of subject matter upon the learners. The emphasis should be placed upon the *understanding* and *ability to use* which is developed within the pupil. The Committee does believe, however, that the key to such understandings and abilities to use scientific facts and principles is dependent upon an adequate determination of the essential basic concepts of science. (National Society for the Study of Education, 1932, p. 250)

The needs of the learner were important, but the physics group saw no way to meet those needs other than through the study of the organized discipline of physics. Appeals to student interest and socially relevant applications would be used to lead the students to an understanding of the organized discipline of physics itself.

Subject-matter understanding would also be enhanced by organizing the content of physics around a very small number of central concepts. The committee suggested two basic themes: the indestructibility of matter and energy and the fact that all physical phenomena are based upon energy transformations. Organization of the courses around basic concepts such as these "would avoid the traditional compartmentalization of physics into short, separate, unrelated sections, almost short courses in themselves, without meaningful interrelations" (National Society for the Study of Education, 1932, p. 255). Under the new approach each separate section of the course would be integrated with all others through its relationship to the basic concepts. In addition, specific learning experiences would be those that would have importance in the lives of the students and would contribute to the development of the basic concepts of physics. There was no need to make the subject overly abstract or distant from the daily experience of students.

Physics content was to be selected both on the basis of its application to the everyday lives of students and on the basis of its relation to the fundamental principles of the science. In addition, the committee advanced the idea that students should be taught the methods of scientific inquiry and practice those methods in physics classes. In many ways the ideas were similar to those that had been promoted earlier in the century, especially by the science committee of the CRSE in 1920. The struggle then, as in 1932, was how to organize the curriculum to appeal to student interest without abandoning the organized study of the discipline.

Criticisms of Actual Teaching Practice

By 1940, however, the state of physics teaching was still one that bore little resemblance to the ideals of either the CRSE's 1920 science committee or the NSSE's Thirty-First Yearbook Committee. In a series of articles on the plight of high school physics, H. Emmett Brown of Columbia University Teachers College laid out the current state of affairs and offered suggestions for the improvement of physics teaching. He focused first on the failure of educators to take into account the principle of *interest* in physics teaching. According to Brown (1940a), teachers continued to include subject matter that held no interest for the student and to exclude material that was interesting. To make his point, he described the content of a typical high school physics textbook.

> Turn to almost any modern text. Chapter 1 in a typical one will deal with measurement. (Why, oh why, must we always begin that way?) Somewhat further on there come a dreary discussion of vector forces probably beginning with a definition of terms, and then going on for eight or more pages to deal with resultants, components, force parallelograms, and all the rest. (Just how close to the interests of a modern adolescent is this sort of material anyway?) This same adolescent *may* be quite interested in the consideration of what constitutes safe speed for his own automobile driving and in the underlying scientific principles but not in the text's tediously academic presentation of accelerated motion and Newton's laws of motion. (p. 157)

Besides the fact that the courses held little interest for students, Brown (1940b) felt that there was an excessive use of mathematics in high school physics. He associated this with a tendency to model the courses after college courses and with a continuing belief that mathematically difficult courses had disciplinary value. Brown argued that the major problem with the use of mathematics in physics teaching was that many teachers had no idea why the mathematics was important, and quantitative work was often assigned merely as a set of tasks to perform without considering the relation of the mathematical problem to the physics principles.

The solution to this problem was to make connections between the quantitative relations involved in physics principles and the experiences of the students. Teachers would show students how mathematical calculations could provide interesting information about their own life experiences. As an example, Brown demonstrated how the formula for kinetic energy could be taught in the context of students' everyday experience.

He observed that most high school physics texts give the formula for the kinetic energy of a moving body. Then the texts provide a number of problems asking the students to calculate the kinetic energy of several different moving objects—and that is where the instruction ends. The formula has been used to obtain an answer but little more has been accomplished. Brown suggested that if the problems were related to the students' own experience they would be much more interesting and instructive. If, for example, the calculation of kinetic energy was used to determine how much force is exerted on an object such as a hammer driving a nail, the student might be more interested and learn more from the experience. In his example, he showed how a ½ pound hammer head moving at 30 feet per second which drives a nail ½ inch into a block of wood exerts an average force on the nail equal to a stationary weight of 168 pounds. Next he asked the students to make the same calculations about the hammer head's striking their own fingernail instead of the intended target. The calculations show that if the finger is resting on a solid object this force could be equivalent to a stationary weight of over a ton and a half. By personalizing the calculations in this way, Brown felt that science teachers could do a great deal to interest students in the study of physics.

Brown's position was that mathematics should be used in physics teaching, but it should be done in such a way that it enhanced the meaning of physics to the student, not treated merely as a set of empty disciplinary tasks to perform. This put the burden on the teacher to make clear the connections between quantitative relationships in physics and the life experiences of the students. Students would also be encouraged to think through quantitative problems to make sure that their understanding of the physics principles and quantitative relationships were sound. In addition, students would be asked to draw conclusions from sets of real data so that they could see numbers as important in the study of physics.

Chemistry

Perhaps one of the most distinctive characteristics of chemistry teaching during the first half of the twentieth century was its stability, both in content and in the percentage of high school students who chose to take the course. Unlike the biological sciences, it did not have to accommodate a variety of distinct subject matters under one course, and unlike physics it did not experience the wrenching declines in enrollment. In 1890, approximately 10% of all high school students in grades 9–12 were enrolled in chemistry classes. In the following years, chemistry enrollments declined only modestly, to 7.4% by 1915 and to 7.1% by 1928. Enrollments in chemistry remained at about 7.5% until the late 1950s, when they rose to 8.1% in 1959 and to 9.3% in 1965 (U.S. Bureau of the Census, 1975). By the 1981–1982 school year, they were at about 8.6% of total grade 9–12 enrollment (Welch, Harris, & Anderson, 1984). Chemistry, like physics, was taught throughout this period as either an eleventh- or twelfth-grade subject. Debates about which of these should be taught first were only slowly resolved in favor of chemistry during the next half century. As late as 1947–1948, about as many twelfth-graders were taking chemistry as eleventh-graders, although the ratio of seniors to juniors taking physics was about two to one (U.S. Office of Education, 1950). Also like physics, chemistry was typically a course for college-bound students, and this as much as anything influenced the content and methods of the course.

Chemistry for Social Relevance

As with the other sciences, chemistry teaching was not immune from the pressures to become more relevant, more applied, and more practical, nor from the pressures to make use of student interest to stimulate learning. And, as with the other subjects, chemistry teachers did not find it easy to balance these new demands with the older conceptions of good teaching.

Early attempts to move high school chemistry away from the traditional college preparatory emphasis and toward a more practical and useful course gave people such as Foord Von Bichowsky reason to be optimistic about the future of chemistry teaching. In a 1913 article, he wrote:

> Chemistry, in the high school of today, is breaking away from college science. It is becoming an end in itself. This is in accord with the prevailing tendency to equip the high school student for a life of usefulness, irrespective of whether that end be reached through the university or in the work shop. (p. 772)

Following these early efforts to organize instruction along more practical lines, the goals of social relevance became formalized in the statements of the science committee of the Commission on the Reorganization of Secondary Education in 1920, the Report of the Committee on Chemical Education of the American Chemical Society (ACS) in 1924, and the Thirty-First NSSE Yearbook Committee in 1932. Each of these groups struggled with the appropriate balance between social relevance and the practical applications of chemistry on the one hand, and the organized study of the subject on the other. The ACS Committee on Chemical Education, perhaps more than the others, relegated the social applications of chemistry to a secondary position. In fact the Thirty-First Yearbook Committee was quite critical of the "standard minimum course" in Chemistry that the ACS had described in 1924. The American Chemical Society established an outline of content to be used in high school chemistry and then listed two optional categories of content "not to be required for college entrance" (American Chemical Society, 1924, pp. 92–93). It was in these last two categories that the illustrative material concerning everyday uses of chemistry was placed and where such major unifying concepts as the periodic table and the electronic structure of matter appeared. In the estimation of the NSSE Yearbook Committee, this ACS-recommended outline—which they admitted had considerable influence on high school chemistry teaching—was largely descriptive chemistry and not in keeping with the new ideals of science education. As evidence of the influence of the ACS approach, a study by Cornog and Colbert (1924) showed that descriptive content occupied 55.8% of the material in the five most commonly used chemistry textbooks in 1924. Second in frequency, at 25.2% was content dealing with useful applications, whereas only 13.1% dealt with chemical theory.

Central Unifying Themes

Whereas the science committee of the CRSE had placed most of its emphasis on the applications of the sciences to the real-world experiences of students, and the American Chemical Society had opted for descriptive chemistry, the NSSE Yearbook Committee focused on ways to make the subject matter of chemistry itself meaningful to students by focusing on a limited number of unifying themes of the disciplines and by relating applications to theory. The committee proposed two possible fundamental generalizations. The first generalization was that chemical substances change during chemical reaction to form substances that behave differently than they did before the reaction occurred. The second generalization was that there is a quantitative relation between the amounts of substances that react and the amounts of substances that are produced in a chemical reaction. According to the committee:

> Pupils in high-school chemistry courses should develop better *understandings* of those fundamental concepts, major ideas, laws or principles of chemistry that will enable them *better to interpret* natural phenomena, common applications of chemical principles, and industrial applications and uses of the principles of chemistry. (National Society for the Study of Education, 1932, p. 259; emphasis in original)

Summary

How much progress had been made during the progressive era in determining what was important in science education? How much progress had been made in creating courses that would accomplish these goals? A number of important ideas were generated between 1920 and the 1950s, but in large part there was almost as much confusion at the end of the period as there was at the beginning. Seemingly intractable problems remained to be solved. In a 1945 article, David Aptekar of Mackensie High School in Detroit said:

> Critical reflective analysis of our courses indicates that many of us are victims of the "traditional approach" to the teaching of exact sciences.

Our sequence of presentation of subject matter, as outlined in current secondary school texts, follows an order of presentation that has been in mode for at least twenty years. . . . A fair criticism of our present courses is that they are too nearly limited to a "giving back" by students of information which we, or our textbook writers, deem essential. Many times we fail to distinguish between learning and memorizing. (p. 33)

In addition, there were the continuing complaints of excessive college influence on the high school curriculum; there was the difficulty of determining the appropriate use of the laboratory to accomplish important science goals; there were changes brought about by the emergence of standardized tests; and there were questions about what constituted legitimate strategies for determining what the goals of science education should be. It is these issues that will be examined in the next chapter.

Chapter 6

School Science Seeks Its Own Identity

Besides firmly establishing chemistry, biology, and physics as the predominant areas of school science and consolidating the various approaches to general science, science educators focused on four other issues during the progressive era. These included the role of the laboratory, college domination of school science, the development of standardized science tests, and the use of large-scale surveys to determine appropriate goals for science teaching. These four issues are the focus of this chapter.

The Laboratory

The science laboratory was a development of the latter third of the nineteenth century. It represented a major change in the way science was taught and a fundamental break from earlier book study of the sciences. Early laboratory work was justified primarily because of its ability to develop observational and inductive reasoning skills and because direct contact with the physical world was considered to be a unique characteristic of science study. Science educators were so enthusiastic about the potential of the laboratory to develop the powers of the mind that the laboratory became the central focus of science instruction. Often, however, the laboratory exercises did not move beyond the simple verification of scientific principles or the tedious observation of natural phenomena for purposes of mental discipline. In fact, it was the formal nature of the laboratory that was blamed in part for the declining enrollments in science courses during the early part of the twentieth century.

Between 1900 and 1920 the movement to make the sciences more practical, real, and relevant to the lives of the students included a new conception of the laboratory. The laboratory was to have a true inductive spirit. It was to be used to solve problems—problems that were interesting and real to the students and problems that had social relevance. Along with this new idea for the laboratory came the development of the project method of teaching, which used a variety of instructional practices, including laboratory work, in the solution of real-world problems. The project method as a general instructional approach was introduced by William Heard Kilpatrick in 1918 in an article that appeared in the *Teachers College Record,* entitled simply "The Project Method."

Use of the Project Method

Under the project method, socially relevant problems, rather than the disciplines themselves, were to become the basis for organizing the curriculum. Any content that was learned would come from the solution of real-world problems. The science class was an ideal place to utilize the project method because of the availability of the laboratory, and the popularity of the project method in educational circles gave considerable support to the idea that the laboratory should be used for genuine inquiry activities.

Although generally convinced of the value of problem solving in science teaching and the importance of linking scientific concepts to the world of the child's experience, educators did not agree on whether the content should be organized around socially relevant problems or around the principles of the disciplines themselves. Kilpatrick's project method placed organized disciplinary science in a clearly secondary role, advocating the organization of science courses around socially relevant problems, not the principles of the discipline. John Dewey, on the other hand, insisted that the ultimate aim of science instruction through problem solving was the mastery of a body of organized principles that had been logically arranged by scientists over the years. As Dewey (1938) said:

> Anything which can be called a study, whether arithmetic, history, geography, or one of the natural sciences, must be derived from materials which at the outset fall within the scope of ordinary life experience. . . . But finding the material for learning within experience is only the first step. The next step is the progressive development of what is already experienced into a fuller and richer and more organized form, a form

that gradually approximates that in which the subject-matter is presented to the skilled, mature person. (pp. 73–74)

Charles Pieper (1920) of the University High School in Chicago favored this emphasis on scientific rather than social problem solving. He said the course in chemistry "will be a course of solving chemical problems, of establishing chemical concepts. It will be a thoroughly scientific course" (p. 409). These chemical problems would be presented to the students or generated out of their own discussion. Then, with the problem before them, the students would seek evidence for its solution "by demonstration, experimentation, reading, consulting authorities, and in any other way possible" (p. 409).

Regardless of whether it was for scientific or social purposes, by 1920 progress had been slow in moving science laboratories in the direction of student problem solving. According to George Twiss (1920), the number of science teachers who were using inductive approaches to science teaching was very small compared to those who were utilizing book recitations and formal laboratory activities. One practical problem with using the laboratory for problem solving was that, for scheduling purposes, the laboratory periods were fixed at certain days of the week. This meant that it was almost impossible to have the kind of free interchange between the laboratory and the classroom that was essential to make the problem-solving approach work. Ruch (1920) said that the inductive method required that laboratory work precede the textbook work, and this was very difficult to accomplish when the laboratory was scheduled as it was. This led to using the laboratory mainly for confirming the principles presented in the lecture, a method that he called "the exact reverse of that demanded by induction" (p. 426).

Demonstration Versus Individual Laboratory Work

One significant threat to the development of an inductive approach to science teaching was the high cost of the laboratory. The laboratory took up space, required equipment and supplies, and used up a good portion of the time available in the schedule. Although these concerns were minor when few students attended school, they became significant as secondary school enrollments grew almost out of control. When an inductive, problem-solving approach was used, many felt that an inordinate amount of time was required and that little could be shown for it. There were two major competitors to the individual laboratory method. One of these was the paired or group laboratory experience, and the other was the teacher demonstration. It was the latter that posed the greatest challenge to the laboratory.

In 1920, educational researchers had few tools with which to conduct their investigations. Some standardized tests had been developed in the individual subjects, but these were hardly adequate for determining the effectiveness of group versus individual laboratory work or individual laboratory work versus teacher demonstrations. But, in spite of the lack of research tools, a number of experiments were attempted, which generally showed that teacher demonstrations were at least as effective as laboratory work in increasing student knowledge of science facts and principles. The effect of this research was to put the supporters of the science laboratory on the defensive. For example, N. Henry Black (1930) of Harvard University felt that science educators had gone overboard in their enthusiasm for laboratory experiments and had neglected what he called "the older form of instruction, namely, lecture-table demonstrations" (p. 366). He felt that demonstrations were needed to arouse interest in the subject and to make the subject clear. According to Black, physics concepts were difficult for students to grasp and demonstrations helped students visualize those concepts. In addition, he felt that the demonstration was a great time saver.

After a thorough investigation of the relative merits of the individual laboratory and the demonstration method in chemistry, W. W. Carpenter (1925) concluded that at least some laboratory work should be replaced by teacher demonstrations. He did not believe that all individual laboratory work should be eliminated nor that schools in the future should be built without laboratories, but he did think that more of the present laboratory exercises should be conducted by the teacher as demonstrations and only a few by the students themselves.

Similarly, the Thirty-First NSSE Yearbook Committee concluded that "in the interests of economy both of time and of money, it seems desirable to perform more laboratory exercises by the demonstration than by the individual method" (National Society for the Study of Education, 1932, p. 106). The committee did recognize, however, that not enough research had been done to determine all the benefits of laboratory instruction:

> It is very probable that experimenters have not yet been able to measure the more valuable outcomes of laboratory instruction, as a number of critics have pointed out. If there are valuable outcomes, the added expense needed to secure them may be justified, but just how valuable the laboratory experience as a whole may be, we do not yet know. (p. 270)

Although evidence against the laboratory was weak and the results were inconclusive, when the issue was framed as an economic one, the less expensive demonstration method looked appealing indeed. In their discussion of the changes brought about by the research on laboratory work, the NSSE Yearbook Committee said that school administrators watched for the results of these studies with great interest. When the results suggested that the demonstration method might lead to equal if not greater learning outcomes, administrators moved quickly to replace the individual laboratory method with the demonstration method. The Yearbook Committee said that the policy was carried out "with enthusiasm and in some cases with such complete thoroughness that certain large city high schools were constructed with no provisions whatever for individual experimentation by pupils" (National Society for the Study of Education, 1932, p. 98).

Double Versus Single Periods

Another solution to the costliness of laboratory work was to reduce the time spent in the laboratory by switching from double-period to single-period labs. L. W. Applegarth (1935) of Whiting High School, in Whiting, Indiana, conducted a study to determine the effectiveness of the two methods. Applegarth's conclusion was that the single-period lab was just as effective as the double-period lab and that the single period would result in time savings for both teacher and student. Applegarth's article, however, was accompanied by an Editor's Note warning the reader that what was measured in the study was primarily the retention of facts. "Our pupils may memorize a few facts in one laboratory period as well as in two but can we put across the higher educational objectives if we are pinched for time with individual pupils in the laboratory where some of our best work should be done?" (p. 627).

Others, such H. Clyde Krenerick of North Division High School in Milwaukee, were happy with the switch from double- to single-period laboratories because it enabled them to make a better connection between the lab and lecture room activities. With a single-period lab, no special scheduling provisions had to be made; a laboratory period was just like any other period. Therefore a teacher could have students do lab work any number of days per week, and it was always possible for the laboratory work to precede the text or lecture work and thus be used in the spirit of inductive problem solving that many preferred. Krenerick (1935) said: "The students are given an assignment and the next day they go directly to the laboratory and perform the experiment without previous classroom discussion" (p. 468).

Value of the Laboratory Debated

With the emphasis on controlled experiments to determine the value of laboratory work and pressures to demonstrate the cost-effectiveness of the laboratory, it became very easy to lose sight of the reasons that laboratories were being used in science instruction. The issue had become simply "the laboratory," regardless of how it was used, compared to "the teacher demonstration," regardless of how it was used. To their credit, the Thirty-First NSSE Yearbook Committee analyzed the variety of reasons that laboratory work might be utilized in science teaching, and they tried to think through the advantages of actual laboratory work or some other instructional device for accomplishing those purposes. They identified seven purposes of laboratory work:

1. The development of simple laboratory techniques, such as weighing, glass bending, microscopic manipulation, etc.
2. Providing and establishing for the pupil himself principles which have long since been well established and generally accepted.
3. Using the laboratory as an instrument for object, or "thing," teaching, according to the historical concepts of Pestalozzi, Comenius, and Basedow.
4. Using the laboratory for the purpose of developing better understanding and interpretations of the principles of science, as a means of better illustration.
5. To produce training in scientific method.
6. As a means of possible training in the experimental solution of the pupil's own problems.
7. The use of the laboratory as a workshop for the study of science problems which arise in the science class or in the life of the pupil. (National Society for the Study of Education, 1932, p. 270)

The Yearbook Committee concluded that the first of these goals, the development of laboratory techniques, could be accomplished in the laboratory, but that if this was to be a major goal of science teaching, then simpler activities should be assigned to students, and they should be given more direct drill in the handling and manipulating of equipment and materials. If verification of principles was to be the goal, the committee felt that this goal could be better met by the teacher at the demonstration table. It was easier and more efficient for the teacher to demonstrate the truth of some principle or relationship than it was for the student to try to do so. The committee was somewhat doubtful about whether the laboratory should be considered the primary means of teaching the scientific method. They argued that the scientific method was not just a single method but rather a set of methods and that more than laboratory work was involved. The committee felt that the best use of the laboratory was for the solution of the students' own science problems and for those science problems that developed in the classes in those subjects. Concerning the use of the laboratory for genuine problem-solving activities, the Yearbook Committee said: "It is the very essence of the original reason for the existence of every laboratory, from that of the alchemist seeking to transmute base metals into gold to that of the modern investigator seeking to split the atom" (National Society for the Study of Education, 1932, pp. 271–272).

Along the same lines, Francis Curtis provided an analysis of three major goals of the laboratory for the NSSE Yearbook Committee. The first of these three goals he called "teaching the pupil to manipulate" or permitting the pupil to "learn to do" (National Society for the Study of Education, 1932, p. 100). He said that if knowledge of laboratory techniques and procedures was the primary goal, then this might be accomplished just as well through classroom observations. But if the goal was to have students acquire manual dexterity and skill, then the individual laboratory method was essential. The second stated goal of the laboratory that he analyzed was that the student should learn to interpret experimental data. With regard to this objective, he said that the students might actually find their own manipulations to be a hindrance rather than a help to interpretation. Curtis felt that the student might get caught up in the details of the investigation and so lose sight of the point of the problem. If interpretation was the prime objective, a demonstration by the teacher might prove to be more valuable because the teacher could direct the students' attention to the key elements of the problem. The third goal Curtis referred to as "teaching the pupil the concept of the scientific method" (p. 100). By this he meant the actual method of the research scientist, including both the manipulation of materials and the interpretation of results. This he felt could be achieved in part by either individual laboratory work or by the demonstration method. He questioned, however, whether the goal itself was too specific to be included in a general liberal arts program, focused as it was on the actual practices of research scientists.

To Curtis, the laboratory had limited usefulness, its main virtue being its ability to teach students certain laboratory procedures. Skills used in the interpretation of data could be better developed by the demonstration method, and the actual conduct of experiments was not considered appropriate for general educational purposes.

Another approach to determining the value of the laboratory was to ask students how they felt about it. Joseph McGee (1935) of Seymour High School in Connecticut presented testimonials from students claiming to like chemistry laboratory work and saying that it was the most interesting part of the course. As one example: "Katherine A. writes 'I think chemistry could be made more interesting by having more laboratory work. It seems to me we do not experiment enough. We all, I am sure, would find it more worthwhile to study it if we did'" (p. 701).

In a study conducted in the Cleveland public schools in 1924, teachers were surveyed concerning their goals for teaching science and students were surveyed concerning their knowledge of those areas, what they considered important to know, and ways to improve the science courses. For biology, chemistry, physics, and general science the students listed additional practical or laboratory work more frequently than any other way to improve the courses (Cleveland Schoolmasters Club, 1925).

The themes that were identified early in this period concerning the merits of the laboratory were repeated throughout the 1930s and 1940s. Comparisons of the effectiveness of laboratory activities and classroom demonstrations, threats to the laboratory by administrators concerned about efficiency, and the potential for the laboratory to be used as a place to conduct genuine problem-solving activities were just some of the subjects that were discussed during these years. Leonard Ford (1940) of Mankato State Teachers College summarized these issues:

> Leaders in the field of education and curriculum planning are bringing about a reorganization of the high school course of study. . . . The phase of science teaching which has undergone the greatest reorganization is the student laboratory work. The tendency seems to be to do away with this part of science teaching. Laboratories have been a constant source of irritation to some administrators because they are expensive and because the double laboratory periods upset an otherwise smooth running curriculum. Further, the charge is made that the laboratory serves to prepare for further college work in this field and few students go on to college. The techniques learned in laboratory manipulation serve no useful purpose. (p. 556)

In response to these challenges, Ford said that we live in a physical world "of material objects that we must touch, smell, hear and see" (p. 557). Laboratory work offers us contact with that world. According to him, classroom demonstrations are helpful in bringing the student some contact with the physical world, but they can never re-place individual student laboratory work.

Also in 1940, H. Emmett Brown pointed out that many of the so-called experiments used in physics and chemistry were essentially the same as those that Harvard had listed in 1887 as appropriate for college admission, and that they merely required students to follow a set of instructions that offered no other problem for the students to solve than to get through the required activity. Thus students often simply went through the motions in cookbook style, recorded what was expected of them even if it was not what they actually got as results, and in general made a mockery of the activity.

Brown (1940c) suggested that many of the experiments on the present list had to be replaced by problems of genuine interest to the students.

> All verifications, proofs of laws (as though it ever were possible to "prove" a law in science from a few sets of hurriedly assembled measurements), detailed and overly precise quantitative experiments and experiments dealing with apparatus which has neither historical interest nor modern usage, are certainly in this category as far as individual experimentation is concerned. Neither must we hesitate to try new ways of using the laboratory, either for fear of failure (remember the meager value of traditional laboratory work) or because of the fancied demands of the College Entrance Examination Board or other standardizing body. Success is only waiting our bold venture! (p. 462)

College Domination of the High School Curriculum

Brown's call for high school teachers to free themselves from the influence of the College Entrance Examination Board represented an attitude expressed over and over again during the first half of the twentieth century. Because of the nature of its development, the high school's relationship to the colleges had always been somewhat strained. Initially the high school acted as a sort of "people's college" to provide a more practical "higher" education to a number of students who had no interest in the classical program of the colleges. In this role it sometimes found itself in direct competition for students with the collegiate institutions. The high school and college also found themselves offering many of the same courses, especially as the colleges started to add more of the modern courses, such as history, literature, and the laboratory sciences, to the curriculum. As it began to assume a clearly intermediate position between elementary and collegiate education, the high school was forced to assume an important college preparatory role. This preparatory role had been a source of contention and irritation to the secondary schools at least since the late nineteenth century.

Before the various standardizing committees, such as the NEA's Committee of Ten and its Committee on College-Entrance Requirements, had attempted to make sense out of college entrance requirements, high school people were annoyed by the detailed and widely varying admission requirements of the colleges. Looking at the issue from the point of view of the colleges, their applicants were coming from such disparate educational backgrounds that they had to state very specifically what would be required for admission. Some applicants were coming out of the academies, some from the Latin grammar schools, some from the high schools, and some with little if any formal education. For this reason, admission requirements were stated not simply in terms of courses to take but in terms of books to read, pages of specific books to study, and exercises to complete, so that anyone, regardless of previous background, could prepare for college. The requirements set by the various standardizing committees helped to ease the transition from high school to college, but they also formalized the preparatory role of the high school.

It was this role that came to be strongly resented during the early years of the twentieth century as the high school began to grow rapidly and began to serve an increasingly large number of students who would not go on to college. It became more and more difficult to justify the Committee of Ten's claim that the same courses could be used equally well for both college preparation and preparation for life. Secondary education was moving toward practical and applied courses, whereas collegiate education was still focused largely on developing an understanding of the subject, on intellectual development, and on professional preparation. Even though the high school and college dealt with the same subject matter, they were beginning to part company on the reasons for teaching that subject matter. However, since college faculties did most of the early textbook writing and organizing of the courses in high school science, the high schools found themselves in the position of being forced to teach courses that very closely resembled the college courses, both in content and in purpose.

College-Style Courses in the High School

In his account of the development of biology teaching in the Chicago public schools, Worralo Whitney (1930) illustrated how college faculty influenced the teaching of high school courses in science in the nineteenth century. He dated the beginning of the teaching of biology as a distinct laboratory-based subject in Chicago to 1892, even though he recognized that botany and zoology had been taught as book subjects before that date. He said:

> The use of biology as a subject to be taught in colleges and universities was quite new at that time and still more a novelty as a subject in the high school curriculum. Consequently Mr. Boyer [the teacher assigned to set up the course] had no high school experience with the subject to help him in installing the course. Professor Martin of Johns Hopkins was giving one of the first courses in biology given in this country, if not the very first. His course was copied after Huxley whose pupil and assistant he had been. The course consisted of lectures on a series, in evolutionary order, of types of animals and plants representing the principal and most important groups. Laboratory work accompanied these lectures which were very exhaustive but gave little attention to related forms of animals or plants. This, then was all Mr. Boyer had to guide him in planning the course for biology in the high schools. (pp. 148–149)

Whitney's account made college domination of the high school curriculum seem unavoidable. Nevertheless, high school people were irked by the relationship, and they were outspoken in their criticism. Speaking of the history of the development of biology teaching in the late nineteenth century, George C. Wood (1913) of the Boys' High School in Brooklyn, New York, said:

> Nothing then being known of the practical bearings of the subject in its relation to human life and organized society, the educators fell back upon that phase of the subject with which they were acquainted—the theory of evolution—a theory which had become a part of their very bone and fibre. The result was the ludicrous and at the same time pathetic college biology in the first year of the high school course within the teaching memory of most of us. The excuse for this heart-rending procedure was that the study of structure was of great "disciplinary" value. What a boy gained by the study of the number of legs on a crayfish was "carried over" and made applicable to any other experience. (p. 241)

Herbert Roberts (1913) of the Kansas State Agricultural College reported the opinions of a number of high school teachers concerning current biology courses. He said one high school teacher wrote that "college biology in high schools is the curse" (p. 148). According to Roberts, what was needed were science teachers who could teach science so that lay persons could understand it. Instead what existed were teachers who taught high school students the same thing they themselves had learned in college.

John Woodhull (1915), who had been a key supporter of general science in the high school curriculum, remarked sarcastically that "perhaps the thing most to be feared is that the colleges may accept General Science and place it in the preparatory group" (p. 232).

These early complaints against high school courses that resembled their collegiate counterparts in both content and method continued throughout the next several decades. George Twiss (1920) blamed the colleges for perpetuating a deductive approach to teaching even as science educators were encouraging high school teachers to use inductive methods. "How can we expect these high school teachers to teach inductively when nearly all of their college teachers, and nearly all their text books have taught them by methods that are almost exclusively deductive?" (p. 10). Twiss said that what had been forgotten by college teachers who understood their content so thoroughly was that their own understanding had been arrived at inductively. Teachers had to realize that students also had to gain command of these general principles inductively through their own concrete experiences and through their own mental processes. The student "must have perceived in the various concrete cases the common features which the general principle describes; else he can have no real command of the principle" (p. 10).

Amer Ballew (1930) of the Austin High School in Chicago pointed out the inappropriateness of using university methods in high school biology courses, focusing on the misuse of laboratory drawings:

> Many of our present day methods in biology have been directly handed down from the university. The university has emphasized morphology with its inherent representative drawings. High school teachers have, in many cases, bodily transplanted this method to secondary school biology. The time has passed when a high school course in biology consists simply of a somewhat simplified edition of a similar course in the university. Present day psychology and education have quite definitely shown that the objectives and methods at the secondary school level are quite distinct from those of the university level. (p. 496)

Fifteen years later, David Aptekar (1945) of the Mackensie High School in Detroit talked about ways to break out of the traditional teaching mold and to begin developing a scientific attitude in students, making better use of the laboratory as a place of discovery, and focusing on content that was relevant to the lives of the students. But he was concerned that the colleges would not find this approach acceptable. "In practicing scientific thinking in classrooms and laboratories the amount of subject matter would suffer greatly. From present indications it is questionable whether colleges would be satisfied" (p. 35).

Differing Emphasis on the Applications of Science

How real was this perceived difference between the approaches of the high schools and colleges to teaching science? Did college professors really want high school students to come to them like storehouses filled with factual information? Were the values of high school and college faculties as different as many of these comments would lead us to believe? The major purpose of collegiate science teaching in the early twentieth century was to advance the discipline and only incidentally to teach the practical applications of the organized subject matter. It was not until approximately 1945 that any significant discussion of college science teaching for purposes of general education and social relevance took place. Close behind the advancement of the subject matter was the belief that the study of science developed intellectual power. In 1929, Archer Hurd surveyed science faculty at the University of Minnesota and found that their list of important laboratory functions still included a significant number of generalized mental functions, including memory, powers of observation, scientific thought, and ability to draw conclusions.

In 1932, the Thirty-First NSSE Yearbook Committee discussed this persistent belief in mental discipline on the part of college faculty.

> Only brief mention has been made so far in this discussion of the disciplinary, or training, values of college courses in science. These have not been forgotten by science teachers, however, most of whom still cling to their personal beliefs in the matter, all studies of transfer of training notwithstanding. (National Society for the Study of Education, 1932, p. 312)

This belief in the disciplinary power of the sciences was not unique to college faculty, however. Throughout the education literature there were continued references by both high school and college faculty to the ability of the sciences to develop mental power. What was different between the two groups was that high school faculty were under more pressure than college faculty to move away from the notion of generalized mental skill development and mastery of a discipline toward specific real-world applications. It was around this issue of applications versus intellectual development that the differences centered.

A study conducted in 1927, for example, showed that only a small percentage of the space in college biology texts was devoted to the practical applications of the subject. In ten textbooks examined, the amount of space given to scientific generalizations was 78% or more in each of the texts, whereas the amount of space devoted to practical applications of those generalizations was less than 10% in all cases (National Society for the Study of Education, 1932, p. 318). This lack of emphasis on practical applications represented one of the major differences between collegiate and secondary science education.

The Scientific Study of the Curriculum

Another development of the early part of the twentieth century that had a significant impact on educational practice was the scientific study of the curriculum. There were two related aspects to this development that had noteworthy effects on science education. The first was the creation and use of standardized tests to measure education outcomes. The second was the use of both large-scale surveys of opinion and content analyses of popular media such as magazines and newspapers to determine the science content that was most appropriate to teach.

Standardized Testing

We have already seen how standardized tests were used to compare the effectiveness of individual laboratory work and teacher demonstrations and how the outcomes of those studies were used to make instructional decisions. In the 1920s the interest in testing was so great that virtually every aspect of educational practice was submitted to scientific test. The scientific measurement of educational outcomes became a kind of panacea for everything that was wrong with education. The faith that scientific testing would provide answers to all the unanswered questions in education was expressed by Charles Pieper (1920). After discussing a variety of approaches to the teaching of chemistry that had developed over the years and the advantages of each, he apologized for not being able to be more definite about which methods were really best. He said:

If I have indulged in glittering generalizations, it must be granted that they have been made upon the basis of experience. There is little experimental evidence in the modern sense of the term. Experimental teaching with carefully devised testing of the results must come. . . . If we will but select a certain set of fundamental concepts and topics or problems and then try experimentally the various combinations of methods, we shall be able to verify the effectiveness of the best method. (p. 415)

Standardized tests of science knowledge were relatively new in 1920. In fact, standardized testing in education in any form was still in its infancy in 1920. Alfred Binet's test of intelligence had been brought to the United States in 1908, and it was revised for use in this country as the Stanford-Binet by Lewis Terman at Stanford in 1916. Summarizing the tests that were available in science at that time, G. M. Ruch (1920) said:

The growth of standard tests is a feature of modern educational progress in many school subjects, although little, comparatively, has been done for high school subjects. A few beginnings have been made, notably the Starch test for physics, although this has not attained as much attention as it deserves. Grier has a range of information test for physiology and zoology, and Downing one for secondary science in general. F. T. Jones devised a test for physics and chemistry, and within the past year Hanor A. Webb and J. Carleton Bell have each attempted tests for chemistry. Lackey and Witham have tests for elementary geography. (p. 432)

With tests in hand, educators were able to attack the many problems awaiting them. One of these problems was the heterogeneous mix of students in the science classrooms. With standardized test scores as evidence, educators would be able to sort students according to ability and create more homogeneous science classrooms. Stephen Rich (1925) put it this way:

Now that we have at least reasonably adequate instruments for testing achievement in chemistry, the way is open for the solution of some of the more urgent problems in which the totality of such achievement is a factor. In particular, the practical problem of reducing the unhomogeneity of the chemistry class may now be attacked, since the extent and degree of that particular factor—the despair of many a chemistry teacher—may be measured. Is it too much to hope for an extension into this field of the methods of classification by intelligence and achievement tests that have already shown their value in the elementary schools? (p. 149)

Henry Gerry (1925) of Teachers College of the City of Boston was also pleased that educators were able to "abandon the speculative art and replace it with scientific measurement" (p. 157). This ability to make accurate measurements would place education in the realm of science itself and provide "scientific solutions to the educational problems that present themselves daily" (p. 157). These problems included large questions, such as whether individual laboratory or teacher demonstrations were more effective, and smaller-scale issues, such as diagnosing specific problems that individuals were having with particular aspects of a course. Gerry also saw the tests as being useful for determining whether teachers were meeting important goals that had been established for the schools:

> General aims for secondary schools have been set up by the Commission on the Reorganization of Secondary Education and these have been made more specific for natural science in a second report. A supervisor needs to know if these objectives are being approached or if the teacher has some less well defined and less essential goals. This is difficult, if not impossible, to determine by occasional visits to the class or by conversations with the teacher. Answers may be secured, however, through the aid of appropriate tests designed to reveal the extent to which the aims are being realized. (p. 167)

Archer Hurd (1925) noted that his use of standardized tests in physics had largely eliminated subjective judgment in the marks he gave to his physics pupils. S. R. Powers (1924), who had authored the Powers Test of Chemistry, believed that standardized tests could be used to determine what course content was of functional value to the students. If the students learned the material, as indicated by scores on the standardized tests, it was of value to them, and if they did not learn the material, it had no value to them. Reporting on the results of a study he had conducted, Powers (1925) concluded that much of what was taught in high school chemistry was of little value to the students, since in most schools there were few if any students who mastered the subject.

The effect of the development of standardized tests in the science areas was to focus attention on the more easily measurable outcomes of education. Since content mastery was the easiest thing to measure, these content outcomes dominated the science education research. This development was in direct conflict with many of the goals of progressive education and had the effect of retarding movement in that direction. A. W. Stewart (1935) of Kent State University was sensitive to this issue when he discussed the need to develop tests that could be used to measure the ability to apply science principles, not just knowledge of the facts and principles per se:

> A modern and progressive statement of objectives in the course of study accomplishes very little if the resulting achievement is measured by tests that bear no relation to the objectives. . . . One of the most important problems in connection with the building of science tests is that of devising and improving types of tests that will give a valid measure of the pupil's ability to understand and apply the important scientific principles included in his instructional course. (p. 695)

Analyzing Student Needs and Interests

Perhaps more significant than the use of standardized tests in influencing the science curriculum was the use of surveys of student and parental opinion and analyses of magazines and newspapers to determine what content was of most use to the students. Curriculum workers were intrigued by the question of how to determine which content was most important for students to learn. One approach was to ask either the students themselves or their parents what they felt was most important for them to know. Usually the respondents would be presented with a long list of topics and asked to rate the topics as to their interest or usefulness. A second technique was to examine magazines and newspapers to determine what science knowledge was required in order to read them intelligently. It was assumed that science concepts that played an important role in people's lives would appear in the media and that the schools could play a role in preparing its students to read these magazines and newspapers. A third approach was to analyze currently used textbooks in the sciences to determine whether the content in these books was preparing students for life outside of the school.

ANALYSES OF NEWSPAPERS AND MAGAZINES.   A study conducted by L. Thomas Hopkins (1925) of the University of Colorado was typical of the studies of the second type. Hopkins began by saying that a major assumption of his was that "subject matter should enable pupils to perform better those desirable activities in which they are now engaged" (p. 793). One of the activities that high school students engaged in was reading newspapers and magazines. Thus science courses in high school should improve students' ability to read those materials. Hopkins analyzed eight popular magazines and four daily newspapers from Denver, Colorado, to determine their coverage of science content. Researchers read 2,770 articles covering 32,660 inches of space from those publications. They found that biology content was much more prevalent in the magazines and newspapers than content from the other subjects and that the amount of space devoted to the theoretical side of chemistry and physics was negligible.

Based on these results, Hopkins drew a number of conclusions. First, because of its coverage in the popular media he believed that biology should be considered the most important of all the secondary school science subjects for the purposes of general education. Physics and chemistry followed well behind. Second, the relative importance of the subjects should determine the sequence in which they would be taught in the secondary school. Third, because of its importance in everyday life, biology rather than physics or chemistry should be considered the most important course for college entrance.

Hopkins was also able to determine which specific topics were most valuable for students to study in order for them to read newspapers and magazines with understanding. In biology, key topics included "public health, knowledge of animal and plant life, foods, natural resources and evolution" (Hopkins, 1925, p. 799). For physics there was a long list of topics appearing in the mass media that included such things as the automobile, radios, the structure of buildings, electrical power, photography, ship construction, tunnels, cement construction, bridges, highway construction, steam engines, railroad construction, steam turbines, storage batteries, and X-rays. For chemistry important topics included fertilizers, the use of chemistry in promoting health, chemical uses of common metals, and the production and use of alcohol. Hopkins suggested that such topics were not covered in the high school curriculum when he said: "The reader can draw his own conclusions as to how far the content of present courses of study agrees" (p. 799).

In a review of research related to biology content that was covered by magazines and newspapers, W. Edgar Martin (1945) also found that biology was the subject most commonly appearing in the media. The topics that were present most often in order of occurrence were human biology, health and disease, animal biology, foods and nutrition, and plant biology. Martin said:

> On the basis of all the data, therefore, the conclusion seems to be justified, that any reorganization of biology to serve the purposes of general education should be in the direction of a more functional treatment of the materials presented, and a greatly increased supplementation of the textbooks by the use of those materials related to the topics shown to be of importance in the studies surveyed. (p. 550)

The editor of the journal in which Martin's article appeared, however, cautioned against using content analyses of newspapers and magazines to make educational decisions. In an Editor's Note he said:

> The editor is of the opinion that newspaper articles cannot determine the basis for a course in science, the subject itself determines that. However, newspaper interests can point to desirable additions which could be made to the basic things, if time permits. The fundamentals for a course in science still are: To acquaint students with the great basic laws of an orderly world, and to develop a desire to apply scientific procedure and thinking to the problems of life. (Martin, 1945, p. 543)

STUDIES OF STUDENT INTEREST.   Another aspect of these scientific studies of the curriculum was the attempt to determine what was of interest to students. In reviewing studies of student interest in general science topics, Victor Noll (1939) found that electricity, stars, radio, the sun, the moon, and the earth headed most lists. Other popular topics were planets, lightening, plants, and animals. In one of the studies reviewed by Noll, Boomsliter (1936) gave seventh- and eighth-grade pupils and their parents a list of 703 topics and asked which of them they would like to know about or needed to know about. The topics were grouped into categories and rank ordered according to interest and utility. The order from highest to lowest was: health, household arts, gardening, manual arts, general interests, and pure science.

Noll also described a study by Tregoning (1929), who examined the chemistry related reading habits and the out-of-school activities and interests of high school pupils. Twenty popular magazines were analyzed for their chemistry content. In addition, high school students were observed in order to determine the materials they commonly used; they were also asked to list chemical substances that they frequently came in contact with, such as foods, cleaning agents, medicines, and fuels; and the local druggist was asked to provide a list of chemical substances that were commonly sold to high school students. Based on this information, Tregoning found that most magazine space that was related to chemistry dealt with the manufacture and use of chemical materials. He also found that students were most interested in the manufacture of chemical materials and the chemical conduct of materials, and least interested in chemical theories and processes. Noll concluded that students should be given information in those areas that they found most interesting and most useful.

In a study by Watson (1926), a list of 174 topics from three textbooks in physics was submitted to 659 parents of physics students. They were asked to indicate which of the topics were of value to them. It was found that of 35 topics found highly valuable, only 12 were usually stressed in physics textbooks. On the other hand, 33 topics usually covered in physics textbooks were considered to have little value by most parents. The topics found to have most value were: ice cream freezers, windowshade rollers, regulation of clocks, kerosene lamps, kitchen ranges, sewing machines, cream separators, fever thermometers, door locks, and fountain pens. On the list of least valuable topics were telescopes, inclined planes, centrifugal pumps, why an object is apparently lighter in water than out, differential pulleys, microscopes, electric transformers, ammeters, telegraphy, and hydraulic presses. Noll (1939) commented: "Clearly, much of what is being taught in high school physics is of little value or interest to the average layman. That what we teach is not all useless is equally clear, but the time wasted on 'dead material' is large" (p. 140).

Noll, as well as many other educators of the day, believed that studies of this kind were valuable for determining what science content should be taught in schools. Content analyses of newspapers and magazines, assessments of student interest in specific science topics, and parental opinions concerning what was "useful" were key factors in selecting content for the curriculum.

Summary

By the 1940s, science educators were still struggling with ways to create a science program that was true to the principles of progressive education that had been laid down by the CRSE in 1918 but at the same time did not violate the integrity of the science disciplines themselves. As the progressive era neared its end, the focus in science education had shifted noticeably away from disciplinary study and toward social relevance and student interest. The impending war, however, would begin to alter educators' thinking about the importance of science knowledge and would provide the initial motivation for fundamental changes in science education that would begin to develop in the following decade.

Chapter 7

World War II
and the Beginnings of Change

To say that World War II had a major impact on the life of this country is to state the obvious. The war affected both individuals and institutions, not the least of which was education. In the first place, the war encouraged and strengthened the vocational and applied aspects of education that had been gaining momentum since the early part of the century. The war represented a very immediate and practical problem that urgently demanded solution. The war effort required the production of industrial and agricultural products as well as the training of personnel who would be directly involved in fighting the war. The education community felt compelled to respond to these problems with short-term, pragmatic answers. A second effect of the war was that it pointed to the need for a general improvement in the entire educational system. The war revealed through the testing of recruits and officer candidates that more people than expected were deficient in basic literacy and quantitative reasoning skills. It also revealed that more people than expected were in poor health and thus physically unable to join the armed forces. A third effect of the war, which continued into the postwar years, was that it produced personnel shortages in a number of important technical fields. The postwar years in particular were characterized by shortages in scientific, technical, and industrial fields, a situation that required increased efforts on the part of educators to meet the demands for technical workers. A fourth effect of the war was that it showed how important science, mathematics, and technology were in the successful conduct of military efforts. In the postwar years, direct competition with the Soviet Union for international influence and military supremacy often took the form of devising ways to increase the level of science, mathematics, and technical education in schools. Finally, the war strengthened our commitment to the principles of democracy, especially our efforts at universal education and the general education of all American youth.

Given such a range of influences, it is easy to see why educators did not speak with a common voice either during or after the war. Whereas some felt that we had to make school more relevant, practical, and enjoyable in order to stimulate a greater number of students to participate and succeed, others felt that the specialized, technical needs of our society obligated schools to emphasize programs that would encourage the participation and success of the brightest students available.

War-Related Issues

The Problem of Personnel Shortages

The war produced an obvious drain on the science talent in this country. Many science faculty were temporarily drawn away from the colleges to work on military projects or to train military personnel; others left the colleges altogether for better-paying jobs in government or industry; and still others, although they remained in the colleges, switched their research interests from basic scientific studies to applied military work. In addition, the U.S. government decided not to grant special deferments to college science students, a decision that greatly depleted the pool of science talent being developed in the colleges. The combined loss of science students and faculty during the war produced a period of several years when future scientists simply were not being trained in sufficient numbers to meet the demands ahead. In the 1940–1941 school year, there were 375,000 science majors enrolled in college; by 1944–1945 that number stood at just 200,000. Similarly, there were 41,000 college science faculty in 1940–1941 but only 36,000 in 1944–1945 (President's Scientific Research Board, 1947, Vol. 4).

The drain of science talent soon became apparent. When, in 1946–1947, the number of returning G.I.'s swelled the number of college science majors to 600,000, only 50,000 science faculty were available to teach them. Many scientists had left academia for government and industry work, and those who were left to teach had overcrowded classrooms, poor facilities, and little time for basic research. The question of how to reduce the deficit in science personnel became a policy issue of national proportion in the years immediately following the war. In response to this need, President Truman issued an executive order in 1946 to create the President's Scientific Research Board, which would study and report on the country's research and development activities and on science training programs. The board was headed by John R. Steelman and included the Secretaries of War, the Navy, Commerce, Interior, and Agriculture as well as various federal commissioners and other executive branch administrators.

The board began its report with these words:

> The security and prosperity of the United States depend today, as never before, upon the rapid extension of scientific knowledge. So important, in fact, has this extension become to our country that it may reasonably be said to be a major factor in national survival. (President's Scientific Research Board, 1947, Vol. 1, p. 3)

The Research Board argued that science was important for both military and economic reasons. Because the United States faced economic competition from abroad and because other countries, especially the Soviet Union, were investing heavily in science and technology, it was imperative that the United States press ahead in the area of science. The board placed most of its emphasis on the improvement of science teaching at the college and university level. Board members felt that the problem was not an insufficient number of potential scientists in the college classrooms but an insufficient number of science faculty who could offer quality instruction given large class sizes, low salaries, and inadequate research support. The percentage of all scientists who were working in the colleges had declined from 58% in 1941–1942 to 43% in 1944–1945 as more and more scientists chose government and industry jobs over lower-paid college work. In addition, the number of Ph.D.'s granted in science dropped to 776 in 1945 compared to 1,900 in 1941. Without sufficient numbers of high-quality scientists in higher education, the education of future scientists would suffer. In response, the board recommended higher salaries for college faculty, an increase in funding for research and development activities in the colleges, and the establishment of the National Science Foundation to coordinate research grants to higher education institutions.

Science for the Scientist and the Nonscientist

Even though the immediate solution to the problem of a shortage of scientists was perceived to lie in making the job of college science faculty more attractive, the board also recognized the importance of providing a general science education for all students, K–12 and beyond. Not only would a quality program at the early levels stimulate interest in science and increase the number of potential scientists, but a successful program of scientific research in the United States depended on the support and understanding of the wider nonscientific population. For help in determining the effectiveness of science teaching at all levels of education for both scientists and nonscientists, the board asked the American Association for the Advancement of Science (AAAS) for assistance. In response, their Cooperative Committee on the Teaching of Science and Mathematics issued a report entitled "The Present Effectiveness of Our Schools in the Training of Scientists." This report was incorporated into the report of the President's Scientific Research Board.

Throughout their report, the AAAS committee emphasized the dual role of science education.

> While it is the primary object of this report to deal with the production of professional scientists, account must be taken of the degree of comprehension of science by the general population. For in a democracy it is upon the popular attitude toward science that the attractiveness of the profession, the resulting selectivity for those finally entering the profession, and the degree of support obtainable for their work will depend. (President's Scientific Research Board, 1947, Vol. 4, p. 113)

Several of the problems that the committee addressed were related to these two roles of science education. At the secondary school level, the problem was that too few students were taking science courses, especially in the physical sciences, and there were too few science teachers available to do a good job with those who did want to take the courses. In some schools, there was no one available to teach physics or chemistry. In addition, little was being done to encourage students with talent in mathematics and science to prepare for work in science fields, and many students with talent were unable to attend college because of financial reasons. At the college level, the committee focused on proposals for making the job of the science faculty more attractive, on early identification of science talent through standardized testing of incoming freshmen, on scholarship programs to insure that all talented students had a chance to attend college, and on ways to improve the general scientific education of nonscience students.

Science for general education purposes had long been a goal of secondary schools, and general science courses as well as general biology had been the most common vehicles used to achieve that goal. By the mid-1940s, a number of colleges had started to take an interest in this general education function of their curriculum as well. In 1945, the Harvard Committee on General Education, which had been commissioned by Harvard president James B. Conant, published its report, *General Education in a Free Society* (Harvard Committee, 1945). In the report, the committee said:

> From the viewpoint of general education the principal criticism to be leveled at much of present college instruction in science is that it consists of courses in special fields, directed toward training the future specialist and making few concessions to the general student. Most of the time in such courses is devoted to developing a technical vocabulary and technical skills and to a systematic presentation of the accumulated fact and theory which the science has inherited from the past. Comparatively little serious attention is given to the examination of basic concepts, the nature of the scientific enterprise, the historical development of the subject, its great literature, or its interrelationships with other areas of interest and activity. (pp. 220–221)

In response to these criticisms, Conant (1947) himself offered a solution in his book *On Understanding Science.* Conant recommended that nonscientists be taught the principles of science through a study of its historical development. The intent of such an approach was to develop an understanding of the scientific process and the human aspects of the scientific enterprise rather than the structure of the discipline as a set of ordered facts.

For both the secondary schools and the colleges, science for general education came to mean developing an appreciation of the way science was conducted, the importance of science in society, the historical development of scientific thought, and the relationships between science and society. It also meant deemphasizing science as a structured body of knowledge. Speaking of the importance of the history of science in courses for general education purposes, the AAAS committee said: "Much more use should be made of the history of science with its adventure and dramatic action, which appeal strongly to young people's interests and arouse their imagination" (President's Scientific Research Board, 1947, Vol. 4, p. 86)

In a similar way the Educational Policies Commission (1944) report, *Education for All American Youth,* supported the historical approach to the study of science.

> These scientists are thought of as living men, facing difficult problems to which they do not know the answers, and confronting many obstacles

rooted in ignorance and prejudice. In imagination, the students watch them at work, and look particularly for the methods which they use in attacking their problems. . . . Thus the methods of science are taught as instruments which men have created and used to solve some of humanity's most important problems. (p. 132)

Even though science's role in the solution of "humanity's most important problems" was usually discussed in the context of general education for the nonscientist, the AAAS Cooperative Committee recommended that the human aspects of the science enterprise become a part of the specialists' education as well.

It is recommended that courses be given [in college science programs] in which a conscious effort is made to clarify the nature of scientific thought, the cooperative aspects of scientific investigations, the ethical implications of the free exchange of ideas and the important effects of scientific discoveries on society. We also recommend that courses be required in the history of scientific thought, in the philosophy of science and in general philosophy, so that the science specialist may recognize the social implications of scientific endeavor. (President's Scientific Research Board, 1947, Vol. 4, p. 143)

Low Enrollments in Secondary School Science

In part, the focus on the human aspects of science was intended to increase overall enrollment in science courses, especially in the physical sciences. The problem of low enrollments in the physical sciences was one that had grown progressively worse throughout the first half of the twentieth century. By the late 1940s, most students' science experience included both a general science and a general biology course, but only a few were taking chemistry and physics. A common response to the problem of low enrollments in chemistry and physics was to question whether the physical science courses as taught were appropriate for general education purposes. And often the response was to suggest ways to make the courses more relevant, useful, and appealing to students. A solution that had achieved some popularity before the war was to offer any one of a number of generalized physical science courses, with titles such as "Senior Science," "Consumer Science," "Survey Science," "Physical Science," and "Fused Physical Science" (National Society for the Study of Education, 1947). With the support of the reports of the Educational Policies Commission (1944, 1952) and the work of the Harvard Committee on General Education, the idea of generalized physical science courses began to be revived after the war. The AAAS Cooperative Committee joined these other groups in their support of a general physical science course, including the creation of such a course in their list of recommendations for the improvement of science teaching (President's Scientific Research Board, 1947, Vol. 4). The AAAS committee recommended that all students take one year of general physical science and one year of general biology in addition to a course in general science. For those with special talents in science, they recommended three years of specialized science beyond general science.

Status of the Teaching Profession

Still another problem facing the science education community in the years following the war was the status of the teaching profession. Salaries were unattractive, there were shortages of qualified science teachers, and there was a belief that the professional training of many teachers was substandard. The AAAS committee recommended both better teacher education programs and higher pay to combat the shortages of science teachers. According to the committee, teacher education programs should include science coursework from a range of the sciences, not just in one specialized area, and should deal with the applications of the sciences to important aspects of the world in which we live: "Teachers need to learn from first-hand observation the applications being made of science and mathematics in manufacturing, agriculture, mining, medicine, research, and the like" (President's Scientific Research Board, 1947, Vol. 4, p. 107).

In addition, the President's Scientific Research Board (1947, Vol. 3) surveyed 567 scientists to determine their ideas about the needs in science education. At all levels, these scientists called for better-trained teachers (in both grasp of subject and in pedagogical techniques), higher pay for teachers, more rigorous training in basic subject matter, more emphasis on practical application rather than theory, and less specialization.

In that survey, less than half of the respondents felt that high school teachers were doing a good job of preparing their students for successful college work in science. According to John Steelman, criticism of high school teachers was the most frequent comment made about the high school science program: "That they themselves do not know enough about their subject; that they are pedagogically incompetent; that they are uninterested in their work and in the welfare of the students" (President's Scientific Research Board, Vol. 3, p. 238). In the opinion of the scientists who responded, a number of things could be done by colleges to improve the preparation of future science teachers. These included

1. More and better courses in education (20%)
2. Better grounding in subject matter (16%)
3. More stress on basic principles (10%)
4. More practical and less theoretical work (9%)
5. Better college teachers (9%)

The one thing that everyone seemed to agree on was that the quality of secondary science teaching needed to improve. Whether improvements would come from more study of science theories, more study of the applications of science, or more study of educational theory was less certain. The simple fact was that science teachers were poorly prepared, and *something* had to be done to make them better prepared.

The Soviet Threat

During the years following the report of the President's Scientific Research Board, many of the problems identified in that report persisted. Science personnel shortages, perceived threats to national security by the Soviet Union, shortages of science teachers, and low enrollments in secondary school physical science courses headed most lists of problems. Even as late as 1955, concerns about the possibility of a U.S. decline in world influence because of personnel shortages in science and technical fields were openly voiced. Brigadier General Arno Luehamn's (1955) speech to the Central Association of Science and Mathematics Teachers provided a flavor of that concern:

> The problem I propose to discuss is where and how we are going to obtain the hundreds of thousands of technically trained young men and women who will be needed to manufacture and operate the fantastically complex equipment which comprises the civilian economy of the United States and, no less, the Military forces. . . .
>
> The factor which favors the U.S.S.R. in the technical race I am talking about is the very great emphasis which the Russians place on science. . . .
>
> The rapid adoption and improvement of the turbojet engine for their MIG fighters, the achievement of an atomic bomb capability in four years instead of the much longer time estimated by our scientists

. . . these serve as convincing evidence that Russia has a great and growing technology. (pp. 725–727)

The Soviet Union was investing heavily in science and technology
in the postwar years, and their apparent superiority in these areas
was something that frightened many in the United States. An improved educational system was seen as one way of correcting for the
apparent deficit.

The Gifted and Talented in Science

One part of the strategy to improve our technical capabilities vis-
à-vis the Soviets was to make better use of the gifted and talented
youth of this country. The issue of making special provision for students with talent in science was one that began to emerge in the postwar years and one that the AAAS Cooperative Committee, in conjunction with the President's Scientific Research Board, addressed in
their report. Sensitive to possible charges of favoritism in the education of the specially talented, the AAAS committee pointed out that
it was the talented who were not receiving their due treatment under
the present system.

> Theoretically our educational creed stresses the nurturing of all youth,
> but actually some of our talented youth are deprived of the opportunity
> to develop to the best of their ability. We must provide opportunity for
> all youth to develop those talents which are basic to the exercise of lead-
> ership in a democratic society. (President's Scientific Research Board,
> 1947, Vol. 4, p. 61)

The AAAS committee supported better identification and guidance
of gifted students and recommended that studies be made of the various curricular and administrative arrangements that were being
used to serve gifted and talented youth.

Between 1947 and 1957 numerous groups and individuals lent
their support to the suggestions of the President's Scientific Research
Board that the most talented students receive attention so as to build
an adequate supply of scientists and technicians for our domestic as
well as military efforts. In 1953, the AAAS Cooperative Committee
on the Teaching of Science and Mathematics, in cooperation with the
U.S. Office of Education, published a report on gifted education entitled *Education for the Talented in Mathematics and Science* (U.S. Office
of Education, 1953). No less concerned about national security in
1953 than in 1947, the committee said: "The present struggle for the

very existence of our freedoms causes the need for the improvement of the instruction in science and mathematics to become increasingly important" (p. 1). According to the committee, technological advance, upon which the very survival of our democratic way of life depended, required additional specialists, but they were not being produced.

One answer lay in increasing enrollments in science courses from the ranks of the gifted and talented. In their report, the committee devoted several pages to ways of attending to the special needs of talented science and mathematics students. The list included the creation of separate schools for the gifted, honors classes, use of a two-track system so some could advance more rapidly, acceleration through the curriculum, supervised work experience outside of school, individualized projects, class projects, small-group projects, use of the gifted student as an assistant in class, math and science clubs, and contests and exhibits. In none of these suggestions, however, was there any discussion about how to change the science courses themselves to make them more appropriate for the talented student. The main problem was seen as too few of the best students taking existing science courses and the solution lay in devising ways to get more of them in those courses.

In 1955, Paul Brandwein published a book entitled *The Gifted Student as Future Scientist* in which he discussed the characteristics of gifted students, ways of identifying them, and proposals for increasing the number of talented students in science. Although most of his proposals involved organizational change, he also suggested that one way to increase science enrollments from among the gifted and talented was to offer "functional" general science courses to stimulate interest in the specialized courses. But, as was the case with the AAAS Cooperative Committee, Brandwein devoted only limited attention to the curriculum itself. The courses were on the books. The only question was how to encourage more students to take them.

One of the reasons that the period following the war was particularly interesting was because it provided insights into what other segments of the society besides professional educators thought of science education. Scientists had been largely uninvolved in discussions about science education since the turn of the century. Then it was commonplace for people such as Charles Eliot, Ira Remsen, and John Coulter to be involved in the debate on education. Fifty years later, scientists began asserting themselves again, and, along with representatives of the military, they created a new dialogue on education.

What was most striking about this dialogue was that for the most part its content was much the same as that of professional educators of the previous 40 or 50 years. The only new ideas that were advanced were that to protect our national security special provision should be made for gifted and talented students and that science had a legitimate general education role in higher education. The ideas of progressive education, especially the emphasis on applied and functional studies, were still strong in the late 1940s and early 1950s, and this was reflected even in the writings of the scientists themselves.

Science Education at the End
of the Progressive Era

As we have already seen in previous chapters, there had been continuing pressure to increase the practical and applied aspects of all high school subjects and to diminish the importance of the organized content of each subject throughout the first half of the twentieth century. A comment by George Counts (1926) reflected this attitude:

> There is one rather severe criticism which may by applied to the entire science program in the high school with the exception of the course in general science. Most of the courses seem to lack human interest. The materials are organized about the interests of scientists rather than about the interests of high school boys and girls or of ordinary persons. . . . The offerings in a given science aim to give the individual a comprehensive view of the subject matter of that science rather than that insight and technique which will be of greatest value to him in meeting the problems of everyday life. (p. 75)

In 1939, just two years before our entry into the war, Victor Noll tried to assess the impact of these attempts to reduce the emphasis on the structured content and increase the emphasis on applied aspects of the subjects. What he found, especially in chemistry and physics, was that although some changes had been made in some locations, a good deal of traditional teaching was still going on. Referring to a study by Malin (1932), Noll observed that "many of the same things are taught everywhere and that these are the same that have been taught for many years. The common gases are taught in nearly all schools, as are valence, nomenclature, and writing of formulas and equations" (Noll, 1939, p. 130).

Summarizing the state of affairs in all the science areas, Noll

(1939) observed that some progress in the direction of "reorganization" was being made in biology and chemistry but little if any in physics. In biology the changes were toward "a more functional treatment with increased emphasis upon the problems arising out of the relationships of living things and especially of man to the environment" (p. 145). In chemistry the nature of commercial applications and industrial processes was now included in the curriculum. And in physics there was some evidence that more practical applications to the home and everyday life were beginning to be included in textbooks.

Functional Science

The "functional" treatment of science that Noll spoke of continued as a theme of science education throughout the 1940s, and it became a major thrust of the National Society for the Study of Education's Forty-Sixth Yearbook, *Science Education in American Schools* (National Society for the Study of Education, 1947). Here again, the emphasis was away from the mastery of structured subject matter and toward real-world applications. All of the objectives of science instruction, including a knowledge of scientific phenomena, an understanding of concepts and principles, skill in the scientific method, and positive science attitudes, were to be taught so that they would *function* in the lives of students. Concerning knowledge objectives, the Yearbook Committee said:

> The information learned must result in altered thinking and in altered behavior. It must make the pupil (and later, the adult) more intelligent and readier for adequate adjustment whenever that information is relevant to life situations. (National Society for the Study of Education, 1947, p. 26)

The learning of organized content was to be a secondary goal, not an end in itself. The comments of the Yearbook Committee concerning chemistry content could apply equally well to the other disciplines.

> Associated with the strength inherent in the organization of chemistry as a subject are certain pitfalls. One of the most crucial is the tendency to look upon the organization as the important item per se. In doing this we may seem to present chemistry content as something to be memorized and may forget that it is only a framework which gives direction to

growth and understanding. (National Society for the Study of Education, 1947, p. 201)

The Role of Specialized Science

Although there were a number of attempts such as that by the Forty-Sixth NSSE Yearbook Committee to make the specialized subjects such as chemistry and physics functional, reform-minded educational theorists of the first half of the twentieth century had, for the most part, focused their efforts on the general science course. When they spoke of applied or functional science, they did so primarily with regard to the perceived educational needs of the masses of students who entered the school system with no plans to continue on to college and little if any interest in the specialized sciences. The specialized courses were intended mainly for the college preparatory students and the few others who found them appropriate. Both this traditional college preparatory curriculum and the applied general curriculum were established parts of the high school science program by the postwar years. Rather than being two separate tracks, however, as some had called for, the college preparatory program was simply a continuation of the applied general curriculum. The transition was smooth and based on the decision to continue the study of science by taking physics and/or chemistry in the eleventh and twelfth grades.

As I noted in Chapter 5, biology played a transitional role in the curriculum. It was a specialized course but also served a general education function because of the obvious relevance of the subject to such practical concerns as health and hygiene as well as agricultural production. By 1949, 20.8% of all grade 9–12 high school students were enrolled in general science at any one time and 18.4% in biology. The general education versus college preparation line was drawn in the upper high school years, when chemistry and physics were taught. Throughout the first half of the twentieth century, approximately 7.5% of all high school students were enrolled in chemistry at any one time, and physics enrollments, which were high at the beginning of the century, were down to 5.4% by 1949 (U.S. Bureau of the Census, 1975).

Attempts to revise the secondary school curriculum left this distinction between college and non-college preparatory science well intact. For example, when the Educational Policies Commission (1944) of the NEA issued *Education for All American Youth*, it advocated a program that would be based not on the traditional academic subject areas but on "areas of common learning." But, responding to the possible objection that the traditional subjects were being neglected, the commission wrote:

> There were some who feared—quite mistakenly, as it turned out—that this course would put an end to the systematic study of bodies of knowledge, such as the sciences, mathematics, history, and languages. This objection was withdrawn, however, when it was shown that there would be ample time in the total program for any student who wished to do so, to complete all the courses in the subject fields required for admission to college or university, even by those institutions which still hold to their prewar requirements. (p. 238)

Similarly, the Harvard Committee's (1945) report, *General Education in a Free Society*, left room in the curriculum for college preparatory physics and chemistry and supported the distinction between the general education function of general science and biology on the one hand and the specialized function of chemistry and physics on the other. In the recommendations for a high school curriculum in science, the report suggested that all students take a general science course, followed by a course in general biology that would most likely be "the last formal science instruction that many students not going on to college will obtain" (p. 159). Students going to college, but having no direct interest in the sciences, could also stop at this point. "Those who plan advanced work in science and mathematics in college should go beyond secondary-school biology to a year of chemistry or physics or both" (p. 160).

As long as this distinction remained, most science faculty were content. When, however, it appeared that ideas for generalizing the content of physics and chemistry might be successfully implemented, there was concern. Sherman Wilson (1940), talking to the chemistry section of the Central Association of Science and Mathematics Teachers in 1939, discussed the threat that "a sort of glorified general or integrated science may take the place of chemistry and physics" (p. 115). Wilson believed that this would seriously handicap the science program and that it would take years to recover from such a loss of organization. He said:

> You are a specialized group. You know that chemistry and physics have been taught in our high schools for more than fifty years. You know the value of these subjects and you may feel that their future is secure. But what are the facts? Statistics show that the percentages of the total number enrolled in standard science courses have been falling off. At present only about seven per cent are taking physics and chemistry. And, if this

integrated idea keeps up, we may all be teaching scrambled science. (p. 115)

When Paul Hurd (1953) suggested that physics did not "fit into either the high school or the college pattern of modern education" (p. 439) and recommended a general physical science course for all students based on principles of physics, chemistry, astronomy, geology, and meteorology, George Mallinson (1955), at that time the assistant editor of *School Science and Mathematics*, came to the defense of physics and pointed out the "unequivocal need for physics . . . throughout the public school" (p. 212).

Challenges to the established academic subject areas in science were thwarted throughout the first half of the century despite low enrollments and despite (or maybe because of) the clear college preparatory function that these courses performed. Their future was secured for at least the next several decades, however, when in the early 1950s the tide began to turn away from the ideals of progressive education and toward traditional educational values. The great debate in American education between traditionalists and progressives sharpened its focus when a simple resolution was passed at a meeting of vocational educators in Washington in 1945.

Life Adjustment Education

Progressive educators continued to advance an educational program that emphasized the everyday activities and interests of youth. Although progressive education had its share of critics who advocated a more traditional system of intellectual training, the dominant pedagogy in the United States during the first half of the century was based on the premise that good education should be oriented toward the everyday activities of students and that it should prepare students for life in society. This belief in the importance of the "life adjustment" function of education reached its culmination with the adoption of a resolution at a meeting of vocational educators in 1945. The resolution, offered by Charles Prosser, said in effect that the educational system was able to provide vocational training for about 20% of the school population and college preparatory work for another 20%, but that the remaining 60% were without a specific program. In Prosser's words:

> We do not believe that the remaining 60 percent of our youth of secondary school age will receive the life adjustment training they need and to

which they are entitled as American citizens—unless and until the administrators of public education with the assistance of the vocational education leaders formulate a similar program for this group. (U.S. Office of Education, 1951, p. 15)

In the postwar years, the U.S. Office of Education eagerly supported the development of life adjustment education, as did many state departments of education, as a way of continuing our commitment to democratic education for all. The U.S. Commissioner of Education, John Studebaker, appointed a National Commission on Life Adjustment Education for Youth in 1947 and a second national commission in 1950 to promote the concept. If one thing was to characterize the movement, it was the almost complete abandonment of traditional subject matter in favor of activities that would "prepare students for life." Democratic living, personal and social growth, and human relationships were considered more important for most of the students in high school than were the traditional subjects of science, mathematics, English, history, and languages.

The programs that were developed in the name of life adjustment education provided the targets that critics of contemporary education needed to gain the advantage in their debate with progressive educators. To many lay persons in particular, there was such an obvious anti-intellectual character to many of these programs that it became easier and easier for the traditionalists to win the day.

One of the largest and most comprehensive of the life adjustment programs was the Illinois Secondary School Curriculum Program (ISSCP), organized by the Illinois State Superintendent of Public Instruction. As part of this program, a follow-up study was conducted to determine how well the schools in the state were meeting the real-life needs of its secondary school youth. The survey that was sent to schools focused attention on 55 problems of youth. Charles W. Sanford (1950), of the College of Education at the University of Illinois, discussing the positive implications of this approach for science and mathematics study, said:

Examples of several problems on this list which seem to be closely related to science and mathematics are "the problem of acquiring the ability to care for one's health and of developing good health habits. . . . The problem of learning how to drive and care for an automobile. . . . The problem of ridding one's self of religious and racial prejudices" as well as numerous problems in the general areas of "Managing Personal Finances Wisely" and "Making Effective Use of Educational Opportunities." (pp. 312–313)

Also part of the ISSCP efforts reported by Sanford was a program at the Oak Park Township High School in Oak Park, Illinois, in which the general science course was being replaced by a health science course. The course was divided into four units: "The Human Body—a Machine," "The Young Person at Home," "The Young Person at School and in the Community," and "The Young Person at Leisure." Concerning this program, Sanford (1950) said:

> A Health Council is very active, teachers and pupils collaborate in determining health needs, physical examinations are administered and followed up with the cooperation of parents, student diets receive particular attention, building changes are continuously improving the health environment, a high order of coordination obtains between the school and community agencies, and so on. (p. 312)

Given the obvious nonacademic focus that many of these programs took, it became more and more common in the late 1940s and early 1950s to find traditionalists leveling scathing attacks against life adjustment education. Mortimer Smith wrote two books: *And Madly Teach,* published in 1949, and *The Diminished Mind* in 1954. Arthur Bestor's *Educational Wastelands* appeared in 1953. In addition, numerous articles were written for the public media castigating educators for the decline in education standards, their failure to transmit the cultural and intellectual heritage of the race, the abandonment of formal subject matter, anti-intellectualism, and the retreat from learning in our public schools.

Smith (1954) said that social skills should not take the place of intellectual training and the cultivation of intelligence. He believed that our very existence as a free democratic society depended on the extent of our knowledge and on our ability to think. Practical usefulness in the curriculum was legitimate, but "a school program which teaches little beyond how to fix a fuse, drive a car, set the dinner table, and enhance your personal appearance, isn't useful enough if your aim is the development of maturity and intelligent citizenship" (p. 3). Furthermore, it should be the challenge of schools to teach *all* students the knowledge, values, and modes of thought of our cultural heritage, not just the small percentage who plan to continue their studies in college.

According to Bestor (1953), schools existed to teach children to think. In fact, schools and colleges were the only institutions that we could count on in our society to furnish intellectual training. Therefore, it was critically important that these institutions do their job well.

The primary job of schools was the deliberate training of disciplined intelligence. Other goals, such as developing a sense of satisfaction that comes with understanding something new, meeting the vocational needs of students, supporting good health and physical development, or encouraging moral conduct, were secondary aims as far as the school was concerned. These might not be secondary goals as far as the society as a whole was concerned, but they were secondary goals of the school. The school could legitimately deal with these other functions, but it was to do so within the context of its primary mission, namely the development of intelligence.

According to Bestor, the vehicles for developing intelligence were the academic disciplines. It was true that the disciplines had become more and more abstract and theoretical as they had developed over the years, but at the same time they had become more practical and powerful. According to Bestor (1953), "the disciplines represent the various ways which man has discovered for achieving intellectual mastery and hence practical power over the various problems that confront him" (p. 19). It was because of their power to organize ideas that the disciplines developed, and it was because of this power that they should be taught in our schools. Bestor cautioned, however, that the disciplines should be taught for the power they conferred and not as a set of facts to memorize. Liberal education should involve teaching in a meaningful way the logical organization of knowledge through the structured disciplines.

During the early 1950s a seemingly unending stream of attacks was aimed at the American educational system because of its alleged softness and its neglect of our intellectual heritage. The answer was to strive for excellence, to provide more rigorous educational experiences for all students, especially those who had the intellectual capability to do the work. In science and mathematics, this meant getting the scientists and mathematicians themselves involved in the creation of courses for the high school students. Mathematics took the lead in this regard in 1952 when the University of Illinois Committee on School Mathematics met to create a course that would teach high school students mathematical understanding and the way mathematicians think. Scientists followed along the same lines when Jerrold Zacharias met with a group of scientists at the Massachusetts Institute of Technology in 1956 to revise the content of the high school physics course. Both of these courses were to be organized around the central concepts of the organized disciplines, and they were to focus on student understanding of the nature of the disciplines.

The approach that characterized the mathematics group at the

University of Illinois and the physics group at MIT would be repeated over and over again in the years ahead. With support from the National Science Foundation, efforts to revise courses in physics and mathematics were soon extended in unprecedented fashion to similar efforts in chemistry, biology, physical science, earth science, and elementary science. The precipitating factor was the Soviet's launching of the earth-orbiting satellite *Sputnik* on October 4, 1957. The response among educators was immediate and decisive. As Diane Ravitch (1983) said:

> The Soviet launch ... promptly ended the debate that had raged for several years about the quality of American education. Those who had argued since the late 1940s that American schools were not rigorous enough and that life adjustment education had cheapened intellectual values felt vindicated, and, as one historian later wrote, "a shocked and humbled nation embarked on a bitter orgy of pedagogical soul-searching." (p. 228)

Summary

At least among educational leaders in higher education and among the leaders of state and federal governments, if not among the majority of classroom teachers, progressive education was dead by the late 1950s. A new orthodoxy had taken its place. The shortages of technical personnel brought on by the war, the perceived threats to national security stimulated by Cold War competition with the Soviets and culminating in their launching of *Sputnik,* and the persistent claims by critics that progressive education had turned its back on traditional intellectual values moved American education away from the theme of social relevance and toward a mastery of the traditional disciplines.

A half-century of noble efforts to make science meaningful and relevant to all students had produced a science program that was satisfying to neither traditionalists nor progressives. Energized by the excesses of the life adjustment educators, traditionalists would grab hold of the science curriculum and dramatically alter the direction of science education in the decade ahead.

Chapter 8

Curriculum Reform

By the mid-1950s, a number of scientists had begun to take seriously the criticisms that had been leveled at the American educational system. With the support of their professional organizations and the financial backing of the National Science Foundation (NSF), groups of scientists began to investigate ways in which they could help to bring renewed intellectual vigor to the school science programs.

When the Soviet Union launched its earth-orbiting satellite *Sputnik* in 1957, the U.S. government backed these initiatives of the scientists with enthusiasm and financial support. What followed were two decades of federal involvement in science teaching and the development of an approach to science education that was focused on the logical structure of the disciplines and on the processes of science.

Curriculum Projects Supported by the National Science Foundation

Physics

It was appropriate that the course that had experienced the most difficulty attracting students and had suffered the greatest enrollment declines since the beginning of the century would be the first of the science courses to undergo substantial revision. In 1954, in the midst of the debate over the condition of American education, the Division of Physical Sciences of the National Academy of Sciences-National Research Council began to discuss ways to improve secondary school courses in physics. At the same time, other conferences sponsored by the American Association of Physics Teachers, the American Institute of Physics, and the National Science Teachers Association also investigated the need for a revised course in physics at the high school level

147

(National Science Foundation, 1962). These groups concluded that the physics that was being taught in schools was out of date, especially in its failure to include such aspects of modern physics as quantum or wave theories; the courses lacked broad unifying themes; too many technological applications had been added to the courses, so that the concepts of science were inadequately developed; and the textbooks tried to deal with far too many concepts, making it difficult to teach any of them in adequate depth (Little, 1959). The various professional organizations and conferences agreed that professional physicists needed to work with classroom teachers to devise new courses to reverse these trends.

Sometime before the fall of 1956, Jerrold Zacharias, a physicist from MIT, began discussing with other prominent physicists the possibility of creating a new course in school physics. The group applied to the National Science Foundation for funding and received approval for the Physical Science Study Committee (PSSC) project in November of that year. In December 1956, several of the individuals who had been involved in the early discussions and who had drawn up tentative proposals for the new course met at MIT. By the summer of 1957 about 50 university scientists and high school teachers were working on the project. During the following year, eight of the teachers used preliminary versions of the materials with about 300 students. By the summer of 1958, the number of teachers participating in the summer sessions had grown to 300, and in 1958–1959 more than 12,500 students were using the new course materials (Finlay, 1962; Little, 1959).

In an attempt to "restore the primacy of subject matter" (Easley, 1959, p. 5), the new course deliberately excluded most of the technological applications that had been part of conventional physics courses. In addition, a number of subjects normally treated in the physics course were omitted in order to make room for a more in-depth treatment of other subjects and for the inclusion of certain aspects of modern physics. The topics that were excluded, such as the physics of sound, were treated in a series of monographs that could be used as optional supplementary material. The primary objective of the course was to present physics as a coherent set of related concepts as they had developed over the years. Physics was to be seen as a "human activity comparable in significance with the humanities, the languages and the other major studies of high school students" (Little, 1959, p. 2).

The laboratory guide (Physical Science Study Committee, 1960b) included 51 experiments that were to help in developing the concepts found in the textbook. Students were given directions, questions to answer, and hints for completing the work, but they were expected to think through the activities and see on their own the relations between the laboratory work and the theories being studied. A series of films was produced to demonstrate phenomena that could not be shown in the laboratory.

The major difference between the PSSC physics course and those it was meant to replace was that it deliberately, albeit somewhat reluctantly, moved away from technological applications toward what was perceived to be a richer, more in-depth, and conceptually more sophisticated narrative account of the development of physics. The brief descriptions of physical laws, the accounts of how those laws applied in everyday life, and the use of mathematical calculations to demonstrate the relationships between concepts was replaced by much fuller accounts that told the story of science as a human activity. The textbook (Physical Science Study Committee, 1960a) was better written and told a better story, and from the point of view of the student who was motivated to put in the time to read through that narrative account, that was a significant improvement.

Biology

The beginning of curricular change in biology was similar to that in physics. In 1954, the National Academy of Sciences-National Research Council established a committee to examine problems of biological education. This committee, supported by grants from the Rockefeller Foundation and the National Science Foundation, generated substantial interest among research scientists for the improvement of the secondary school biology course (National Science Foundation, 1962, p. 6). The American Institute of Biological Sciences (AIBS), as the principal professional organization of biologists, became concerned enough about the problem of biology education to establish a curriculum study group and to apply to the National Science Foundation for funding for its efforts. This group, which identified itself as the Biological Sciences Curriculum Study (BSCS), began its work in 1959 under the direction of Arnold Grobman at the University of Colorado. The steering committee, composed of high school teachers and administrators, textbook writers, and prominent research biologists, met during 1959 and early 1960 to discuss strategies for the development of a new course in biology.

The committee agreed on a number of important issues. First, there was the concern about content. The content of biology courses as they were taught was thought to be out of date, and the courses failed to deal adequately with such issues as "organic evolution, the nature of individual and racial differences, sex and reproduction in the human species, and the problems of population growth and control" (Glass, 1962, p. 18). Hurd (1970) later described the existing courses as having a

> phylogenetic approach overlain with life forms treated at the organ-tissue level of organization and from a structure-function concept of biology. The . . . course design, sometimes called the "fern-frog" organization, was first laid out around 1860 to take advantage of Charles Darwin's newly proposed theory of evolution. (p. 157)

In addition, and in response to the continuous pleas to make science courses more relevant to the lives of students during the first half of this century, the courses contained a significant amount of material that dealt with technological applications in health, agriculture, and conservation, often giving little if any attention to the underlying scientific principles.

A second concern of the committee was with the way the content was presented in the textbooks. Biology was not being presented as a coherent, integrated, conceptual whole but rather as unconnected fragments, bits and pieces that could be learned without developing a sense of the relationships between groups of concepts. There was too much emphasis on memorization of factual material and not enough on the deeper understanding of biological concepts. In relation to the applications of biology, the older courses tried to show how biology was related to everyday life but failed to adequately develop the understanding of the biological principles to which the applications were related. Similarly, although the idea of presenting unifying themes had been suggested decades earlier and some attempts had been made to incorporate thematic organization as a part of good biology teaching, not enough had been done to actually show the relationships between each new idea and some larger integrating theme. Additional work was needed to integrate the individual concepts with such organizing ideas as the interdependence of structure and function, regulation and homeostasis, and the genetic continuity of life.

A third concern of the committee was with the misimpression that the older courses gave about the nature of biology and their failure to accurately portray the essential character of scientific activity. This was a failure both of textbook presentations and of laboratory work. Textbooks tended to treat biology as a set of stable facts and principles without giving adequate attention to the historical development of the subject, the changing nature of scientific knowledge, or the human side of scientific investigation. Although there had been efforts to include problem-solving activities in the biology curriculum and to emphasize biology as a process of inquiry, laboratory work had often degenerated into descriptive activities and the identification and memorization of structures and processes.

Armed with the power of consensus on these fundamental issues, the BSCS group set out to establish a course that was up to date, that faithfully portrayed the nature of scientific knowledge and process, and that did so in such a way that students came away with a deeper understanding of the discipline of biology than they had in the older courses. The group also agreed that because of the diversity of content and methods used in the life sciences, it would be difficult to suggest a single best way of organizing the course. Therefore they created three versions of the same course, each with its own special focus but with a considerable amount of overlap among them. Blue, Green, and Yellow versions of the course (Biological Sciences Curriculum Study, 1963a, b, c) emphasized the molecular, community, and cellular levels of biology, respectively. The first trial materials were produced in the summer and fall of 1960 and were tested in 100 schools in the 1960–1961 school year. The courses were revised the following summer and tested in about 350 schools during the subsequent school year.

In addition to the textbooks for each course, the BSCS group also produced a student laboratory guide, a set of films to illustrate some of the laboratory procedures that were hard to demonstrate in class, an optional laboratory block program to stimulate original investigations on real problems in biology, a series of "Invitations to Enquiry" that provided teachers with activities to help develop the concepts of scientific investigation, and a special version of the course for the slow learner (Hurd, 1970).

The Biological Sciences Curriculum Study was a massive effort to change biology teaching from the way it had been taught during the previous 50 years. Given the financial backing that the group had and the widespread support of prominent educators and scientists, BSCS was able to make available to the schools a set of curriculum materials of high quality and considerable appeal. If used as they were intended, they held out the hope of correcting many of the less desirable practices of the past. There had been earlier efforts to reform biology education along many of these same lines, but they had not enjoyed the same level of moral and financial support and were generally unsuccessful. One substantive difference between the BSCS curriculum and the proposals of the previous half-century was its move away from technology and other real-world applications toward the structure of the discipline itself. As with the other curriculum projects, this represented the most significant break with the ideas of the past.

Chemistry

At the request of the American Chemical Society, a group of chemists and high school chemistry teachers met in June 1957 to discuss ways of coordinating high school and college chemistry. The group received funding from the National Science Foundation to create a new, updated course in high school chemistry that would have as its primary purpose preparation for the study of chemistry in college. Arthur F. Scott of Reed College was the first director of the project, followed by Laurence E. Strong of Earlham College. Under Scott's and then Strong's leadership, nine high school chemistry teachers and nine college professors of chemistry met in 1958 and 1959 to organize a new course in high school chemistry, which would be called the Chemical Bond Approach (CBA).

According to Strong (1962), "the Chemical Bond Approach Project is an attempt to produce a study of chemistry that will reveal the importance of theory and experiment" (p. 45). Elaborating on that theme, Strong said:

> Chemistry, through most of its history, has been largely descriptive. In the last sixty years, however, there has been an extensive development of theory in chemistry. These two aspects of modern chemistry—the descriptive and the theoretical—provide a possibility for acquainting students with science as a process of inquiry that interrelates the mental and the experimental. (p. 44)

A major goal of the course was to introduce students to logical thinking in chemistry. Students would be expected to think through their laboratory work and use chemical theory to explain their observations. According to Strong (1962), "we attempt to confront the student with the implications of logical arguments based on theory" (p. 48). Much of this was to be done through the discussion of such mental models as atomic structure, kinetic theory, and energy relationships. The unifying theme for the course was the chemical bond, as the title of the project suggested (Chemical Bond Approach, 1962a, b). To encourage initiative and logical thought, students were to be given more freedom in the laboratory and less direction in conducting their laboratory work.

Although the stated goals of the Chemical Bond Approach Project also included "the role of chemistry in society and everyday living" (Hurd, 1970, p. 182), few, if any, of these applications were to be found in the textbook itself. The text material was written at a highly abstract level, with little reference to household or industrial applications of chemistry or to technology. Two goals were emphasized to the virtual exclusion of any others: (1) "To present the basic principles of chemistry as an intellectual discipline and to achieve an appreciation of chemistry as a creative pursuit of human knowledge," and (2) "To develop facility in analytical, critical thinking—especially thinking which involves logical and quantitative relationships" (Hurd, 1970, p. 182).

Two years later, in 1959, the American Chemical Society's (ACS) Ad Hoc Committee on Possible Organization of a High School Chemistry Course met to discuss the creation of a second new high school chemistry course, which would be aimed at a wider range of students than was the CBA course. The ACS committee, headed by Alfred B. Garrett, a professor of chemistry at Ohio State University, had in mind a course that would offer maximum flexibility and adaptability to local conditions but at the same time be well coordinated with the college course. The committee also foresaw a course that would appeal to all students taking chemistry regardless of their future college or career plans, much like the Committee of Ten had suggested more than 65 years earlier. The major problem that Garrett's committee noted concerning the older courses in chemistry was that over the years new topics had been added to them by accretion with no apparent concern for their logical ordering within the total curriculum. In the committee's guidelines concerning the course, they said: "A reduction in the total number of topics covered would make possible a deeper penetration on narrower fronts. As a result the students' grasp of chemistry and of the nature of scientific reasoning and experimentation might be vastly improved" (Merrill & Ridgway, 1969, p. 113). They also noted, however, that such a reconstruction of the course would take a great deal of imagination. The most difficult problem was how to leave out topics that were thought to be indispensable.

As a solution to this problem of perceived indispensability of topics, the committee proposed that the new course be constructed around a core of ideas that represented the central principles of chemistry. Supplementary to this core would be a set of addenda that could be used at local option. This plan would provide for a reasonable amount of conformity across the country yet provide for a good deal of variation from one location to another.

In the fall of 1959, members of the ACS committee and representatives of the National Science Foundation met with Glenn Seaborg, Chancellor of the University of California at Berkeley, to discuss their ideas for the new course and to urge him to take responsibility for heading the project. Seaborg agreed to take on the task and quickly secured the services of chemistry professor J. Arthur Campbell of Harvey Mudd College as director of the project. Campbell suggested the name Chemical Education Material Study (CHEM Study) for the project. A steering committee made up almost exclusively of university and industry representatives met in Berkeley in January 1960. There they decided to assemble a team of outstanding high school teachers, university professors, and industrial chemists to prepare materials for trial during the next school year. A group of 25 people met in April of 1960 at Harvey Mudd College to begin the process of outlining material for the new course. Professors of education and curriculum specialists were not included.

At that first meeting, the group struggled with such basic questions as where in the course to place the material on atomic structure and chemical bonding, how much of the classwork would depend on the students' laboratory experiences, ways to deal with the mole concept, how extensively the course would deal with the subject of radioactivity, and how much emphasis would be placed on industrial practices and practical applications. The group was generally agreed that the course should be geared to the same population that was currently taking chemistry in high school (students in the top half of their class) and that it should be of value both to those planning to continue their study of chemistry in college and to those for whom it would probably be their final science course. The group also agreed that the course should integrate laboratory and classroom work (all labs had to fit into a 45- to 50-minute lab period), that it should avoid presenting chemistry in an arbitrary or authoritarian way, and that students should be encouraged to understand fundamental ideas of the subject rather than to memorize statements of principles and definitions of terms. They also felt that industrial applications should not be completely ignored, and thus they tried to include some reference to applications in the textbook (Merrill & Ridgway, 1969).

The group met again for six weeks in the summer of 1960 to

begin writing the new text materials. Twenty-five schools had been contacted to determine if they would be willing to use the preliminary materials during the 1960–1961 year. These schools, all located within 50 miles of Berkeley or Claremont, became the first group to test the new course. Materials were revised the following summer, and during the 1961–1962 school year 140 teachers used the course materials with about 12,000 students. By 1962–1963, approximately 700 teachers were teaching the new course to 45,000 students. By that time, the National Science Foundation was actively supporting summer institutes to give teachers intensive training with the new course materials, which then included the textbook, teacher's guide, laboratory equipment, and a set of films that had been created in conjunction with the project (Chemical Education Material Study, 1963a, b, c).

One of the more important goals of the CHEM Study course was to give students a better idea of the nature of scientific investigation and the way scientific knowledge was generated, and the laboratory was to be an essential part of the development of that goal. George Pimentel, who had the task of editing all of the text materials for the course, said of the laboratory program:

> The laboratory program was designed (1) to help students gain a better idea of the nature of scientific investigation by emphasizing the "discovery approach," and (2) to give students an opportunity to observe chemical systems and to gather data useful for the development of principles subsequently discussed in the text and classwork. (cited in Merrill & Ridgway, 1969, pp. 33–34)

As important as these aims were to the CHEM Study group, they soon realized that it was not always possible for students to fully develop the evidence in support of a theory in the laboratory. Sometimes experimental evidence had to be presented in the text or through films or teacher demonstrations to provide the basis for the theories that were being developed. In all cases, however, the intention was to give students the idea that theoretical models do derive from experiment and that "the ultimate 'authority' in science is natural phenomena, not the teacher or the textbook" (Merrill & Ridgway, 1969, p. 29).

This issue of authority was one that became a focal point of a number of debates about the new course. Kenneth Pitzer, a member of the steering committee, felt that the group's original outline was too authoritarian in that it dealt with too many abstractions that were beyond the grasp of students and failed to confront the students with experimental evidence until too late in the course. He felt that the CHEM Study project was making the same mistake as the CBA course by placing too much emphasis on theory that could be presented only as authoritative pronouncements.

> I believe that the Chemical Bond Approach outline is subject to criticism for its heavy emphasis on material which is not experimentally accessible to the student at the high school level . . . and which is therefore merely given by authority. (cited in Merrill & Ridgway, 1969, p. 132)

Speaking of the parts of the proposed CHEM Study course that dealt with atomic structure and the periodic table, and with molecules and chemical bonds, he said they were

> based almost entirely upon this type of *experimentally* inaccessible material and also to a very large degree upon *theoretically* inaccessible material. I fail to see any significant number of high school chemistry experiments which can be directly tied to this material, and I would be very reluctant to see practically the entire first semester pass before a chemical reaction is related to the main thread of classroom instruction. (cited in Merrill & Ridgway, 1969, p. 132)

In the final version of the course, the "authoritarian" argument was met by deferring a detailed treatment of both atomic structure and bonding until relatively late in the course and by using a more thorough treatment of combining volumes of gases as the experimental basis for the atomic theory early in the course.

In the end, the textbook that was created was fundamentally different from those that had preceded it, and it was significantly different from the CBA text as well. Perhaps the most obvious difference between the earlier texts and the CHEM Study text was the latter's limited reference to the applications of chemistry in industry and the home. The older books were filled with hundreds of illustrations of industrial products, manufacturing practices, and applications of chemistry in the everyday lives of students. A text published in 1951 by Garrett, the head of the ACS committee that originated the CHEM Study project, for example, had almost 200 pictorial references to such applications (Garrett, Haskins, & Sisler, 1951). The 1963 edition of the CHEM Study text, on the other hand, contained only 25 illustrations that related to something from the student's life experience or to an industrial application. The lead chamber process for the manufacture of sulfuric acid and the preparation of sodium and chlorine from molten sodium chloride were two examples of industrial applications that were illustrated in the CHEM Study text. The CBA text contained even fewer such illustrations. The 1964 edition of the text had no more than ten illustrations that related to technology, chemistry in the home, or even to naturally occurring chemical substances or events. The CBA text writers limited their illustrations to a diagram of a steam turbine, several photographs of naturally occurring crystals, the industrial production of sodium and chlorine from molten sodium chloride, and an illustration of heterogeneous and homogeneous substances.

Besides the movement away from technological and everyday applications in the new courses, the second obvious difference between the new and older texts was that the new texts tried to tell a story that was interesting, conceptually integrated, and based on experimental evidence. The older texts, on the other hand, tended to be more encyclopedic in nature, with statements of facts and relationships presented with little of the evidence or logical connections accompanying those statements.

Other Curriculum Projects

Following the initiating efforts of the groups in biology, chemistry, and physics, many other curriculum projects were undertaken during the 1960s with the financial support of the National Science Foundation. Projects in the earth sciences, physical sciences, engineering, and elementary science soon followed, all of them pursuing much the same philosophy as the projects in biology, chemistry, and physics.

Earth science courses that were developed with NSF support included Time, Space, and Matter (TSM) and Earth Science Curriculum Project (ESCP). TSM was developed by the Secondary School Science Project (1966) at Princeton University and tested at selected school sites beginning in the 1962–1963 school year; a final version was published in 1966. The development of ESCP was under the control of the American Geological Institute. Work began on this program in 1962, and a final version was published in 1967. Both of the earth science courses were activity oriented, focused on the methods of science, and demonstrated the relationships among the different science areas through a broad conceptual schemes approach.

Still another ninth-grade science course that was produced with NSF support was Introductory Physical Science. Work began on this course in 1963, and it was published in 1967. Development of the course was under the direction of Educational Services Incorporated of Massachusetts, the same organization that had directed the PSSC physics course. The textbook integrated laboratory activities and explanatory text material in a course that was largely activity oriented.

Three programs that were developed for the elementary school with NSF support included Science—A Process Approach (SAPA), Elementary Science Study (ESS), and Science Curriculum Improvement Study (SCIS). SAPA was first published in 1967, ESS in 1969, and SCIS in 1970. Science—A Process Approach was developed under the auspices of the American Association for the Advancement of Science (1967). The course utilized a highly structured approach to teaching specific processes of science, such as observing, classifying, measuring, and predicting, while it deemphasized the mastery of specific science facts. Statements of behavioral objectives were used to guide the work of the students and teachers. Elementary Science Study, created by the Educational Development Center (1969) in Newton, Massachusetts, emphasized independent exploration of science phenomena by children. The nonsequential, open-ended units utilized a discovery approach and students were given a great deal of freedom to explore on their own the materials that were provided. The teacher's role was to guide the activities without taking too active a part in trying to arrive at conclusions for the activities. The aim of the Science Curriculum Improvement Study (1970) was to create in students a functional understanding of science concepts and an open inquiring mind. The course focused on both the processes and products of science and made extensive use of the laboratory. The teaching strategy was the "learning circle" developed by Robert Karplus, creator of SCIS. The learning circle included an exploration, concept invention, and an application stage that was reminiscent of the teaching models proposed earlier by Herbart and his followers.

Theoretical Support
for the Curriculum Reform Movement

For the most part, what came to be known as the curriculum reform movement was led by college science professors with the help of school teachers. Education faculty played a secondary role if they were involved at all. There were, however, a number of educational theorists who lent their considerable support to the movement and played an important part in generating momentum for the changes that were occurring. One of these was Joseph J. Schwab, a well-known curriculum theorist from the University of Chicago, and another was Jerome Bruner, the noted psychologist from Harvard University.

The Structure of the Disciplines:
Jerome Bruner and the Woods Hole Conference

The Woods Hole Conference was a ten-day meeting of scientists and educators who had been called together by the National Academy of Sciences. The group of 35 met in September 1959 to discuss the new developments in science and mathematics teaching that were taking place across the country and to offer guidance for future developments in this area. The group was headed by Jerome S. Bruner, a psychologist from Harvard University, and included representatives from education, history, and psychology, as well as the sciences and mathematics. The conference report was written by Bruner and published in 1960 under the title *The Process of Education*.

The group's reason for considering these issues was much the same as the reasons that had led to the creation of the curriculum groups themselves. In 1959, national security was a primary justification for serious consideration of our educational programs, especially programs in science and mathematics. We lived in an age of technological complexity, we had an unmet need for additional scientists, and the Soviet Union was ahead of us in the space race. It was believed that all of these factors imperiled our national security.

Few of the conclusions of the Woods Hole group were definitive; rather they pointed out promising ideas and called for additional research. Discovery or inductive learning, for example, was described as a potentially valuable way to teach the fundamental ideas of a field, but it was felt that research was needed to determine the proper balance between using authoritative assertions in teaching and having students discover principles by themselves (Bruner, 1960).

The group was particularly intrigued by the new emphasis that the curriculum committees in science were placing on teaching the structure of the disciplines and giving students a sense of the fundamental ideas of a discipline as early as possible. Speaking of the math, physics, and biology curriculum projects, Bruner (1960) said:

> The main objective of this work has been to present subject matter effectively—that is, with due regard not only for coverage but also for structure. The daring and imagination that have gone into this work and the remarkable early successes it has achieved have stimulated psychologists

who are concerned with the nature of learning and the transmission of knowledge. (p. 2)

Ten of the 35 members of the Woods Hole Conference were psychologists, and the fact that their ideas about learning and knowledge fit so well with those of the curriculum makers added greatly to the success of the curriculum projects.

Bruner (1960) described "structure" as the fundamental principles of a field and the relationships among those principles: "Grasping the structure of a subject is understanding it in a way that permits many other things to be related to it meaningfully. To learn structure, in short, is to learn how things are related" (p. 7). He illustrated what he meant by structure through the example of "tropisms" in biology. A tropism is the tendency of organisms to react in predictable ways to stimuli in their environments. According to Bruner, if students were brought into contact with several examples of organisms responding to light, temperature, salinity, and so on and the unifying principle of tropism explained, then other, similar events could be meaningfully related to that more general principle. Tropisms were part of the structure of the discipline of biology.

Learning the structure of biology or chemistry or physics meant learning the discipline in the way that scientists understood the subject. It meant learning content that had been organized by the adult mind. This conception of the discipline included not only the principles of the field but also the modes of inquiry and the attitudes of scientific investigation. According to Bruner, the current practice of teaching the conclusions of the sciences without providing a sense of the scientists' spirit of discovery produced knowledge unrelated to the essence of the subject itself.

Teaching the fundamental principles of a discipline required a deep and thorough understanding of the subject on the part of the teacher, and it required that textbooks provide comprehensive explanations of important physical phenomena. Bruner felt that the lead being taken by noted scientists in the development of the new curriculum projects was one important way to insure that the fundamental ideas of the subjects would be taught again.

There were several advantages to teaching the structure of the disciplines compared with less comprehensive and more fragmented approaches. First, Bruner believed that students would find the subject more *comprehensible* if they were presented with the fundamental ideas. New ideas could then be made to fit into a pattern. Related to this notion of comprehensibility, learning the structure of a discipline was expected to aid in *memory* of the subject. Bruner (1960) said:

Perhaps the most basic thing that can be said about human memory, after a century of intensive research, is that unless detail is placed into a structured pattern, it is rapidly forgotten. What learning general or fundamental principles does is to ensure that memory loss will not mean total loss, that what remains will permit us to reconstruct the details when needed. A good theory is the vehicle not only for understanding a phenomenon now but also for remembering it tomorrow. (pp. 24–25)

The third, and perhaps most important, of the advantages noted by Bruner was the idea that learning the structure of a discipline was at the heart of the transfer-of-learning issue that had been debated for at least the last century. Nineteenth-century conceptions of transfer had focused on the development of such mental abilities as analysis, judgment, and memory through the study of the academic disciplines. Studies by Edward Thorndike (Thorndike & Woodworth, 1901; Thorndike, 1924) convinced educators that such general transfer was unlikely and that skills had to be taught directly. According to Thorndike's view, a rigorous study of mathematics, or physics, or Latin would not develop a person's general mental abilities. Bruner (1960), however, argued that with a slightly modified conception of transfer, it could be shown that general skills could in fact be taught through the subject fields. The key was to teach the facts of the subject within the context of the general principles of that field.

In essence, it consists of learning initially not a skill but a general idea, which can then be used as a basis for recognizing subsequent problems as special cases of the idea originally mastered. This type of transfer is at the heart of the educational process—the continual broadening and deepening of knowledge in terms of basic and general ideas. (p. 18)

Bruner did not advocate a return to a nineteenth-century conception of transfer, but neither was he satisfied with the idea that no transfer of learning at all was possible.

In addition to supporting the curriculum reformers' emphasis on a thorough presentation of the fundamental ideas of the discipline and tentatively supporting inductive, discovery learning as an appropriate mode of learning, Bruner and the Woods Hole Conference introduced a number of other ideas that were to have an effect on science education in the years ahead. One of these involved the distinction between analytical and intuitive thought, especially as it related to problem solving in science and mathematics. Whereas analytical problem solving was generally thought to proceed stepwise, with full awareness of the path being taken, intuition, which proceeded with little awareness of the specific logical pathway, seemed to come out of a generalized perception of the total problem. Historically, scientists and mathematicians had stressed the importance of intuitive mental processes for the creative solution of problems in their fields. Although Bruner did not use the word *creativity* in his discussion, much of his description of intuitive thought was what is normally associated with creative behavior. He identified, for example, the need to have a thorough grasp of the fundamental nature of the subject field within which the problem solver was working, the importance of self-confidence on the part of the intuitive thinker, the need to provide students with an opportunity to make guesses based on intuitive hunches, and the likelihood that teaching generalized problem-solving approaches (heuristics) would enhance intuitive thought.

A second idea that Bruner introduced to the educational community by means of his report on the Woods Hole Conference was the idea of stages of mental development as developed by the Swiss psychologist Jean Piaget. Piaget had completed much of his work as early as the 1920s in Geneva, but he had not received much attention in the United States until Bruner and a small number of other psychologists began to work with his ideas in the late 1950s. In addition to describing Piaget's four stages of cognitive development, Bruner applied Piaget's theories of mental development to science teaching and learning in the classroom. One principle, in particular, that was stated by conference member and co-worker of Piaget's, Barbel Inhelder, came to be remembered as the theme of the Woods Hole Conference. Speaking of the teaching of such subjects as geometry and physics, Inhelder said: "Basic notions in these fields are perfectly accessible to children of seven to ten years of age, *provided that they are divorced from their mathematical expression and studied through materials that the child can handle himself*" (cited in Bruner, 1960, p. 43; emphasis in original). Bruner (1960) put the issue even more dramatically: "We begin with the hypothesis that any subject can be taught effectively in some intellectually honest form to any child at any stage of development" (p. 32). The key to success was to translate materials into the logical form that the developing child could understand and to present them in a way that was consistent with the child's level of intellectual development. Once having identified an issue as crucial in the pursuit of some field, "then instruction in these subjects should begin as intellectually honestly and as early as possible in a manner consistent with the child's forms of thought" (p. 54). This development and redevelopment of important topics in later years of school, with each subsequent encounter presented in more abstract terms, constituted what Bruner called the "spiral curriculum."

The Teaching of Science as Enquiry: Joseph Schwab

Joseph Schwab had been a member of the Biological Sciences Curriculum Study and was largely responsible for writing the *Biology Teachers' Handbook* (Biological Sciences Curriculum Study, 1963d), which contained, among other things, a set of "Invitations to Enquiry," intended to assist the teacher in presenting the concepts of scientific investigation.

Just as Bruner had focused on the organized content of science, Schwab stressed the processes by which scientists generated that knowledge. One forum that allowed Schwab (1962) to present his ideas concerning the teaching of science as "enquiry" was the Inglis Lecture at Harvard University in 1961. In that lecture he argued for a fundamentally different approach to science teaching that would more faithfully mirror a changing conception of science itself. Since scientists no longer viewed scientific knowledge as stable truths to be discovered and verified (as many nineteenth-century scientists had believed to be true), but as "principles of enquiry—conceptual structures—which could be revised when necessary" (p. 11), school science teaching should also promote this revised notion of science. According to Schwab, "scientific research has its origin, not in objective facts alone, but in a conception, a construction of the mind" (p. 12). Thus, "the knowledge won through enquiry is not knowledge merely of the facts but of the facts interpreted" (p. 14). Science textbooks therefore should present not merely the conclusions of science but also the factual and theoretical evidence that supports those theories.

In further elaborating this new conception of science, Schwab (1962) distinguished between "stable" and "fluid" enquiry (p. 15). Whereas stable enquiry used current principles to "fill a . . . blank space in a growing body of knowledge" (pp. 15–16), fluid enquiry involved the invention of new conceptions and the development of entirely new principles. What had happened by the mid-twentieth century was that the rate of change in understanding the fundamental principles of science was escalating so fast that the presentation of science as stable enquiry was no longer a faithful representation of the current view of the nature of science. In part this was due to the new importance of science in society. Speaking of the new social importance of science, Schwab (1962) said:

A hundred fifty years ago, science was an ornament of a leisurely society. It was still mainly pursued by amateurs and gentlemen. It was a gratuitous activity of the enquiring intellect, an end pursued for its own sake. . . . It is so no longer. Industrial democracy has made science the foundation of national power and productivity. Science now plays the part once played by exploration, by empire, and by colonial exploitation. (p. 18)

Schwab (1962) went on to say that this new vital importance of science had led in turn to pressures for new discoveries, new principles, and new applications. The new enquirers

are charged, as a class, with the invention of new conceptions, the construction of molecular and probabilistic models, the development of specialized calculuses for radically new treatment of problems of politics, psychology, cellular dynamics, and the classical sciences of physics and chemistry. (p. 20)

Science teaching had not kept pace with this new conception of science. In part, this was due to the transfer of control of textbook writing from the scientists themselves to professional educators during the 1920s, 1930s, and 1940s. According to Schwab (1962), more attention was paid by these professional educators to the needs of individual, community, and social class than to the subject matter itself. Science was taught "as a nearly unmitigated *rhetoric of conclusions* in which the current and temporary constructions of scientific knowledge are conveyed as empirical, literal, and irrevocable truths" (p. 24). This rhetoric of conclusions persuades us "to accept the tentative as certain, the doubtful as the undoubted, by making no mention of reasons or evidence for what it asserts" (p. 24). Data and evidence were not being presented along with the statements of scientific principle, and when they were, they were offered as proof of the truth of the principle. But, more often than not: "The data component of scientific enquiry is . . . treated . . . by the device of silence" (p. 27).

Schwab described the failure of science teaching to keep pace with scientific development as "urgent" and "compelling" because it concerned the very welfare of our nation. According to Schwab, the nation faced three important needs, each of which required that science be taught not as a rhetoric of conclusions but as a fluid, ongoing activity. The first was the need for additional scientists who could probe the frontiers of scientific knowledge. The shortage of technical personnel adequately trained in science and mathematics had been recognized during and immediately after World War II and was still seen as a critical need in the early 1960s. The second need was for competent political leaders who could operate effectively in a world dominated by science and technology and who could develop policy agendas based on the sometimes conflicting claims of scientists. The third need was for a public that was aware of and sympathetic to an ongoing program of scientific research and discovery, a public that realized that scientific knowledge was not final and that was willing to support pure research even if the practical outcomes were not obvious.

The secondary school could assist in the development of properly educated scientists and political leaders, but it was the education of the general public that should be the school's primary concern. Since only a fraction of youth attended colleges and universities, it fell to the high schools to produce a well-educated public. Schwab suggested a number of ways by which schools could foster realistic perceptions of the nature of science. One method was for teachers and students to read and analyze, in either the original or edited form, historical papers that scientists had written. Through this means the students would acquire scientific knowledge that was worth knowing and at the same time develop the attitude that science was an active rather than a static process.

It was not Schwab's primary concern that students develop habits of enquiry themselves, although he felt that it was better to have students practicing methods of enquiry in classrooms than being taught by dogmatic means. Schwab (1962) described the process of using enquiry as a mode of teaching to portray science as enquiry, as "enquiry into enquiry" (p. 65). In these classrooms, students would be led to dissect the textbook and lectures, to look for evidence for the validity of the claims of others, and to be active in a process of analysis. The teacher's job in such a classroom changed from one of presenting information and explaining concepts to one of teaching students how to ask questions, how to look for evidence, and how to evaluate the results of their enquiries.

One of Schwab's preferred modes of enquiry learning was the discussion. He felt that through discussion students learned that many questions have no "right" answers, but rather answers that are *more or less* defensible in light of the evidence. If conducted at the appropriate intellectual level, discussion could be a powerful mode of learning. Schwab offered three reasons for the effectiveness of discussions in teaching. First, discussion evokes much more active engagement in the learning process, and there are more numerous and varied ideas and associations involved. Second, it is a group activity and enlists as reinforcers of learning many of the desired emotional outcomes of working as a member of a group. Third, it affords a situation in which the teacher can establish more effective interpersonal relations and interact much more frequently with many more students in a given learning period than most other teaching methods permit.

How Successful Were the New Programs?

What made the science curriculum projects unusual as an education reform effort was the scale of the endeavor and the extent to which the projects were actually completed and used in the schools. The national scope of the projects, the funding by the federal government, the widespread use of the courses across the country, and the involvement of noted scientists in the creation of the courses all made this effort unmatched in the history of American education. The new curriculum projects offered the opportunity to put into practice a number of principles of good education that thoughtful science educators had been advocating for decades but had been unable to implement successfully on a wide-scale basis.

Research Studies of the Courses' Impact

To determine the extent to which the new courses were used by science teachers, it is necessary to look at research studies that were conducted some years later. In the mid-1970s, for example, the National Science Foundation sponsored a series of studies on the status of science, mathematics, and social studies education. These included (1) a set of case studies of current classroom practices; (2) a review of documents and reports dealing with science, mathematics, and social studies education during the period of 1955–1975; and (3) a 1977 National Survey of Science, Mathematics, and Social Studies Education. From these latter two reports in particular we can learn a good deal about how extensively the new curriculum projects were used.

USE OF THE NEW PROGRAMS.   The results of the 1977 National Survey showed that for the 1976–1977 school year, 43% of the surveyed school districts were using either the Blue, Green, or Yellow versions of the BSCS materials, and an additional 6% were using *Patterns and Processes* (Biological Sciences Curriculum Study, 1966), the BSCS text that had been created for the "slow learner." In chemistry, 15% were using the CHEM Study materials, but fewer than 5% were using the CBA chemistry curriculum. In physics, 11% were using the PSSC materials, and 12% were using the Harvard Project Physics

(1968) course, a second physics course that was specifically designed to appeal to a larger number of high school students (Weiss, 1978). In comparison, data collected by Helgeson, Blosser, and Howe (1978) revealed that the Holt series of science textbooks—*Modern Biology* (Moon, Otto, & Towle, 1963; Otto & Towle, 1965), *Modern Chemistry* (Metcalfe, Williams, & Caska, 1966), and *Modern Physics* (Dull, Metcalfe, & Brooks, 1951)—which had dominated the science textbook market in the pre-curriculum-reform period, still held a large share of the textbook market. In the early 1970s, 40% of high school students were using the Holt text in physics, 50% in chemistry, and 35–40% in biology (Helgeson, Blosser, & Howe, 1978).

The three most popular new elementary science projects were used in 32% of the surveyed school districts—Elementary Science Study (15%), Science—A Process Approach (9%), and Science Curriculum Improvement Study (8%). In addition, one or more of the courses geared to the junior high school student were being used by over 50% of the districts. The most popular junior high school courses were Introductory Physical Science (Haiber-Sham, Cross, Abegg, Dodge, & Walter, 1972), used by 25% of school districts; Probing the Natural World (Intermediate Science Curriculum Study, 1972), used by 12% of the surveyed districts, and Investigating the Earth (Earth Science Curriculum Project, 1967), used by 10% of the districts. Taken together, the data indicated that in the early to mid-1970s approximately one-third of the elementary school districts in the country were using one or more of the elementary science projects and that about 60% of the districts were using one or more of the curriculum projects aimed at students in grades 7–12 (Weiss, 1978).

When looked at in the aggregate, the impact was impressive. Never before had a single curriculum initiative had such a widespread effect on science teaching in this country. But for some of the specific subjects such as chemistry and physics, the impact was less dramatic. Fewer than one-quarter of the school districts were using the new curriculum materials in each of those two subjects. The most significant changes occurred in biology, where almost 50% of the school districts used one or more of the BSCS courses, and in junior high science, where courses in earth science and physical science became viable alternatives to general science.

EFFECT ON COMMERCIAL TEXTBOOKS.   Beyond the direct impact of the new courses themselves, additional students were influenced by the curriculum projects through the inclusion of the new material into other commercially published textbooks during the 1960s and 1970s. These indirect effects of the curriculum projects were the subject of a study reported by Suzanne Quick (1978). She examined three innovations that came from the curriculum reform movement and the extent to which they had been incorporated by publishers into the commercial programs. The three innovations were

> (1) updating and redistributing subject matter content to more accurately reflect the current state of a scientific discipline, (2) organizing content around a few conceptual schemes that are central to understanding a scientific discipline, and (3) using an activity-oriented approach to science instruction. (p. 48)

"Updating content" and "utilizing a conceptual themes approach" were determined by examining each edition of the secondary school science textbook, *Modern Biology*, published between 1956 and 1973. The intent was to look for those revisions that were consistent with changes proposed by the curriculum reformers and those that were not. Incorporation of "an activity-oriented approach" was determined by examining the characteristics of all elementary science programs published between 1954 and 1975.

Quick (1978) noted that the 1963 edition of *Modern Biology* (Moon, Otto, & Towle, 1963) was published one year earlier than the normal four-year cycle of revisions would call for, apparently to coincide with the release of the BSCS textbooks that same year. This accelerated pace of revision continued two years later with the release of another edition in 1965. The 1965 edition (Otto & Towle, 1965), contained the greatest number of content changes of any edition published between 1956 and 1973, and the vast majority of the changes were consistent with the BSCS philosophy. Quick claimed that beginning with the 1963–1965 revisions "close to 70 percent of the subsection changes in *Modern Biology* . . . are alterations that reflect a move toward content redistribution advocated by the BSCS developers" (p. 82).

To test the extent of incorporation of unifying themes in *Modern Biology*, Quick (1978) looked for evidence of inclusion of four themes: (1) the change of living things through time—evolution; (2) the complementarity of organism and environment; (3) the complementarity of structure and function; and (4) a general process theme that Quick labelled "History-Scientific Processes" (p. 87). According to Quick, "subsection changes *inconsistent* with the BSCS approach to theme incorporation dominated in *Modern Biology* revisions until the publication of the 1965 . . . version" (p. 87). After that, most changes reflected the thematic approach of BSCS. Her research showed that the 1965 edition showed the strongest degree of theme incorporation, with 72% of the changes being consistent with the BSCS approach.

Examination of the incorporation of an activity orientation in elementary programs revealed a number of findings. First, Quick found that the *number* of elementary programs that were available to schools increased dramatically during the period of federally sponsored projects—from seven programs in 1954 to 27 programs in 1975. Many of these were produced with accompanying laboratory activities, and some that had been "textbook only" programs added laboratory activities during this time. However, Quick also found that by 1975, 12 of the 27 elementary programs were "textbook only" programs, thirteen were "textbook with lab" and only two were based on manipulatives. Quick (1978) concluded that federal intiatives at this level seemed to have increased interest in elementary science but "the fact that publishers continue to create both traditonal and activity-oriented programs indicates that they perceive strong school-level demands for programs with both orientations" (pp. 113–114).

Although Quick's research was limited to the high school biology course and the elementary science programs, she offered strong evidence that a number of the ideas that were proposed by the curriculum project committees were in fact incorporated into commercially prepared textbooks during the period following their initial appearance. Most notable of these changes were the updating of science content and the greater use of conceptual themes to organize that content into more conceptually meaningful units.

ENROLLMENT CHANGES.   Even though the new materials were widely used and had a way of filtering into the rest of the textbooks in use at the time, as early as the mid-1960s it had become clear to many that the new curriculum projects were not going to solve all the problems in science education. For one thing, the new courses had little if any effect on increasing enrollments in science courses. Although this had never been a primary aim of the new curriculum projects, it had been expected that better courses would be well received by students and that more would elect to take the courses. The new courses were not, however, more popular than the older courses had been. In fact, by 1964 physics educators were so concerned with persistently low enrollments in physics that they began to conduct national studies to determine the reasons for these low enrollments and to look for solutions to the problem (American Institute of Physics, 1964). The results, again, overwhelmingly supported the belief that high school physics courses were too difficult (Young, 1965).

A survey conducted by the CHEM Study group in the fall of 1964 provided information about enrollment changes in chemistry, biology, and physics in schools where the CHEM Study program was available. The survey was sent to approximately 700 schools that had used the CHEM Study materials for two full years or more. Usable data returned by 267 schools served as the basis for the analysis. Several observations were made from these data. First, between 1961–1962 and 1964–1965, the number of students taking chemistry, biology, and physics *of any kind* in these schools stayed essentially constant, with about 13.4% of students in grade 10–12 enrolled in chemistry, 27.4% in biology, and 6.3% in physics. As a percentage of grade 9–12 enrollments, these numbers convert to approximately 10.1% in chemistry, 20.6% in biology, and 4.7% in physics, figures I have noted before. Over the four-year period, there was a substantial increase in the percentage of students enrolled in the new versus the old courses, but the percentage of all students enrolled in science courses remained essentially unchanged. In fact, if we sum the percentages for the three subjects, we find that in 1961–1962, 47.4% of students in grade 10–12 were studying physics, chemistry, or biology at any one time, whereas in 1964–1965, the enrollments were at 46.4 percent (Merrill & Ridgway, 1969, p. 58).

Analyses of the Projects

It was also clear that although the new curriculum projects had a number of strengths that almost everyone welcomed, they also had some significant weaknesses. Paul Hurd (1970) summarized what were generally perceived to be the major strengths and weaknesses of the new courses. He listed the strengths under 14 specific points, the heart of which can be summarized in the following statements:

1. The new curriculum projects contained information that was more up to date and had more scientific validity than the older courses.
2. The new courses engaged students in independent, "discovery"-type investigations, which were considered to be more characteristic of the scientific enterprise and which were believed to lead to more meaningful learning.
3. The new courses presented a more accurate picture of the na-

ture of science by "stressing its nonauthoritarianism, its intuitiveness, its incertitude, its questions and doubts, its motivations, its dependence upon human qualities, its processes of inquiry, and its unifying principles" (p. 95)

4. The new courses were less concerned with "subject coverage" and dealt instead with a smaller number of "significant concepts, taught in depth and in context until the student has some intuitive feeling for the topic" (p. 95).

On the negative side, Hurd identified thirteen specific weaknesses of the courses. Three that were particularly relevant to the nature of the courses and to a theoretical consideration of the nature of the secondary school curriculum in science were:

1. The courses were too difficult for the typical high school student because of their theoretical sophistication and abstract nature.

2. The new courses did not do enough to motivate students to study science. Science was not related to the social world of the students, to their personal concerns, or to practical applications, and for this reason students developed little interest in scientific study.

3. The courses ignored the role of science in everyday life.

Summary

The curriculum reform movement's scope and impact was unprecedented. The courses achieved the sought-after rigor, and they presented the disciplines of science in a more thorough and honest way. They presented the science disciplines as logically structured areas of human investigation, they dealt candidly with the nature of scientific research, and they encouraged students to think and act like scientists within the structure that was established. What the curriculum makers failed to do, however, was to consider a number of fundamental principles of curriculum and instruction. They did not take into account the importance of student interest or the pedagogical need to relate science knowledge not only to broad unifying themes of the discipline itself but also to the experiential world of the student, nor did they sufficiently consider the importance of readiness for learning and the need to postpone abstract learning until the student was capable of dealing successfully with such intellectual complexity. In addition, many of the projects ignored one of the most important reasons for teaching science in any culture at any time, namely, to provide individuals with knowledge and skills that would help them live intelligent lives in the culture in which they found themselves.

By the end of the 1960s, largely out of a recognition of the curriculum projects' failure to achieve some of the more important social goals of science teaching, a new theme began to emerge in the discussions of science educators. Scientific literacy, the relationship between science and society, and the integration of science with the rest of human life and with other academic disciplines were phrases that came to represent a turning away from the intellectual study of the structure of the disciplines for its own sake and a renewed emphasis on the study of science in its relationships to human life and action. In the next chapter we will examine this movement toward the development of scientific literacy and the revitalized emphasis on the relationship between science and society that had been interrupted by the disciplinary studies of the 1960s and late 1950s.

Chapter 9

Scientific Literacy
and the New Progressivism

By the late 1960s and early 1970s attention in education had moved from concerns about keeping pace with the Soviets to concerns about providing an equitable and humane educational environment for all American youth. An unpopular war in Vietnam served as a catalyst to arouse feelings of discontent and even anger with many facets of American life. Persistent and oppressive poverty, especially in urban areas, overt racial prejudice and violent reactions to that prejudice, ever-present gender inequity, and a growing sense that many of our social institutions were needlessly impersonal and bureaucratic led many Americans to search for ways to improve society. Legislation was passed in an effort to remedy the inequities of the past and to insure equality of educational opportunity regardless of race, gender, or physical handicap; federal funding was used to support compensatory education programs in areas of both urban and rural poverty; and social critics offered suggestions for humanizing social institutions.

Given the social atmosphere of the late 1960s and early 1970s, the calls for intellectual rigor, for excellence, and for disciplinary study that had been made little more than a decade earlier sounded strangely anachronistic. Many educators who had been skeptical of the curriculum reformers' emphasis on the structure of the disciplines were quick to point to the failure of these courses to meet the new challenges of education. The new need was for an enlightened citizenry, not an educational elite. To these critics, the science curriculum should be relevant to the lives of a broad range of students, not just those planning careers in science, and the methods of instruction should demonstrate a concern for the differences in ability and inter-

est of each individual student. This sensitivity to individual differences was seen in the widespread popularity of individualized instructional programs and in the expanded opportunities for student
choice in course selection.

The increased attention to student interest and the renewed focus on the social relevance of the curriculum were reminiscent of several fundamental principles of progressive education that had been
so widely condemned in the 1950s. The similarities between the values of the two periods led Diane Ravitch (1983) to refer to the educational emphasis of the 1970s as the "new progressivism." In science
education, the term "scientific literacy" was used to describe an education in science for all youth that was relevant to their lives and that
focused on socially important issues. It was said that all students
should become scientifically literate if they were to deal effectively as
adults with such important social concerns as hunger, overpopula-
tion, and energy shortages. For many science educators, scientific literacy became the watchword of the 1970s. But the term lacked pre-
cision and, because of this, was used to describe a wide assortment of
educational goals. In this chapter, an attempt will be made to clarify
what was meant by scientific literacy, what its relation was to other
educational goals, and how the concept developed through the decades of the 1960s, 1970s, and 1980s.

Scientific Literacy

A key proponent of science education for scientific literacy was
Paul DeHart Hurd of Stanford University. Hurd was one of the first
people to use the term, in an article entitled "Science Literacy: Its
Meaning for American Schools" (1958). Hurd used the term *science
literacy* to describe an understanding of science and its applications to
our social experience. He said that science and its applications in
technology had become so dominant a force in our society that it was
difficult to discuss human values, political and economic problems, or
educational objectives without a consideration of the role played by
science. As he put it: "More than a casual acquaintance with scientific
forces and phenomena is essential for effective citizenship today. Science instruction can no longer be regarded as an intellectual luxury
for the select few" (1958, p. 13).

In 1963, Robert Carlton, executive secretary of the National Science Teachers Association, asked a number of scientists and science
educators what the term *scientific literacy* meant to them and how they
felt it could be increased. In their definitions, most of the respondents

focused on greater content knowledge in a broad range of science fields. Only a few spoke of the relationship between science and society as Hurd had. Gerald Holton, professor of physics at Harvard University, described two facets of scientific literacy: "(1) some narrow-area contact—knowing and keeping up with at least one chosen, even though small, part of science, and (2) range-contact—trying to keep in touch with a variety of other scientific developments" (quoted in Carlton, 1963, p. 33). Hugh Odishaw, executive director of the Space Science Board of the National Academy of Science, said: "Scientific literacy can be defined as a comfortable familiarity with the development, methodology, achievements, and problems of the principal scientific disciplines. A thoughtful reading of some fifty books could establish such familiarity" (quoted in Carlton, 1963, p. 34). And Howard Meyerhoff, chairman of the Department of Geology at the University of Pennsylvania, said that scientific literacy implied not "omniscience" but rather "familiarity with scientific methods and . . . sufficient knowledge in the several fields of science to understand reports of new discoveries and advances" (quoted in Carlton, 1963, p. 34).

Still another conception of scientific literacy was that it was a set of skills and knowledge that enabled one to read and understand the science that was discussed in the popular media. In a study reminiscent of the student interest surveys of the 1920s and 1930s, Koelsche (1965) identified 175 science principles and 693 science vocabulary words in a sampling of newspapers and magazines. Koelsche believed that schools could provide students with a working knowledge of most of these terms and principles and that "the lists constitute desirable subject matter for scientific literacy" (p. 723).

In a 1967 article, Milton Pella reported on a study conducted at the University of Wisconsin in which 100 published science education articles were examined to determine what educators meant when they used the term *scientific literacy*. He found six referents that were used most frequently:

1. Interrelations between science and society (used 67 times)
2. Ethics of science (used 58 times)
3. Nature of science (used 51 times)
4. Conceptual knowledge (used 26 times)
5. Science and technology (used 21 times)
6. Science in the humanities (used 21 times)

Pella then evaluated the extent to which the new NSF-supported science curricula dealt with issues of scientific literacy and found them wanting because of their failure to include adequate mention of technology, social applications, and the relation between science and the humanities.

Norman Smith (1974), a retired NASA aerospace research scientist, defined scientific literacy as an understanding of the events around us, the ability to verify the truth of claims made by lay persons and the popular media about science, and the ability to evaluate the relevance and importance of scientific developments and projects in relation to the needs of society. According to Smith, we were bombarded daily by television, radio, newspapers, magazines, and our own experiences with " opportunities to test our mettle as seekers and promoters of scientific literacy" (p. 34). Smith provided a list of twelve examples of energy-related issues that invited discussion and enhanced scientific literacy. Here are two such examples:

1.   In a letter to a newspaper editor, a man complained that the city buses tended to be overheated in the winter. That, he said, was a waste of valuable energy. *Was his latter statement correct? If his complaint had referred to subway trains, would your answer be the same? . . .*
9.   Automobile companies have reported that they are beginning to make more parts from plastic or aluminum instead of steel in order to reduce the weight of their cars and thereby improve gasoline mileage. *From the standpoint of energy and resources required to produce these three materials, how would you evaluate this switch? From the standpoint of overall energy saving?* (pp. 34–35)

Although definitions of scientific literacy varied from writer to writer, it was clear that to most people the concept implied a broad and functional understanding of science, much like that emphasized by the Thirty-First NSSE Yearbook authors, not the "structure of the discipline" approach of the new curriculum projects. Science knowledge was to be used to answer important questions that people encountered in their everyday lives, not just to answer questions about theoretical science. It meant that science should be understood as an important social force, not simply as a set of abstract principles familiar to experts.

Hurd, especially, believed that more than anything else scientific literacy meant understanding the coherence of science and society. Speaking of ways to accomplish the goal of scientific literacy in contrast to the goals of the curriculum reformers, Hurd (1970) said that science had to be taught "in a wider context than the processes and concepts of which it is formed" (p. 109). Besides the intellectual side of science teaching, it was also important that aesthetic and social values be taught. In fact, according to Hurd, the social context of science was the *only* appropriate context for science teaching for general educational purposes.

The theme of scientific literacy gained additional prominence when the National Science Teachers Association (NSTA) identified it as the most important goal of science education in its position statement on "School Science Education for the 70s." The statement, approved by the NSTA Board of Directors at its annual meeting in July of 1971, began with the words: "The major goal of science education is to develop scientifically literate and personally concerned individuals with a high competence for rational thought and action" (National Science Teachers Association, 1971, p. 47).

As the goal of scientific literacy was elaborated in the position statement, it became clear that the NSTA was taking a very different stand on science education from that taken by the curriculum reformers only a decade earlier. The scientifically literate person was described as one who "uses science concepts, process skills, and values in making everyday decisions as he interacts with other people and with his environment" and "understands the interrelationships between science, technology and other facets of society, including social and economic development" (National Science Teachers Association, 1971, pp. 47–48). Learning objectives were to be analyzed on the basis of their consistency with the nature of science, but also on the basis of their "desirability and potential usefulness by thoughtful lay citizens" (p. 49) and for their potential interest to students. In addition, science programs were to be evaluated for their student-centeredness and their ability to "foster student liking for science in general and for independent investigation in particular" (p. 49).

What was clearly evident in the NSTA's position statement were the themes of social relevance, student interest, the relationships between science and other areas of the curriculum, the interdependence of science and technology, and the human aspects of the scientific enterprise. What was abandoned was the idea that the structures of the science disciplines should be studied largely for their own sake. The goal of education was to teach those aspects of science that would help students understand the world around them and that would provide them with the tools for acquiring new science knowledge in the future. The NSTA statement was a strong reaffirmation of the principles of progressive education that had been elaborated time and again by leaders in science education during the first half of the twentieth century.

The Science-Technology-Society Theme

Although the term *scientific literacy* continued to be used to describe a wide range of progressive educational goals throughout the 1970s and early 1980s, the importance of the relationship between science and society came more and more to fall under the rubric of science-technology-society (STS). One of the first persons to formally propose that science education be oriented around a science-technology-society theme was James Gallagher, in a 1971 article entitled "A Broader Base for Science Teaching." Gallagher argued that the new curriculum projects took a limited view of science, focusing as they did on the conceptual schemes and the processes of science. Gallagher wanted learners to become familiar with the social interactions of science as well as with the structured disciplines themselves.

> For future citizens in a democracy, understanding the interrelations of science, technology, and society may be as important as understanding the concepts and processes of science. An awareness of the interrelations between science, technology, and society may be a prerequisite to intelligent action on the part of a future electorate and their chosen leaders. (p. 337)

In 1982 the NSTA board of directors adopted a position statement entitled "Science-Technology-Society: Science Education for the 1980s," and by the mid 1980s the science education literature was filled with discussions of the STS theme. The close relationship between the STS and scientific literacy themes was evident in the NSTA position statement. The following two excerpts make the point:

> Many of the problems we face today can be solved only by persons educated in the ideas and processes of science and technology. A scientific literacy is *basic* for living, working, and decision making in the 1980s and beyond. . . .
>   The goal of science education during the 1980s is to develop scientifically literate individuals who understand how science, technology, and society influence one another and who are able to use this knowledge in their everyday decision-making. The scientifically literate person has a substantial knowledge base of facts, concepts, conceptual networks, and process skills which enable the individual to continue to learn and think logically. This individual both appreciates the value of science and technology in society and understands their limitations. (National Science Teachers Association, 1982).

According to STS advocates, science education in the 1970s and 1980s was to be humanistic, value-oriented, and relevant to a wide range of personal, societal, and environmental concerns. Three approaches in particular, namely, humanistic education, values education, and environmental education, deserve special attention as part of the science-technology-society thrust.

Humanistic Education

Humanistic education was advocated by a number of science educators who believed that science teaching should do a better job of portraying science as a human activity and should be more concerned about the emotional response of learners. Humanism is a belief in the importance of human beings, especially those qualities that make each person distinctively human and enable individuals to experience meaningful lives. As such, a humanistic orientation is one that considers the feelings and emotions of people to be just as important as their knowledge and intellectual skills. Ann Howe (1971), writing about the new elementary curriculum projects of the 1960s, provided a flavor of the humanistic approach.

> The objectives which are most commonly mentioned for elementary science education today are for children to learn the processes of science, to learn how scientists work, to learn basic scientific concepts, and to gain increased ability for intellectual functioning. It is rare to find any mention of how or where people fit into this scheme of concepts, processes and skills. I believe there is another dimension which should be included in science programs for children—an understanding of themselves as a part of, and in relation to, the reality around them. . . .
> We should consider what it is that gives meaning to people's lives and how science education may contribute to that end. . . .
> The world needs people who can think *and* feel; people who know the earth and also love it; who know much about the forms of life and respect all life; who know what the stars are made of and can still look up at them and wonder. (pp. 143–145)

Similarly, Ehrle (1971) advocated a humanistic approach to science education when he discussed the many problems that our society faced in the 1970s and beyond, including "the information explosion, the people explosion, the deterioration of the environment, the question of war and/or peace, the persistence of racial and ethnic injustice, [and] the realities of our dehumanizing technocracy" (p. 22). Likewise, William McElroy (1970), director of the National Science Foundation and former president of AIBS, believed that one way to humanize science was to pay attention to the affective, nonrational aspects of the enterprise. According to McElroy: "The science community should consider more carefully . . . emphasizing man as an emotional and feeling creature as well as a reasoning one" (p. 517). He felt that there was an "extreme emphasis" on rational thinking in the science community and that this approach needed to be counterbalanced by more humanistic approaches.

Still others described humanistic science teaching as a third phase of science education that had evolved from earlier emphases on teaching about the products and the processes of science. To them humanistic science education was akin to humanistic, or third-force, psychology, which had developed as an alternative to Freudian and behavioristic approaches. According to Bybee and Welch (1972), for example: "The primary focus of humanistic psychology is on the experiencing person, with an emphasis on distinctively human qualities such as choice, creativity, valuation, self-realization, and self-actualization" (p. 20). In science education, a humanistic approach was one that (1) did not omit the human factor when teaching about the scientific enterprise, (2) included the connections between science and the humanities, and (3) used humane teaching methods, including the provision for student choice and a commitment to providing students with meaningful experiences and personal involvement.

Values Education

An expectation of the humanistic approach to science education was that students would have an opportunity to examine what they thought and felt about value-laden science issues and would be able to communicate their values to others. Not only would the science that was taught be related to important social issues, but students would be given an opportunity to wrestle with moral dilemmas concerning those issues and would be given instruction in the valuing process.

Harmon, Kirschenbaum, and Simon (1970) argued that values issues must become thoroughly integrated into the teaching of science so that no science class would be taught without an opportunity to consider the values implications of the science content.

> With nuclear holocaust just outside the window and the polluted atmosphere already seeping in, we simply cannot afford to train a generation of students who know the *how* and *why* of scientific phenomena, but do not have a process for inquiring into the values issues raised by the topics they study. (p. 17)

The authors argued that any science subject could be taught on three levels—the facts level, the concepts level, and the values level. As examples of the values dimension that could be present in the teaching of Newton's laws of motion, the authors offered the following values questions: "What do you believe automobile manufacturers should be doing to save lives? Would you be willing to start a petition drive on that subject?" (p. 18). Other topics that they felt lent themselves to values discussion included lead poisoning, energy conservation, soil erosion, and air and water pollution.

The values dimension was considered an important part of scientific literacy in a science-technology-society context because of the need for citizens to make informed decisions regarding critical issues that affected their lives. Bybee, Harms, Ward, and Yager spoke about this decision-making aspect of values education in 1980. They felt that a discussion of controversial issues had to become a greater part of science teaching. Questions such as the limits that should be placed on technology or on the activities of scientists needed to be addressed. In addition, science students needed to evaluate dilemmas that were brought on by scientific and technological development, such as the effects of increased agricultural production on the environment. They also needed to think through the consequences of various decisions that might be made.

Most strategies for teaching students about values issues during the 1970s and 1980s followed the same basic rule: *Present the students with the dilemma, give them rational processes for thinking through the dilemma, but do not try to impose your own values on them.* There was an understandable sensitivity to the need to remain "value neutral" when dealing with controversial issues in a pluralistic society where individuals often clashed sharply over differences in political and religious belief. As a consequence, debate was acceptable, information gathering was important, and disagreement was expected, but closure on an issue was generally discouraged. Students were encouraged to work though these value dilemmas with the expectation that they would refine their own values as they were confronted with opposing values and as they saw the conflicting values applied in the context of critical social issues. In addition, students were often taught about the valuing process with the expectation that they would apply this process when they were faced with important value dilemmas in the real world. Critics of these approaches argued that overemphasizing the right of individuals to hold their own beliefs about fundamental issues led students to think that one value was as good as another. The balancing of this tacit moral relativism with the desirability of teaching particular values was not dealt with in any significant way in the science education literature during the 1970s or 1980s. Most literature presented values education as important without discussing the difficulties implicit in achieving the goal of informed, values-sensitive citizens.

Environmental Education

Perhaps one of the greatest forces behind the movement toward a science-technology-society approach to science education in the 1970s and 1980s was the tremendous growth in environmental awareness that took place during this time and the attendant commitment of individuals to protecting and preserving their life space. Issues of energy conservation, environmental pollution, and the survival of the planet were concerns that affected all inhabitants of the earth and were intimately tied to a wide range of science fields and technologies. Virtually every science education writer who advocated scientific literacy within an STS context raised environmental/ecological concerns as a potential subject matter for school science.

Bybee (1979) went so far as to argue that ecology would soon become an organizing theme for both society and science education.

> Our future support and growth will be based on ecology, which is a set of biological and psychological principles, and will become a social metaphor all of which will guide the formation of policy. In the short period of 20 years ecology has become a household word. Ecology will increasingly influence our ideas, values, and growth as we continue the transformation from a mechanistic-industrial-technical paradigm to an organismic-environmental-community paradigm. (p. 107)

Science education was considered to be especially important in this ecological society because the new society would have science at its core. Bybee suggested four goals of science education that were related to the new paradigm. These goals were (1) the full development and nurture of the individual, (2) the protection, conservation, and improvement of the environment, (3) appropriate use of natural resources, and (4) the development of a sense of community from the local to the international level. This ecological perspective, combined with the elements of humanism mentioned earlier, and the development of decision-making skills for informed citizenship, became the centerpiece for the STS movement in the 1970s and 1980s.

But besides being an important part of the STS movement, environmental education also existed as a separate entity. Throughout the entire twentieth century and earlier, science education had concerned itself in one way or another with a study of the natural environment, although none of these earlier efforts occurred in the context of the environment as a critical social issue. Nature study, outdoor education, and conservation education taught students about the outdoor world and encouraged them to respect and preserve it, but courses such as these did not deal with the environment as a source of social problems to be solved. As Troy and Schwaab (1982) put it:

> Man has been educating himself about the environment for a long time, perhaps since his earliest presence on earth. However, formal environmental education is considered a relatively new academic discipline. It may have experienced its true birth around the time of Earth Day, April, 1970. (p. 209)

The beginnings of the modern environmental movement in education can also be marked by the initial publication of the *Journal of Environmental Education* in 1969 and by congressional passage of the Environmental Education Act (Public Law 91-516) in 1970. This legislation defined environmental education as

> the educational process dealing with man's relationship with his natural and man-made surroundings, and includes the relation of population, pollution, resource allocation and depletion, conservation, transportation, technology, and urban and rural planning to the total human environment. (Environmental Education Act, 1970, p. 1312)

By the 1980s, however, environmental education had gained only a very tenuous status in the schools. Troy and Schwaab (1982) pointed out that whereas most state education departments had developed environmental education courses or curricular materials, there were many disagreements in the field concerning the definition of environmental education, especially whether it was to be considered a separate subject or to be integrated into the entire K–12 curriculum. The authors said that environmental education efforts were characterized by "a lack of organization and little sense of direction" (p. 215) and that the curricular guidelines issued by local, state, and national education offices were "vague and often disregarded by those who are best able to implement them" (p. 215).

Regardless of the status of environmental education as an organized field of study, the environmental perspective did find its way into the science curriculum during the 1970s and 1980s, either

treated informally to illustrate other science principles or as an organizing principle for the science curriculum itself. Comments by a
number of science educators during this period pointed to that fact.
For example, Moon and Brezinski (1974) said that environmental
education was "fast becoming a major focal issue of this decade" (p.
371). They believed that the efforts that had been expended during
the curriculum reform movement were now being redirected into
"more broadened interdisciplinary approaches to the biosphere"
(p. 371).

Speaking specifically of energy education, Glass (1983) said that
the energy shortages of the 1970s had caused Americans to be more
aware of the need to be responsible users of energy resources. This
new awareness showed itself in the form of a new curricular emphasis, namely, energy education. The effort was led by projects such as
Energy and Man's Environment and the NSTA's project for an energy
enriched curriculum. In addition, many materials were developed to
be used along with lessons in a variety of disciplines at all levels of
schooling.

Controversy About Social Issues as Organizing Themes

During most of the 1970s and 1980s there was little criticism of
the STS approach to science education or of the STS interpretation
of scientific literacy. However, when Hofstein and Yager argued
forcefully and unambiguously in 1982 that the science curriculum
should be *organized* around social issues rather than around the concepts of the disciplines, a heated controversy arose.

Hofstein and Yager (1982) challenged the assumptions of more
traditional, disciplinary-based science educators when they said:

> Rather than including information merely because it is basic to the dis-
> cipline, the decisions should be made on the basis of relationship to real-
> life problems, thoughts, and interpretations. There needs to be a cul-
> tural validity to school science as well as a scientific validity. Courses in
> science should be bounded not by discipline lines, but by a specific con-
> text, or relation to current issues and concerns. (p. 542)

Hofstein and Yager (1982) were advocating a curriculum whose
logic would be based on social issues, not the logic of the organized
disciplines. According to this view, content should be selected not be-

cause of its disciplinary value but because of its utility in helping students deal with real-world problems. As they put it:

> The use of societal issues as organizers for the science curriculum of the '80s has many advantages. First of all, it helps delineate content that can be useful for improving the quality of life. . . . This means that knowledge considered fundamental to the discipline in the past may be omitted from the curriculum. (p. 542).

Hofstein and Yager (1982) said that the curriculum reformers of the 1960s were wrong to assume that "science would be inherently interesting to all students if it were presented in the way it is known to scientists" (p. 542). They argued that the discipline-centered curriculum projects that focused on an understanding of science for its own sake was motivating to only a small segment of the society and that an issues approach would appeal to a much wider group of students.

Hofstein and Yager (1982) illustrated the use of societal issues as organizers for the science curriculum with numerous examples. They suggested that the industrial production of fertilizers could be the basis of a unit to show the relationship between science and technology. The interdependence of science and government was another issue upon which science instruction could be based. In addition, there were the relationships between science and the arts, especially such things as the electronic synthesis of sounds and the portrayal of science in literature. Finally, there were those science issues that are related to the personal needs of people.

> Information is needed regarding controversial areas such as abortion and family planning; use of energy in homes; planning for proper food preparation and use; care and maintenance of the body; stress and mental health; life style and its effects upon others; pollution rights *and* responsibilities; disease prevention and cure. (p. 545)

In these examples, a number of key elements of the new progressivism became clear. First, the science to be taught was science in relation to important aspects of contemporary life—chemistry in the context of agricultural production, for example. Second, science content was to be relevant to the personal needs of individuals both because of the utility of such knowledge for the well-being of society at large and because of the motivational power of such personally relevant knowledge. Third, science was to be taught in a larger interdisciplinary context—not simply as an isolated body of knowledge but as part of the entire body of human knowledge, which encompasses the arts, literature, mathematics, and the social sciences. Fourth, the relationships between the scientific enterprise and other aspects of life in a democratic society were to be made clear to students. The effect of science on the qualify of life, the ethical dilemmas raised by scientific discovery, and the importance of public support if science were to flourish all should have their place in the science education curriculum.

What was discomforting to opponents of this approach was not the emphasis on social relevance but the call to *organize* science courses around contemporary social issues instead of around the concepts of the sciences themselves. Kromhout and Good (1983) responded to the proposal to use societal issues as organizers of the science curriculum in an article entitled "Beware of Societal Issues as Organizers for Science Education." Although Kromhout and Good did not object to the use of socially relevant problems to motivate students and to lead them into a coherent study of science, they saw the use of societal issues as fundamental organizers of the science curriculum as part of a widespread flight from science that was occurring in the United States—and that needed to be stopped.

To illustrate their concerns, Kromhout and Good (1983) pointed to one science curriculum, the Individualized Science Instructional System (ISIS), that was organized around a study of socially relevant issues. They suggested that the modules of the program were interesting and motivational and could teach basic analytical skills and terminology to students; however, "since the units are organized around a particular socially important problem . . . they are independent of each other by design, and therefore are unable to convey any real understanding of the structural integrity of science" (p. 649). The authors argued that today's technological problems, being temporary, will fade away and that the societal-issues approach will not provide students with skills for dealing with technological problems of the future. "Thus our position is that if the *organization* of science courses is to be dictated by social issues, it will be counterproductive in the struggle for scientific literacy" (p. 649). The authors also expressed their concerns that under such an organization of science, the "basics simply do not get taught" (p. 649), that an orderly systematic approach to content acquisition was needed if science was to be learned effectively, and that "societal issues normally do not provide that logical, orderly framework" (p. 650).

In response, Yager (1983) pointed out that Kromhout and Good were successful products of the system that they advocated and did not realize that only a very small percentage of students were successful with a systematic disciplinary study of science. For science education to have an impact on the vast numbers of students who did not have aspirations to become scientists, Yager believed that a new structure of science education was essential.

The debate was further fueled when Yager suggested that the interface of science and society should become *the* organizing paradigm for the discipline of science education. During the late 1970s and early 1980s, science educators had discussed at length the apparent loose organization of the "discipline" of science education and the question of whether science education should be called a discipline at all. It was suggested that for science education to be considered a discipline, organizing paradigms were needed to guide both research activities and graduate instruction. In 1982, for example, Yager, Bybee, Gallagher, and Renner presented a list of problems in science education that had been identified by science educators, the apparent causes of those problems, and their possible solutions. The main concerns included declining graduate enrollments, decreasing faculty size, limited research productivity on the part of faculty, and decreased external funding of the major science education research centers in the United States. When representatives of the 28 largest science education centers in the country were asked to propose solutions to the perceived problems, the following statements were prominently mentioned on their lists:

> Establish research paradigms and insist that all research arise from these. . . .
>   Establish a theory base for science education to guide science teaching at all levels as well as the teaching of science education and research in science education. (Yager et al., 1982, pp. 391–392).

These discussions led to a number of suggestions regarding unifying theories for the discipline and appropriate research paradigms. In 1983, while he was president of the National Science Teachers Association, Yager said there were many advantages to be realized if the interface of science and society were to become the framework and rationale for the discipline of science education. According to Yager (1983), this framework would provide a scholarly context for the efforts of science educators, and it would give greater meaning to research efforts in science education.

A year later, Yager (1984) was even more explicit about science and society as an appropriate organizing theme for science education:

> Science education is defined ... as the discipline concerned with the study of the interaction of science and society—i.e., the study of the impact of science upon society as well as the impact of society upon science. Their interdependence becomes a reality and the interlocking concept for the discipline. Research in science education centers upon this interface. (p. 36)

Although most science educators did not find it necessary to identify a single organizing theme or research paradigm for science education, viewing such efforts as overly defensive, some suggested themes of their own. The strongest alternative proposal for a unifying theory for the discipline came in a statement by Good, Herron, Lawson, and Renner (1985). These researchers suggested that science education was "the discipline devoted to discovering, developing, and evaluating improved methods and materials to teach science, i.e., the quest for knowledge, as well as the knowledge generated by that quest" (p. 140). This definition of science education was based on what these authors called a scientist's definition of science—that science is both the knowledge of the physical world and the processes of seeking that knowledge. Science education is involved with the methods and materials for passing on this knowledge to students of all ages. To Good and colleagues, the science-and-society theme overemphasized the political and sociological aspects of the field and virtually ignored theories of learning. Under the science-and-society definition, they argued, mathematics and foreign language education should likewise become the study of the impact of those subjects on society and the impact of society on those subjects. They continued their argument by saying:

> Physics education is not the study of the impact of nuclear energy on society, nor is it the impact of society on nuclear physics. Chemistry education is not the study of the impact of chemical dumping on society, nor is it the study of the impact of society on chemical dumpers or on the chemists who synthesized the chemicals in the first place. Biology education is not the study of the impact of gene splicing on society, nor is it the study of the impact of society on genetic engineers. This, of course, is not to say that these sorts of issues are unimportant, yet surely they do not constitute the essence of science education. (p. 141)

Yager (1985) responded quickly to these suggestions by Good and colleagues, saying that their notion of science education as the transmission of scientific knowledge and processes made science education " 'administrative'—less than a discipline—an inquiry without a domain of its own" (p. 143). He wrote:

Such views as those espoused by Good et al. illustrate the elitist view of science teaching and science learning. They suggest that the only rightful domain for science education is that of helping people learn what scientists know and that the only legitimate research is concerned with the way people learn. . . . It would seem that this definition would better fit the actions of future or would-be scientists, i.e. persons needing to know what scientists now know so that they can produce new knowledge about the universe. . . . Good et al. seem to reject the idea of appropriate science experience for all learners. They seem unimpressed with the research that demonstrates the failures of traditional science teaching and learning science as primarily a means for gaining passage for further formal study. (p. 144)

Summary

In time, the heated debates about the nature of science education subsided. The issue of whether discipline-based or socially relevant science should be the focus of science education efforts, however, remained unresolved. The argument that science instruction should be appropriate for all students, not geared primarily to the needs and interests of future scientists, was one that had been widely discussed throughout the first half of the century. Then the reaction was to nineteenth-century disciplinary studies; in the 1980s it was to the structure-of-the-discipline approach that had characterized the curriculum reform movement of the 1950s and 1960s. In both instances, a major reason that was given for modifying traditional science instruction was the continuing decline in science enrollments. Since the majority of students had avoided taking traditional, disciplinary-based science courses, the solution in the 1980s, as before, was to offer science that could help people in their everyday lives, that would allow them to make a contribution to the well-being of society, and that was interesting to the students.

Concurrent with the themes of interest, relevance, and social benefit, however, both in the 1980s and in the 1930s, were those themes suggesting that the organized study of the disciplines of science and of the processes of scientific investigation were essential elements of any respectable program of science education. As the debate between Good and Yager illustrated, this issue represented an important and often emotional point of disagreement between science educators in the 1980s, a disagreement that was not easily resolved.

Chapter 10

Process and Product
in Science Education

As we saw in Chapter 9, there was abundant evidence of a resurgence of progressive ideas among science educators during the 1970s and 1980s. But there was just as much evidence of continued support by science educators for the basic ideas of the curriculum reform movement of the late 1950s and early 1960s. Taken together, these were the most obvious themes of science education research and writing during the postprogressive period, and as we have already observed, these two areas of interest sometimes found themselves in sharp conflict. The idea that science educators should concern themselves with the way students learned the basic concepts and processes of science often found itself in competition with the idea that the proper role of science educators was to focus on the applications of scientific knowledge to the solution of social problems.

In the previous chapter I looked at the theme of social relevance as embodied in neo-progressive thought; now I will look at the efforts of science educators to understand how students learn the processes and products of organized science. I will examine ideas about how students learn fundamental science concepts and how they learn to solve science problems; I will also note the variety of ways that have been suggested to teach these concepts and modes of thought.

To a large extent this work has been based on psychological principles of learning, in contrast to the more sociologically based work dealing with the application of science to society. Psychological principles of learning and student behavior have held an important position in science education research, as they have in all areas of education, since psychology became organized as a discipline in the late nineteenth century. William James, for example, summarized many of the key elements of the new nineteenth-century psychology in his very popular *Talks to Teachers on Psychology* (1899). Edward Thorndike's (1913) writings on the psychological principles of education similarly affected educational thinking throughout the entire first half of this century. Beginning in the late 1950s and early 1960s, coincident with the curriculum reform movement, the writings of Jerome Bruner, Robert Gagne, and David Ausubel, as well as the growing influence of Jean Piaget, kept the psychological tradition in education alive and flourishing, and by the late 1980s hope was growing that the secrets of learning and memory previously hidden because of the physical complexity of the human brain would start to be uncovered by neuroscientists.

It was largely the ideas of research psychologists such as Bruner, Ausubel, Gagne, and Piaget that affected thinking about teaching and learning in science through the 1960s, 1970s, and 1980s, and it is within the context of this body of psychologically based research that I will examine the development of ideas regarding how students learn science concepts and how they acquire the ability to utilize the scientific mode of thought.

During this period of time, most writing on science education and research on science learning focused on four major areas of interest:

1. The ways to develop the intellectual skills that are generally associated with a scientific mind—skills such as careful observation, objective evaluation of evidence, and the ability to draw inferences from data.
2. The ways to develop in students a clear notion and appreciation of the nature of science as a process of inquiry into the natural world, complete with an appreciation of its methods, values, and importance as a human activity.
3. The ways students gain mastery of science facts, concepts, and principles in a meaningful way and in a form that can be remembered and used in the future.
4. The development of a particular type of instruction—known alternately as "inquiry teaching," "discovery learning," and "the heuristic method"—to accomplish one or more of the previous three goals.

None of these research areas was new; they could be observed in the writings of science educators at least a hundred years earlier. But they become elaborated within a psychology of learning that was new, or at least more fully developed than that of the nineteenth century.

Developing the Scientific Mind

It had long been a goal of science educators to develop in students ways of thinking that mirrored the way scientists think about the natural world. Development of these intellectual skills was important for two reasons. First, anyone who might become a scientist obviously had to learn to think like a scientist, and second, for those who would not become scientists, scientific thinking provided an effective way of dealing with their everyday world. Discussing these two justifications, Gauld (1982) said:

> The tendency to be accurate, intellectually honest, open-minded, objective, and to demand reliable empirical evidence before making decisions may be most clearly seen in the problem solving activity of scientists . . . but they also represent predispositions appropriate for solving problems in everyday life as well. (p. 111).

When science educators talk about general thinking skills that can be taught in science classrooms, they use such terms as *problem-solving skills*, *critical thinking ability*, *reflective thinking*, *science process skills*, *the scientific method*, and *scientific inquiry*. What these terms have in common is that they represent a way of thinking about the world that is clear, rigorous, and logical. But besides being viewed as a general mode of thought that applies to both everyday living and to formal scientific investigations, scientific thinking can also be viewed as a specific mode of thought that is closely bound up with the structure and methodology of a particular discipline. Whereas *general* modes of scientific thought involve careful observation, the ability to control variables, the disposition to suspend judgment, and the ability to draw logical inferences from available evidence regardless of the object of inquiry, *specific* modes of thought involve the ability to place observations within a particular conceptual framework, the ability to make use of certain laboratory apparatus and instruments, and the ability to design experiments to produce data that advance our knowledge in a particular area of science.

Much of the writing that dealt with teaching the scientific way of thinking during the 1960s, 1970s, and 1980s pointed to the failure of schools to give adequate attention to this goal taken in either its general or specific sense. In their review of the first 60 years of the journal *Science Education*, Champagne and Klopfer (1977) identified this failure as one of the major themes of science education writing. They said that although educators showed a great deal of agreement concerning the role of reflective thinking and problem solving in children's learning of science in schools, the belief was often not matched by school practice. "A contemporary issue of some magnitude in science education is this disparity between belief and practice regarding reflective thinking and problem solving" (p. 437).

The Scientific Method and Scientific Thinking

The curriculum projects of the 1960s encouraged the development of scientific thought by placing the student in the role of scientist. The student was expected to investigate problems in science as a scientist would and to arrive at conclusions based on data that he or she had collected. The process was not to be conceived of as a narrow, restrictive adherence to a stepwise process, however. Science involved doing one's best with the resources at hand. In fact, much of the writing of the 1960s was critical of an earlier portrayal of the methods of science as a five- or six- or seven-step process that was supposed to lead inevitably to the successful solution of science problems. The steps as they were usually presented included (1) defining the problem, (2) constructing hypotheses, (3) experimenting, (4) compiling results, and (5) drawing conclusions (National Society for the Study of Education, 1947).

One response to the sometimes mindless adherence to a rigid series of steps in the scientific method was for science educators to produce lists of science process skills that were considered more open and flexible. It was frequently said that there was not just one scientific method but many methods that could be used in the solution of science problems. Science educators also argued that working scientists themselves did not follow the scientific method in lockstep fashion but rather used whatever resources they could to solve problems.

One group that generated an alternative list of science processes were the developers of the elementary science program, Science—A Process Approach (SAPA). In the SAPA program eight scientific processes were taught in grades K–3 and six more in grades 4–6. The first eight included (1) observing, (2) measuring, (3) using number relationships, (4) using space/time relationships, (5) classifying, (6) inferring, (7) predicting, and (8) communicating. The second group included (1) formulating hypotheses, (2) controlling variables, (3) ex-

perimenting, (4) defining operationally, (5) formulating models, and
(6) interpreting data (American Association for the Advancement of
Science, 1967). In the years ahead, process statements such as these
proved to be an attractive and useful alternative for describing the
methods of science and the activities of scientists.

General Versus Context-Specific Scientific Thinking

I already mentioned that scientific thinking could be viewed as
both a general and as a context-specific process. One question that
arose was whether it was possible to teach a generalized set of thinking or problem-solving skills that could be used in a variety of contexts or whether the modes of thought in a discipline must be taught
within the context of that discipline. Increasingly, science educators
came to the conclusion that problem-solving ability depended on a
knowledge of the concepts that were relevant to the area of investigation and of the specific processes used in that subject field.

Butts (1964) said that rather than viewing scientific problem solving as a general procedure that is applicable to all situations, it might
be better to view problem solving as "what one does when one brings
to a problem patterns of ideas and inquiry methods specific to a particular discipline" (p. 116). Lawson, Karplus, and Adi (1978) expressed a similar sentiment with respect to the teaching of proposi-
tional logic. According to them, instruction that is intended to
develop thinking "should allow students opportunities to generate
and test hypotheses within the context of the discipline being taught"
(p. 477) rather than in isolation. Pushing this point concerning the
importance of a conceptual context in scientific thinking even further,
Freundlich (1978) said:

> Random or inappropriate problem solving behaviors often indicate an
> undeveloped conceptual system. In the classroom, where the problem
> situation is often artificial, such behavior often signals that the "prob-
> lem" is not, to the pupil, genuine. It is formulated within a conceptual
> system he was supposed to have acquired, but has not—it is actually
> quite alien to him. The pupil, then, has no criteria for judging the ap-
> propriateness of problem solving procedures. (p. 21)

The point that scientific thought occurs within a context of concepts held by the individual was well made. However, numerous attempts to teach thinking as a general skill persisted through the
1960s, 1970s, and 1980s. As already noted, the elementary curriculum project, Science—A Process Approach, which was built on the

idea that science processes could form the basis of science instruction, was one such example of efforts to teach science processes separate from an overarching conceptual context.

Intuitive Versus Analytical Problem Solving

Another issue that arose when trying to teach problem-solving skills centered on whether scientific thinking was fundamentally analytical or fundamentally intuitive. Most definitions of the scientific method, most lists of science processes, and most descriptions of critical thinking pointed to highly analytical skills. It had long been recognized, however, that progress in science was due just as much to apparently spontaneous bursts of insight, especially in the generation of hypotheses, as it was to rigorous hypothesis testing.

In support of the view that greater importance should be placed on hypothesis-generating activities, Rachelson (1977) said that there was too much emphasis on the "logical, observable, and the repeatable" in science teaching (p. 115). Students were being taught the technical skills involved in conducting experiments, but not enough time was being spent on the creative activity of formulating hypotheses. Similarly, Taylor (1962) said:

> We suspect that the heart of the "scientific method," the core of scientific progress, is much better described by the usual steps in the creative process than by the traditional textbooks' descriptions of the specific sequences in the scientific method. The latter tend to almost entirely emphasize the verification stages. In addition, descriptions of the scientific method have become so abstract that teachers and students have lost sight of the vital human-being-in-action part of the scientific method. (p. 599)

Adding support to the importance of creativity in scientific endeavors, Moravcsik (1981) wrote that creativity is a key element in science: "Without it, science . . . turns into a sterile manipulation of set rules and their embellishment without any tangible output whether in a conceptual or a practical sense" (p. 222). Moravcsik suggested three ways that science educators might orient their science instruction to produce students inclined toward creativity:

1. Banish memorization as much as possible from science teaching, and replace it with understanding through problem solving.

2. Replace the excessive reliance on textbooks with renewed stress on experimentation.
3. Make the content of science secondary to the teaching of research methods and attitudes.

Others argued that no attempt at all should be made to teach a scientific method of thought. DiVincenzo (1976) wrote:

> Educators persist in thinking that nature's rarest gift (creative thought) can be nurtured by introducing students to a litany about scientific method. We must realize that students come equipped to discover just as puppies come equipped to swim. . . . Students need not be schooled in reasoning theory to perform acts of discovery. Discovery, like swimming, will come to pass if and when conditions are right. (p. 491)

Although they recognized that scientific thought had both an analytical and an intuitive dimension, many science educators felt that too much emphasis was placed on the analytical and not enough on the spontaneously creative, intuitive side of scientific thinking.

Piaget's Influence

As pointed out in Chapter 8, in the late 1950s, Jerome Bruner and a number of other psychologists in the United States began to discuss the work of Jean Piaget in the context of science education. In fact, Bruner's (1960) *Process of Education* contained one of the earliest descriptions of Piaget's work on human mental development to be read by many American educators. Beginning with that early introduction, Piagetian ideas had an enormous impact on theory and practice in science education, especially on how science educators looked at the development of human reasoning ability.

In a 1979 issue of the *Journal of Research in Science Teaching* devoted to a discussion of major research paradigms in science education, Lawson provided an account of Piagetian theory as it applied to science education research. In this account, Lawson (1979) described two types of reasoning strategies that matched Piaget's developmental stages and that were relevant in science education. The first he called "descriptive reasoning strategies" (p. 508) because they had the description of experience as their major aim. These strategies included the skills involved in such mental activities as seriating, classifying, and measuring. In Piagetian terms, descriptive strategies like these are based on a set of concrete mental operations and the stage is referred to as the "concrete operational stage." The second type he called "hypothetico-deductive reasoning strategies" (p. 508) because they function in complex problem solving that is deductive in nature. Included are such mental skills as the isolation and control of variables, proportional reasoning, correlational reasoning, and probabilistic reasoning. This is referred to by Piaget as the "formal operational stage."

According to Piagetian theory, individuals develop the ability to perform mental operations in a fixed temporal sequence through physical maturation, direct instruction, and involvement with their environment over time. The process of mental development involves the transformation of new knowledge to fit into existing mental structures (assimilation) and the alteration of existing mental structures to accept the new knowledge (accommodation). The mental operations that develop are coherent, generalized abilities that could, once acquired, be used with facility in any number of contexts. Since these mental structures are relatively stable and not easily changed, it follows that students should be presented with material that matches their level of cognitive development. Some moderate-level challenges might be helpful in order to keep the developmental process moving along, but there is no reason to expect students to use rational thought processes that involve operations that they have not yet acquired and are not expected to acquire for some time.

Lawson (1979) talked about this issue of developmental readiness, pointing out how both combinatorial and probabilistic reasoning are essential cognitive skills for dealing with Mendelian genetics:

> A topic such as genetics would cause a severe comprehension problem for students with little or no facility with these aspects of formal thought. Such students, of course, may be quite capable of the verbal parroting of key words and phrases (e.g., gene, dominant, recessive, crossing over), but this verbal knowledge would be no part of their useful bag of knowledge. . . . This is why science educators, who have a developmental perspective on teaching, object to the introduction of theoretical concepts such as these to students who are not developmentally ready. (p. 511)

Lawson, Karplus, and Adi (1978) provided additional examples of the dependence of science understanding on formal operational thought. They pointed out how proportional relationships are part of such topics as gravitational acceleration, air pressure, diffusion, and the chemical law of definite composition; how combinatorial reasoning was required for an understanding of the nature of probability; and how correlational reasoning was essential for determining whether relationships exist between such variables as smoking and lung cancer or between CO_2 concentration and phytoplankton density.

Besides the issue of developmental readiness, a second implication of Piagetian theory arises from the fact that the operational schemata appear to be neat packages that can be developed in the abstract and separated from the content of science. Thus, it is easy to think of trying to develop students' abilities of correlational reasoning, proportional reasoning, controlling variables, and so on as discrete mental skills apart from the content of science. Piaget's work did in fact have the effect of focusing attention on scientific reasoning as the aggregation of these mental skills. Linn (1982) addressed this point when she wrote: "Piaget's theory has profoundly influenced science education research. Following Piaget, researchers have focused on content-free strategies, developmentally based mechanisms, and structural models of each stage of reasoning" (p. 727). Lawson (1982) similarly recognized this limiting quality of the Piagetian influence and supported Linn's suggestions concerning students' development and use of formal reasoning. "Linn . . . calls for research into practical issues such as the roles of task-specific knowledge and individual differences in performance, roles not emphasized by Piaget in his theory and research. From a science teacher's point of view, this is good advice" (p. 743). These suggestions were not always heeded, however, and much research as well as classroom teaching focused on the development of generalized mental skills that would be applicable in a variety of content settings.

The Nature of Science

It is one thing to say that students should learn the scientific method—that they should learn the scientific way of thinking—but it is something else to agree on what that method or way of thought is. To a large extent, the definitions of scientific method and the lists of science processes that were discussed during the 1960s and 1970s were based on conceptions of science that had their origins in inductivist and empiricist philosophies that had developed in the seventeenth century. Whereas earlier scientists and philosophers of science such as Bacon, Boyle, and Newton may have had what we in the late twentieth century consider to be extreme views about the power of inductive thought, the basic process that they described was one that most science educators were comfortable with and, for the most part, accepted. This process places foremost importance on sense impressions as the source of raw data about the world upon which our science knowledge builds. The data are systematically organized into categories, the organized data lead to inferences, the inductive inferences are tested, and conclusions are drawn.

Questions about the appropriateness of portraying the scientist as a coldly rational inductive empiricist were generally based on the work of philosophers such as Kuhn (1970), Feyerabend (1975, 1981), and Toulmin (1961, 1972). The contribution of these philosophers was that they showed how scientists have engaged in science activities as human participants and not as completely objective and detached observers. Summarizing the new conception of science, Hawkins and Pea (1987) said that the postmodern critique of the nature of scientific knowing involved a view of science

> in which scientists shape, not only document, their objects of study. . . . Progress in science is best viewed as constructed knowledge within communities of knowers rather than descriptive of a reality mirrored through particular human procedures. The consequence is that scientific progress is not viewed as a smooth cumulative process, but as revisionary within communities of scholars. (p. 292)

When Freundlich (1978) argued for the necessity of an adequate conceptual background for solving problems, he based his argument on the ideas of the new philosophers of science: "When solving a problem, such background theories are *always* at our disposal. If they weren't, we wouldn't have a problem to begin with" (p. 20). Thus it is the case that "*all* description, *all* observation, is made in terms of concepts embedded in a general conceptual system" (p. 20). Likewise, Norris (1985) called on the new philosophy of science when he argued that observation had to be connected with the background theories of the observer. Finley (1983) made a similar point in his discussion of the failure of science educators to make use of the newer conceptions of science saying:

> If, as recent philosophers have suggested, processes as fundamental as observation are dependent upon the conceptual knowledge of the observer and if conceptual knowledge varies from discipline to discipline, the methods and processes of those disciplines must be different. Similarly, if we fail to recast our view of the nature of science, and continue to overemphasize a discovery approach to instruction, we are likely to

continue to expect that students will inductively formulate concepts and generalizations. It is unlikely that a child would ever inductively discover the full meaning of science concepts—even a concept as fundamental as mass. Such terms have rich meanings in the context of the sciences and unless we intend for our students to understand them within the limits of their sensory impressions, instruction based on discovery will not be successful. (p. 53)

Albert Einstein (1950), writing about the excessive faith on the part of nineteenth-century scientists in the inductive method, said: "There is no inductive method which could lead to the fundamental concepts of physics. Failure to understand this fact constituted the basic philosophical error of so many investigators of the nineteenth century" (p. 78).

Science educators were slow, however, to apply this new view to science teaching. Duschl (1985) pointed out that the new curriculum projects of the 1960s took no account of the new philosophies of science. He said that at the same time that the very definition of the nature of scientific inquiry was being challenged and changed by historians and philosophers of science, the scientific community itself, which was responsible for many of the changes in the science curriculum during this time, "effectively ignored [these] developments" (p. 551).

For the most part, science educators were oblivious to the development of the nonempiricist philosophies of science. This was a problem for science education both because it gave students a limited view of the nature of science and, more important, because it perpetuated the myth of totally objective and nonspeculative science among future scientists themselves. As Gauld (1982) said: "Teaching that scientists possess these characteristics is bad enough but it is abhorrent that science educators should actually try to mold children in the same false image" (p. 118).

Concept Learning

While some science educators were devoting their energies to answering questions that dealt with the teaching of science processes, others were more concerned with the way that students mastered science concepts, that is, how students came to understand the products of science. It is, of course, somewhat artificial to try to separate these two lines of research, since science product and process inevitably go hand in hand. We have already seen how a number of science educators argued that science processes could not be taught outside the context of the relevant science content and how scientific knowledge was always generated within an existing conceptual framework. Nevertheless, there was an area of research that focused specifically on the acquisition of science concepts—the mastery of science content—just as there was an area of research that focused on the acquisition of science processes. As with science process research, research that was conducted on concept acquisition during the 1960s, 1970s, and 1980s was done largely within a psychological framework.

Although the understanding of science concepts and principles had always been a goal of science educators, one of the major contributions of the curriculum reformers of the late 1950s and early 1960s was to improve written science materials in such a way that science concepts were presented in a fuller, more conceptually meaningful way. Instead of offering brief reference-book-style descriptions of phenomena, the new textbooks were written to tell a story that was interesting and understandable. Jerome Bruner (1960) was a major contributor to this approach, as was Joseph Schwab (1962). Differences of opinion presented themselves, however, in a number of areas. First, a distinction could be drawn between those who felt that the best way to develop conceptual understanding was by means of carefully organized instruction that was presented directly to students and those who felt that students acquired a mastery of science content, at least in part, through direct and independent interaction with the materials of science themselves. Also, within the direct instruction, or reception learning, camp, some looked at concept learning as the progressive linking of ideas outward into increasingly more inclusive concepts, while others viewed learning as the mastery of discrete bits of knowledge and the hierarchical development of that knowledge into more general concepts. The first of these direct instruction views was represented by David Ausubel's reception learning theories and the second, by Robert Gagne's hierarchical schemes.

Reception Learning

David Ausubel (1968) took the position that direct didactic instruction was the most effective way to teach concepts to children. This conviction was based on his notion of human mind and how it develops. Ausubel argued that mental development was a process by which new concepts were continuously brought into the conceptual framework of the mind. Old conceptual structures are modified to accept the new concepts as those new concepts are assimilated with the old. Ausubel believed that this process was most effectively accomplished through the direct and orderly presentation of ideas to young developing minds by a teacher who understood the logical connections between the concepts of a particular discipline. Thus, from the point of view of the student, this approach was one of reception learning.

Joseph Novak of Cornell University was the major advocate of Ausubelian theory as applied to science education, and it was Novak who provided a discussion of reception learning in the *Journal of Research in Science Teaching* in its special issue on major research paradigms in science education. Novak (1979) defined reception learning as a form of learning in which concept labels and the regularities they represent are taught explicitly by the teacher. This is in contrast to discovery learning, in which regularities are discovered by the students themselves. For reception learning to be effective, the concepts had to be meaningful to the students. Meaning is accomplished through the interconnectedness of concepts. In distinguishing between rote and meaningful reception learning, Novak, Ring, and Tamir (1971) said that in *meaningful reception learning* new knowledge "is associated with ideas or concepts in the learner's cognitive structure" (p. 485), whereas in *rote reception learning* no associated conceptual base is formed and there is no connection with prior concepts.

The obvious task of educators was to organize instruction in such a way that material could be learned meaningfully, that is, learned in relation to something else that the student knew. When no relevant concept was available in the student's cognitive structure, then the learning could be of a rote kind at best. If the relevant concept was not stable or well differentiated, then the learning would be only partially meaningful. The key to meaningful understanding was that a new concept be tied to a preexisting concept. According to Ausubel (1968), "the most important single factor influencing learning is what the learner already knows" (p. vi).

New knowledge is not, however, merely added to existing knowledge but rather is assimilated into existing relevant concepts. In that process of assimilation, both the original concept and the new knowledge are altered, and the interconnections between concepts become more complex. The richer these interconnections, the more one can learn on a related subject and the easier it is to solve problems in that area. In areas where existing concepts are limited and undifferentiated, learning is difficult and slow. In contrast to the Piagetian view, Ausubel's theory says that older children are capable of solving more complex problems than younger children, not because of some "unique cognitive capability" or structure but "because the overall level of differentiation and integration of their concepts is much more elaborate" (Novak, 1978, p. 5). The more elaborate and differentiated the cognitive structure is, the more effective will be subsequent learning.

The theory also suggests that it is easier for someone to understand a specific piece of information if the larger principle to which it relates can be made obvious. Thus, the *direct teaching* of significant organizing principles becomes a major goal of instruction, in contrast to approaches that try to have students build their understanding of these organizing principles *inductively* from many discrete encounters with related material. One specific instructional practice that is an outgrowth of this idea is the use of *advance organizers*. Advance organizers are brief introductory instructional episodes organized by the teacher to facilitate meaningful learning. The advance organizer is intended to organize relevant concepts so that new material will be more easily assimilated into the existing conceptual structure.

Ausubel also argued that once a child's mind had developed to the point where comprehension of abstract concepts was possible, verbal instruction should supersede the use of physical objects in teaching. According to Ausubel:

> In older children, once a sufficient number of basic concepts is consolidated, new concepts are primarily acquired from verbal rather than from concrete experience. Hence, in secondary school it may be desirable to reverse both the sequence and the relative balance between abstract concepts and supportive data. There is a good reason for believing, therefore, that much of the time presently spent in cookbook laboratory exercises in the sciences could be much more advantageously employed in formulating precise definitions, making explicit verbal distinctions between concepts, generalizing from hypothetical situations, etc. (Ausubel & Ausubel, 1966, p. 410)

Hierarchical Learning

Robert Gagne is the person most often associated with a theory of learning called "hierarchical learning." Like Ausubel's reception learning, hierarchical learning was identified in the 1979 issue of the *Journal of Research in Science Teaching* as one of the major research paradigms in science education. In his *Conditions of Learning* (1977) Gagne described and gave examples of several learning hierarchies. He said:

> Many subjects taught in schools have an organization that can readily be expressed as a learning hierarchy. The rule, or set of rules, that is the

learning objective may be shown to be composed of *prerequisite* rules and concepts. The learning of the intellectual skills which are the "target" of instruction is a matter of *combining* these prerequisite skills, which have been previously learned. (p. 143)

As an example, Gagne (1977) used the intellectual skill of calculating horizontal and vertical components of forces using vector diagrams. He identified three prerequisite skills for being successful at this learning task. Students should already know how to "(1) use rules to verify the conditions for equilibrium, (2) represent the magnitude and directions of forces as parts of triangles, and (3) employ trigonometric rules to represent the relationships in a right triangle (sine, cosine, tangent, etc.)" (p. 143). If these three prior learnings are available to the student, then the new learning can proceed easily. If not, then the new learning is impossible. Carrying the idea of essential prior skills one step further, each of the prerequisite or subordinate skills may themselves be analyzed to identify other rules or concepts that are needed for them to be learned.

Gagne is also recognized for his cumulative learning model—the idea that the acquisition of specifically learned rules is a cumulative process. This idea is a direct outcome of the notion of learning hierarchies. According to Gagne (1977):

> The specific rules that are learned make possible the learning of other more complex rules that are increasingly general in their applicability. Human intellectual development may be conceived as resulting from the learning of many specific intellectual skills which enter into the learning of other more complex and more general intellectual skills. Cumulative learning ultimately results in the establishment of capabilities that make it possible for the individual to solve a great variety of novel problems. (p. 152)

The idea that intellectual development results from the learning of many discrete intellectual skills leads naturally to systems of managed instruction in which learning material is broken down into small segments and arranged sequentially. In fact, a good deal of Gagne's more recent efforts have been devoted to the refinement of such instructional design technologies (see, for example, Gagne, Briggs, & Wager, 1988). Also, most systems of individualized instruction that are based on the mastery of a sequence of performance objectives derive from such ideas.

Jones and Russell (1979) traced the origin of the hierarchical learning paradigm to programs that were used to train military personnel during World War II. These programs were organized so that even individuals who had no prior experience with a given target skill could eventually master it if the material were broken down into small enough pieces and sequenced properly. These approaches made use of clearly stated objectives, repetition, reinforcement, small bits of new information, and attention to sequence.

Although there was some criticism of the application of this model to education because of its perceived rigidity, the practice of describing knowledge in terms of hierarchies of prerequisite skills, carefully stating behavioral objectives prior to instruction, and arranging instruction for the sequential mastery of small segments of new information was common in science education during the time period in question.

The Learning Cycle

An instructional strategy that was less highly teacher directed than the two previously examined approaches was the learning cycle developed by Robert Karplus (1977) for use in the SCIS elementary science program discussed in Chapter 8. The learning cycle followed the major steps in the process of intellectual development proposed by Piaget. As noted earlier in this chapter, Piaget (1964) suggested that cognitive development is a function of four processes. The first three are physiological development, personal interaction with one's environment, and social transmission or direct instruction. The fourth process Piaget called "self-regulation," the process by which an individual is first faced with and subsequently transforms new knowledge to fit into existing mental structures. Self-regulation is also described as a movement from a state of cognitive conflict or disequilibrium to one in which cognitive order and equilibrium is regained. Disequilibrium provides the energy by which reorganization of mental structures takes place.

The learning cycle involves a set of instructional steps linked to this notion of cognitive development. According to Karplus (1977): "The learning cycle consists of three instructional phases that combine experience with social transmission and encourage self-regulation. . . . These three phases are *exploration, concept introduction*, and *concept application*" (p. 173). The three phases were described by Karplus as follows:

> During *exploration*, the students gain experience with the environment— they learn through their own actions and reactions in a new situation. In

this phase, they explore new materials and new ideas with minimal guidance or expectation of specific accomplishments. The new experience should raise questions or complexities that they cannot resolve with their accustomed patterns of reasoning. . . . As a result, mental disequilibrium will occur and the students will be ready for self-regulation. . . . The second phase, *concept introduction*, provides social transmission—it starts with the definition of a new concept or principle that helps the students apply a new pattern of reasoning to their experiences. . . . The concept may be introduced by the teacher, a textbook, a film, or another medium. This step, which aids self-regulation, should always follow exploration and relate to the exploration activities. . . . In the last phase of the learning cycle, *concept application*, familiarization takes place as students apply the new concept and/or reasoning pattern to additional situations. (pp. 173–174)

The learning cycle makes use of a number of principles of concept learning that have already been discussed. For example, it provides for direct teaching of concepts by the teacher—either by demonstration, lecture, reading, or other teacher-planned and -organized activities. Thus, in this second phase, it favors the direct expository method suggested by Ausubel. This phase is preceded, however, by an exploratory phase in which the student can become familiar in a firsthand way with the objects of learning. Thus direct teaching of a concept is not attempted until the student has had a chance to explore the materials and develop some familiarity with them. In addition, in accordance with Piagetian theory, the student is expected to experience some cognitive conflict, or disequilibrium, and the desire to achieve equilibrium in this phase. This provides the energy that makes the direct teaching of the concept successful. It should be pointed out that during the exploratory phase, there is no expectation that students will discover the meaning of the concept in question on their own. Although such independent discovery may occur, the model does not depend on it for its success or advance it as one of its features. The third phase provides for a further strengthening of the concept through the application of the newly acquired material to new contexts. This idea is in keeping with Ausubel's idea of networks of concepts that increase in meaningfulness as they appear in more and more new contexts.

Inquiry Teaching

If a single word had to be chosen to describe the goals of science educators during the 30-year period that began in the late 1950s, it would have to be *inquiry*. Inquiry teaching was intimately associated with the NSF curriculum projects and was viewed long afterwards as an educational ideal worth striving for, even if that striving was often unsuccessful. Unfortunately, confusion often surrounded the inquiry goal because inquiry came to be used in at least two different ways. On the one hand, it was used to describe a specific aspect of the nature of science. Since science was in part a process of inquiry, inquiry skills, it was argued, should be taught to students. In this sense, inquiry teaching meant providing students with facility in the scientific way of thinking, providing an accurate picture of the way scientific knowledge is generated and has been generated in the past, and developing in students basic scientific attitudes. If this were as far as things went, there would have been little problem. Science educators could have devised a variety of strategies for accomplishing these goals. These might have included lectures about the methods of science, reading of scientific papers to see how scientific knowledge had been generated over time, and actual practice in the role of an inquiring scientist. But inquiry teaching also came to be associated with a particular method of teaching—a method of teaching not only the processes of science but also the concepts of science. Inquiry teaching came to be associated with a set of instructional practices and beliefs about learning that are generally referred to as inductive in nature. Inductive approaches are based on the premise that students can be inquirers in the classroom and generate meaning more or less independently by examining a variety of available learning materials. Under this approach, the teacher acts as a guide and a facilitator of learning rather than as an authoritative dispenser of information. Other instructional practices that are associated with this meaning of inquiry teaching include discovery learning, teaching by the problem-solving method, and heuristic teaching. In this section I will first look at some of the statements made about inquiry teaching and then at comparisons that have been made between inquiry (inductive) and expository (deductive) teaching strategies.

Claims and Criticisms

In a 1964 article, James Rutherford said:

When it comes to the teaching of science it is perfectly clear where we, as science teachers, science educators, or scientists stand: we are unalterably opposed to the rote memorization of the mere facts and minutiae of science. By contrast, we stand foursquare for the teaching of the scientific method, critical thinking, the scientific attitude, the problem-solving approach, the discovery method, and, of special interest here, the inquiry method. (p. 80)

Rutherford was also one of the few people to distinguish between the inquiry aspects of science and inquiry as a pedagogical method. Inquiry as it appears in the method of science he referred to as "inquiry of content," and inquiry as a method of teaching he referred to as "inquiry of technique" (p. 80).

David Newton (1968), on the other hand, did not distinguish between science as inquiry and the pedagogical technique of inquiry teaching. He was simply opposed to all aspects of the new orthodoxy in science teaching. He was particularly upset that this "new philosophy" in science education had "swept aside all criticism of itself either from within or from without the profession" (p. 807). He said that to find fault with the method or to question either inductive teaching or discovery learning was similar to "vilifying mother, apple pie or the DAR" (P. 807). Newton argued that a purely inductive science classroom was dishonest for four reasons: First, it was not consistent with the nature of the learner. Adolescents need the security of authority. He believed that given the many other insecurities in a young person's life, the job of succeeding as an adolescent "becomes much more difficult in an atmosphere of 'discovery' teaching, when the student commonly does not know where he stands and the teacher is 'not allowed' to tell him" (p. 808). Second, the method was not the method used in college teaching and therefore was poor preparation for college science. Third, it was not consistent with the nature of science. He agreed that science was not just product, but neither was it just process. He felt that science educators had gone too far in their enthusiasm for the processes of science to the neglect of the products of science. In his words:

> The science teacher has a right, indeed, an obligation, to help students see that science is more than just a way of attacking problems or a method of understanding the world; it is, just as importantly, an enormous, impressive, and extremely useful collection of facts, principles, and concepts which, because of the way it brings order to the world is both intellectually satisfying and practically useful. (p. 809)

Fourth, inquiry teaching had not been shown to be good pedagogy, even though it was almost heretical to question the technique in the present atmosphere of support for it. He felt that many successful aspects of traditional teaching, most obviously the lecture, were being "neglected and unfairly abused" (p. 810) by the advocates of inquiry teaching.

In 1981, Welch, Klopfer, Aikenhead, and Robinson summarized the role of inquiry in science teaching, basing their conclusions on a number of surveys and assessments that had been sponsored by the National Science Foundation during the 1970s. In addition to being a revealing account of teacher attitudes toward inquiry teaching, the paper also demonstrated how science educators continued to use the different meanings of inquiry teaching interchangeably and how teachers continued to be unclear about the meaning of inquiry teaching.

Welch and colleagues (1981) began their paper by saying: "For many years, the science education community has advocated the development of inquiry skills as an essential outcome of science instruction and for an equal number of years science educators have met with frustration and disappointment" (p. 33). Their analysis of the NSF survey results led them to conclude that there was a considerable discrepancy between belief about the importance of inquiry teaching and actual school practice. They said that "although teachers made positive statements about the value of inquiry, they often felt more responsibility for teaching facts, 'things which show up on tests', 'basics' and structure and the work ethic" (p. 37). They also found that teachers considered inquiry teaching difficult to manage. Teachers mentioned the difficulty of meeting state mandates for laboratory work, the difficulty of obtaining equipment and supplies for the laboratory, and the dangers involved in inquiry teaching, especially in classrooms where there were discipline problems. Teachers also expressed reservations about whether inquiry teaching actually worked for most students. They felt that it caused confusion and was "too difficult for any but the very brightest student" (p. 37). In summary, they said:

> The widespread espoused support of inquiry is more simulated than real in practice. The greatest set of barriers to the teacher support of inquiry seems to be its perceived difficulty. There is legitimate confusion over the meaning of inquiry in the classroom. There is concern over discipline. There is a worry about adequately preparing children for the next level of education. There are problems associated with a teacher's allegiance to teaching facts and to following the role models of the college professors. (p. 40).

Comparisons of Inquiry and Non-Inquiry Pedagogies

The disappointment expressed by science educators at their failure to incorporate inquiry teaching into science classrooms presumed that inquiry teaching was a better kind of teaching than alternative methods. As we have seen with respect to both uses of the term *inquiry*, there had been disagreement over the years concerning this presumption. Whereas almost everyone agreed that it was valuable to portray science as a process of investigation and to teach students how to use the methods of science, others felt that advocates of inquiry teaching had overemphasized the importance of science processes at the expense of the teaching of content. Most of the disagreement, however, was over the effectiveness of inquiry teaching as a pedagogical method. In this regard, numerous studies were conducted during the decades in question to determine the relative effectiveness of inquiry versus expository methods of instruction. The inquiry methods that were compared carried different labels from study to study, but in each case a comparison was made between some aspect of inductive, or discovery, methods on the one hand and deductive, or expository, methods on the other.

DESCRIPTIONS OF INQUIRY AND NON-INQUIRY APPROACHES.   I will begin by looking at the distinctions that researchers have made between these two general approaches to teaching. According to Tanner (1969), an *inductive or discovery method* "is intended to enable the learner to discover or construct principles or concepts, by interacting with instances of those principles or concepts." In contrast, a *deductive or expository* method "is one in which the principle or concept is presented to the learner prior to his working with instances of it" (p. 647). Similarly, Novak (1979) drew a distinction between reception and discovery learning. Reception learning is the kind of learning "where the regularities to be learned and their concept labels are presented explicitly to the learner." Discovery learning, on the other hand, "requires that the regularities in objects and/or events are first discovered by the learner" (p. 483). Novak went on to say that there was a continuum from pure reception learning to pure discovery learning and that most discovery learning was actually a kind of "guided discovery" (p. 483). Guided discovery, as its name implies, is a form of discovery teaching in which the teacher takes an active part in organizing instructional activities so that students can be led to make "discoveries."

According to Kaufman (1971), discovery learning is based on the premise that that which is self-learned is best learned.

> Discovery learning relies on the intuitive behavior of an inquisitive child and his ability to synthesize observable phenomena into a meaningful change of behavior. The advocates of this method of learning see the

child as a dynamic organism constantly absorbing stimuli from his environment and being able to make deductions from this input to bring about learning. . . . Opponents of the discovery process view this method as being the constant rediscovery of the wheel. The function of the school is to transmit and maintain the cultural community of our civilization. If each child is to discover the basic concepts of science the intellectual advancement of mankind will be nil. (p. 73)

At the peak of the controversy concerning the benefits of discovery learning, Schulman (1968) provided an analysis of the discovery method as viewed by some of the major educational theorists of the day. For example, Schulman described Bruner's views on discovery learning as Socratic in nature. According to this view, discovery involves "an internal reorganization of previously known ideas" (p. 35) rather than a discovery of something outside the learner. Others felt that the learner was capable of discovery through independent interaction with the materials of science, and still others believed that such discoveries were possible only through the guidance of a sympathetic teacher.

RESEARCH STUDIES.   A number of studies were conducted to compare the effectiveness of the various forms of inquiry and non-inquiry teaching, but, as we will see, the results that were obtained from these studies were generally inconclusive. A study by Thomas and Snider (1969) to compare the didactic and discovery methods of teaching eighth-grade students found that a group taught by didactic methods scored higher on tests of knowledge but that there were no differences between groups in their knowledge of science process skills or their critical thinking ability.

Another study conducted by Schefler (1965) compared two classes of college-level freshman biology taught by an inductive approach with two taught by the deductive method. For the inductive group, subject-matter concepts were introduced in the laboratory by means of a discovery technique. During the lecture periods following the laboratory, group discussion of the laboratory data was intended to lead to a discovery of the concepts in question. The control groups were introduced to the same concepts in lecture, and the lectures were followed by "illustrative laboratories" that were intended to confirm the previously introduced concepts. The results showed no significant differences between groups in either content knowledge or the students' understanding of the nature of science.

Babikian (1971) conducted a study to determine the effectiveness of a discovery method on learning concepts of buoyancy in liquids

(Archimedes' principle) for 216 eighth-grade students. Three in-structional methods were compared: an expository method, a non-inquiry, verification-oriented laboratory method, and a discovery method. The instructional methods were highly structured, and content presentation was controlled by means of printed manuals of instruction. In the expository method, the concept was stated first and then examples were given for clarification. Students in this group were allowed to ask questions and discuss the concept with the teacher or other students. In the verification-oriented laboratory method, the teacher presented the concept and provided the students with instructions and equipment to verify the concept in the laboratory. The students could ask questions and discuss the concepts being studied, but they worked independently in the lab. In the discovery method, the teacher presented the procedural instructions for the discovery of an unstated concept in the manual and made the equipment needed to discover the concept available to the students. The teacher did not explain the concept, and questions about it were given "yes" or "no" answers only. According to Babikian, the expository and the verification-oriented laboratory methods were significantly more effective than the discovery method for teaching science concepts to eighth-grade students. Significant differences were found in respect to overall achievement, verbalization of concepts, and the application of concepts to numerical problems. There was no significant difference between the verification method and the expository method.

Sakmyser (1974) compared an inductive and a deductive approach to programmed instruction for teaching chemical equilibrium to high school chemistry students. The results showed no differences in the success of the two methods for teaching chemical equilibrium. A similar study by Hermann and Hincksman (1978) also used programmed materials, this time to teach principles of stoichiometry to high school students. The difference in the two treatments was the relative placement of rules and examples in the programmed instructional sequence. In the inductive method, examples of a rule were followed by the rule, while in the deductive method, the rule was followed by examples of that rule. In the inductive approach, the rules were placed in the eighth and ninth frames of a 10-frame set, and for the deductive approach, the rules were placed in the second and third frames. The results showed no long-term differences between the inductive and deductive methods, although immediate retention of the concepts was significantly higher using the deductive approach.

Spears and Zollman (1977) reported a study that compared a structured (verification) with an unstructured (inquiry) approach to teaching the processes of science in the laboratory component of a college-level physical science course. Under the first strategy students were expected to use the laboratory to verify principles that had been presented in the lecture. Under the second strategy students were expected to use the laboratory to freely investigate the principles learned in lecture. For example, in an experiment about the gas laws, the students in the structured laboratory were given the following instructions: "To investigate more carefully this relation (between temperature and volume), place the syringe in water of at least three different temperatures, recording the temperature and volume of the gas" (p. 35). The students in the unstructured laboratory were told simply to investigate the relation between temperature and volume. The students in the unstructured laboratory were free to investigate the relationship in any way they wished. The results of the study showed no significant differences between the two groups except on the Activities of Scientists subscale of the Welch Science Process Inventory, on which the structured laboratory group scored higher. In addition, the researchers observed that "the students in the unstructured laboratory . . . seldom followed the steps of observation, model building (predicting), and testing of the model" (p. 37). What the students did for the most part was describe what they had seen in the laboratory and use the lecture material or the textbook to explain the observations. The researchers felt that the students in the structured laboratory scored higher on the Activities of Scientists subscale because the structured class provided examples of the activities of science, which students were able to recall. In summing up their conclusions, the researchers said that unstructured laboratories might be useful for students who have had prior experience in scientific experimentation but that most college freshman or sophomores taking their first physics course seem to require more structured experiences and more structured training in the scientific process to understand it.

Research studies conducted during this time period on the comparative effectiveness of inquiry and non-inquiry strategies were generally inconclusive. Teachers who chose to use one method over another did so because of personal success with the method or because of a faith in the ultimate superiority of that method. Educational research was unable to offer a definitive answer to the question of which was more effective or which had greater educational value.

Summary

At least since the last third of the nineteenth century, it had been the goal of science educators to equip science students with the methods of science. In more recent times, however, conceptions of what those methods entailed were challenged in such a way that simple descriptions of the nature of science were no longer adequate.

Earlier descriptions of the scientific method as a rigid series of steps gave way to the influence of a number of prominent instructional and developmental psychologists who were able to describe in more detail the components of the problem-solving process. Lists of process skills, such as observation, measurement, and description, replaced the stepwise scientific method. Similarly, Piaget's work provided better descriptions of the component skills involved in problem solving. Piaget's work also brought attention to the questions of how it is that humans acquire the ability to think rationally and how they develop the ability to carry out the logical operations that scientists do. During the time period in question, these goals having to do with the development of scientific reasoning were as important as any other to science educators.

Throughout the 1960s, 1970s, and 1980s, a good deal of energy was also devoted to questions concerning the relative value of learning the processes of science and the products of science. In addition, numerous discussions centered around the strategies that could be used to accomplish those goals. Inquiry teaching was widely touted as *the* educational goal of the period, but, largely because of the confusion over whether inquiry was a method of instruction or a description of the nature of science, inquiry teaching was not incorporated into classrooms to the extent that many science educators hoped it would be.

Chapter 11

What We Have Learned
and Where We Are Headed

In 1893, plans for the secondary curriculum assigned approximately 20% of the total available time in school to science teaching. Those plans would have had most students taking science in each of their four years of high school. Instead, from the early 1900s, when the principle of elective courses took hold, to the present, the percentage of ninth- to twelfth-grade students enrolled in science courses at any one time has been consistently at about 50% of total school enrollment. In other words, the average number of years of science study for all students combined has been approximately two of the four years spent in high school.

If we remove from these calculations the students who take science courses for three or four years, we find that many students take only a single high school science course and that approximately 50% of the students can look at tenth-grade biology as the last science course they will ever take. It has long been recognized that science education for the purpose of general cultural development has been one of the primary roles of the secondary schools. As evidenced by student enrollments, however, our ability to translate this recognized responsibility into effective programs is another issue. Responding to this failing, Helgeson and colleagues (1978) stated:

A review of state requirements, . . . course enrollments from state and national reports, and current reports of various groups regarding educational needs indicate science courses are usually required in only one or two years of the four year high school program. In the opinion of the reviewers, it appears that the role of science in the secondary school curriculum for general education remains unclear. What students should learn also remains unclear. (p. 37)

Perhaps the primary reason that the role of science remains unclear is that there are so many valid and often competing justifications for science in the curriculum. These justifications for teaching science affect what kind of science is taught and the ways in which it is taught. A review of some of the historical reasons for teaching science will help to make this point.

Why Science Is Part of the School Curriculum

One reason for teaching science is that it represents an important part of human knowledge that should not be lost to future generations. In the past 100 years, science has come to be viewed as a fundamental aspect of our culture and is, therefore, an essential part of the curriculum. Similarly, courses in history and in modern literature are now seen as representing essential aspects of our culture, and they are also included without question in the secondary school curriculum. Ancient languages and literature, on the other hand, are viewed as less important to our modern life, and we expect that they will be studied by only a few. Similarly, the study of physics, which once was thought to be one of the key studies in the curriculum, has steadily lost enrollments in the secondary school program such that now only a small minority of high school students ever study physics. Mathematics falls into still another category in that it has been considered essential knowledge for hundreds of years, and it continues to hold a position of esteem in educational institutions everywhere.

Historically, subjects have been retained in the curriculum because they were thought to function in some way to produce socially or personally significant outcomes. The study of a particular subject makes us more aware of the complexities of human interaction and therefore more effective in our social and personal lives; or it makes us better at solving the variety of problems that we face; or it makes us more intellectually competent; or it makes us more economically productive; or it makes us feel good; or it leads to advances in the frontiers of knowledge. Some areas of knowledge function in multiple ways and gain their importance because of the significance of the connections they make with a wide range of human experience. Science is one such area and mathematics is another. Both are thought to be related to intellectual development, aesthetic pleasure and personal satisfaction, economic development, and the advance of knowledge of our physical world.

In the nineteenth century, it was argued that a knowledge of science was important to one's economic well-being and that the study of science assisted in the development of mental powers of observation and inductive reasoning. In the first half of the twentieth century, the study of science was linked to effective living in an increasingly industrialized world, to industrial and economic development, and to the maintenance of the public's health. From the mid-1950s to the late 1960s, science study was associated with the production of scientists who could advance the frontiers of scientific knowledge in order to maintain national security and international prestige. In recent years, economic development, national security, and the ability to think rationally have again come to the foreground. Is there any way that we can learn from the shifts in focus and draw essential lessons for science education from them? Perhaps if we look at some ideas that have persisted over time, we can get a better sense of what is important and what is effective in science education.

The Teaching of Science: What Does It Mean?

When we look at the variety of meanings that the phrase *the teaching of science* has had over the years, the first distinction that comes quickly to mind is the one between science as process and science as product. All areas of study have both a body of knowledge that has been generated and a set of processes by which that knowledge has developed. Both process and product may be the focus of study in the school curriculum, but in most fields one or the other typically gets the greater attention. For example, art and music are usually taught as process more than as product. Through band, chorus, orchestra, and studio art courses, students learn how to make art and they learn how to make music. Courses in art and music appreciation that focus on the products of artists and musicians may also be included, but more school time is spent on musical and artistic performance than on the study of musical and artistic products. In contrast, historical knowledge as the product of research gets more attention in schools than does historiography, the process of conducting historical investigations. The process of mathematical scholarship gets little if any attention in schools, but the product of mathematical research does. Science, perhaps more than any other area of the curriculum, tries to deal with both the products and processes of the subject in the same courses. In art, we are likely to find studio courses separate from art history and art appreciation or theory courses, but in school science the laboratory and lecture room are combined to present science process and product together. Whereas this may be viewed as science's greatest strength when compared to other areas of the school curriculum, it has also presented considerable problems for science educators.

When we speak about science process, we need to further distinguish between the *logical processes* that are used in science, such as making systematic observations, performing controlled experiments, and using inductive and deductive reasoning to arrive at conclusions, and the *technical processes* that are used in science, such as using microscopes, operating electronic equipment, performing titrations, and so on. In addition, we need to distinguish between learning *about* the processes and learning *how to carry out* the processes. One involves knowledge as the primary goal, whereas the other involves skill development as the primary goal. Thus, in organizing science instruction as a study of "process," we need to determine the extent to which we expect students to become proficient in manipulating equipment and science materials, the extent to which we expect them to become proficient in carrying out the logical operations of science, and the extent to which we expect them to have knowledge of those processes.

Another legitimate aspect of any area of the school curriculum is the historical development of that particular field of study. One can study the history of art, the history of music, the history of mathematics, and the history of science. Typically, such courses deal with the historical development of both the accumulating knowledge in the field and the processes of generating that knowledge. These courses in the history and philosophy of the various disciplines are more often part of the curriculum in higher education than in secondary schools, although attempts to include historical studies in secondary science education are well known. In addition, we may study the relationship between the academic discipline and society and how the values and practices of society affect the generation of knowledge in that field. This can be either a contemporary study or a historical study.

We can also focus our attention on the applications of a subject, or we can focus on knowledge of the subject itself. Thus mathematics can be studied as a useful subject that enables us to solve practical problems in economics, science, and sociology, or it can be studied as an organized body of knowledge apart from its applications. In the first approach, the applications become a major part of the mathematics course; in the second, they do not. Likewise, science can be studied in its pure, relatively isolated form or in relation to its technological applications.

This analysis is further complicated by the fact that many of the approaches mentioned above can be seen either as ends in themselves or as means to other ends. For example, applications of science can be the primary content of science study, or they can be used as a motivational tool to increase learning of the organized discipline. Likewise, the history of science can be studied as an important subject matter in its own right or it can be used to make modern concepts more understandable, to interest students in the study of modern science, or to present students with a more accurate view of the nature of science. Even the study of the organized science disciplines can be seen as fulfilling a human need to understand the physical world or, more functionally, as a way of producing more scientists or of helping us solve environmental and health problems.

It is clear as we read through this list that most, if not all, of these ways of interpreting the phrase *the teaching of science* have been suggested over the years, sometimes as the only legitimate approach to the subject. A few, however, have recurred often enough for us to consider them as major or dominant approaches. There are three such interpretations of what it means to teach science:

1. Teaching the science disciplines as structured bodies of knowledge to be learned as logically organized subject matter
2. Teaching science as a set of investigative processes
3. Teaching science as a human activity closely interconnected with its technological applications and with the rest of society

Only occasionally do these three interpretations stand alone in their pure forms; usually they are melded together to create composites having greater or lesser emphasis on one approach or the other. Of the three, teaching science as a structured body of knowledge has been the most dominant focus of school science courses during the past 100 years *as it has been practiced.* Teaching the processes of science and the social applications of science have received considerable attention in the science education literature throughout the entire period, but advocates of science process and social applications have been less successful implementing their ideas in the classroom over the long term. Each of these three approaches will be reviewed in its historical context.

Science as a Structured Body of Knowledge

Why Teach Science Content?

One of the earliest justifications for including science in the school curriculum was that through science teaching the natural world could be made understandable to all who were interested in studying it. Humans are curious by nature, and they desire to know about their world. It is natural for them to want a fuller understanding of the world around them, and education can assist in this process. As noted in Chapter 1, John Stuart Mill pointed this out in 1867 when he said:

> It is surely no small part of education to put us in intelligent possession of the most important and most universally interesting facts of the universe, so that the world which surrounds us may not be a sealed book to us, uninteresting because unintelligible. (cited in Youmans, 1867, p. 30)

This most obvious and fundamental approach to teaching science, which was so popular during the nineteenth century (and which had its occasional apologists in the twentieth century as well), received relatively little explicit attention during the ensuing years. That the fundamental reason for teaching science was to put humans in a deeper relationship with their physical world gave way to more utilitarian reasons for teaching science. Some of these reasons might be considered high and noble and others base and materialistic, but regardless of their aim, each focused on science study as a means to some end other than the satisfaction of the natural desire of humans to know and to understand.

Herbert Spencer (1864), for example, argued that a knowledge of science would assist in such things as rearing and disciplining children, maintaining good health, gaining a livelihood, and improving the memory. Later, during the first half of the twentieth century, science study was justified primarily on the basis of its social utility. It was claimed that knowledge of science would lead to economic development and needed improvements in public health as well as to citizens who were more informed about and better able to function in their increasingly urbanized and industrialized world. Science knowledge was to have social value, and it was to be functional. Still later in the twentieth century, science study was promoted as an essential weapon in our military arsenal and most recently as part of an economic strategy to regain international supremacy in world markets. In addition, many science educators today advocate the teaching of science content for a kind of social utility that is reminiscent of efforts made during the earlier part of this century, with the added urgency of impending environmental catastrophe.

These economic, military, and social utilitarian arguments for teaching science content have become so strong in recent years that the personal or humanistic arguments seem to have been forgotten. When we examine actual classroom practice, however, we are struck by an obvious irony. What many observers of science classrooms report is that the actual teaching of science resembles more the teaching of science "for its own sake" than it does the teaching of science for any particular utilitarian end. In other words, the practice of science teaching is more often aimed at the acquisition of science content with the simple hope that students can understand something previously unknown to them, not with any particular utilitarian end in mind.

Perhaps the reason for this apparent rejection of the social, economic, and military aims is that these aims are too broadly stated and too transient to have any direct impact on the teaching of the sciences in the schools. How, for example, is a teacher to teach chemistry in such a way that our military position in the world is enhanced? How is a teacher to teach biology so that we become more competitive in world markets? Only those immediate and clear social applications such as public health and environmental conservation provide enough direction for actual classroom practice; in fact, when social utility is the primary goal, it is these kinds of specific social ends towards which science teaching has been most successfully directed during the past century.

One justification for teaching science content that enjoyed popularity in a previous era but is no longer given credence today is the nineteenth-century notion that memorization of facts aids in the development of the memory. The practice of teaching facts by rote has been widely condemned by science educators throughout the twentieth century, largely because it was felt that this practice did not lead to understanding and because it had few if any other redeeming features. Curiously, however, the practice of teaching factual information and, perhaps more importantly, of testing for factual knowledge, is one that persists today. Even so-called science literacy tends to be measured not by what people can read and understand, but by what facts they have retained in memory.

What Science Content Should Be Taught?

One of the difficulties that has plagued curriculum developers in science as they try to decide what to include in the curriculum is the fact that there is simply too much material to teach in the relatively short time that is available. Solutions to the problem have included (1) beginning science instruction as early in school as possible, (2) searching for ways to teach more efficiently, so that more can be taught in a shorter time and/or remembered longer, and (3) organizing concepts around general themes that can be learned more effectively than the innumerable details. This problem has grown over the years and will most likely continue to grow with the addition of new knowledge in each of the major science areas.

One partial solution to the problem of "too much to teach and not enough time to teach it" has been the development of what has proved to be a highly stable set of courses with clearly marked boundaries into which curriculum experts in each area can place what they consider to be the most important knowledge in that field. Although this has not answered the question of what specific content should be taught, it has provided for breadth in the science curriculum, and it has avoided the inevitable turf battles that would have developed between the individual science branches had science been viewed more holistically.

Obviously, knowing why a subject is being taught is key to deciding what to teach. Thus course content has been organized around socially relevant issues, around the fundamental principles of the disciplines, and around broad conceptual schemes or organizing principles of the disciplines. The importance of content that is in some way relevant to our present experience is advocated by most educators. It is considered a waste of both student and teacher time to deal with content that appears to have no utility whatsoever either for the present or the long term. The idea that science courses should focus on the basic principles of the disciplines relates to the notion that the disciplines represent the accumulation of human thought and are the most powerful means that we have for understanding our world and using that knowledge to our advantage. Organizing science courses around a small number of central themes is a way of presenting science content so that it is more easily learned and remembered.

How Should Science Content Be Taught?

A third area of interest when analyzing the teaching of science content is the question of *how* science content can best be taught. It is likely that more energy has been expended on this question over the years than on questions of value and content combined.

Most twentieth-century conceptions of mind that have influenced science educators' views of the learning of science have been built on a base of nineteenth-century psychology. According to these views, concepts, which ultimately have their source in sense perceptions, are linked together to form clusters of ideas. The more connections that are made among these ideas, the richer is the conception. The process by which old ideas are modified by the inclusion of new ones is generally referred to as "accommodation," and the process by which the new idea is modified to fit into the existing conceptual structure is called "assimilation." In these models, both the perception and the conception are important. As Kant and numerous writers since have told us, our conceptions depend on what we perceive and our perceptions depend on our existing conceptions.

There are a number of implications of this idea of concept formation for science instruction. First, the basis of all understanding is sense impressions. Only after a sufficient base of ideas derived from sense impressions has been established can those ideas be manipulated verbally to produce new meaning. Thus direct, hands-on experience with natural phenomena becomes an essential part of science teaching. Second, the particular way ideas are organized is important. Ideas that are unrelated to other ideas hold less meaning than those that are richly interrelated, and it is more difficult to take in new information if it is not related to existing conceptual structures or if the requisite conceptual structure is not present. So we often hear maxims like the following expressed by science educators: *Whenever possible, relate new ideas to something the student has already experienced, and if the student has not previously had the prerequisite experience, provide that experience before beginning instruction.* Another says: *Always relate new ideas to something the student already knows.* Adherence to these rules leads to the practice of using the laboratory and the outdoors to provide direct contact with the physical world through the senses and to confirm through personal observation the validity of important scientific principles. Also derived from this conception of mind is the practice of making instruction personally relevant, that is, connected to something with which the student is already at least somewhat familiar. Although Dewey (1916) was hardly the first to advocate such a practice, his "reconstruction of experience" is representative of theories of learning that make use of what the student already knows. Dewey believed that *all* instruction should be organized in such a way that it takes account of what the student knows. Prior student experience is restructured in the mind through the process of interacting with the teacher and the other students. Learning *always* involves present understanding as the starting point. Insistence on relevance of subject matter to enhance meaningful learning has been part of science education discussions since the late nineteenth century and continues to be a large part of good science teaching today.

Two other issues that are related to this idea of concept formation involve the question of readiness, that is, the point at which a child is ready to learn certain kinds of science material, and the question of whether it is more effective to present content to the child in the form that it is understood and organized by the adult or if it is better to have the child *discover* the concepts in a way that is consistent with the child's own mental structures.

DISCOVERY LEARNING.   The question of the effectiveness of discovery as a way of learning has been with us since the nineteenth century. Referred to as "heuristic learning," "inductive learning," "inquiry," "independent problem solving," or "discovery," a major justification for the approach is that through such techniques the child's unique conceptual patterns can come into contact with that portion of the new experience that is most likely to produce meaningful learning. It is argued that teacher-telling is less effective since the teacher can only guess at, or, at best, estimate what part of the learning experience will be effective, or, even worse, present the new material as understood by the teacher and not consider at all what the student already knows. It is also argued that a personal experience with some object or phenomenon is inherently more complex and filled with learning potential than is another person's description of that experience. A teacher simply does not have the time or ability to describe a phenomenon or object as fully as the object or phenomenon can describe itself.

The other side of the discovery argument is that such techniques are too time consuming and that potential gains in understanding or in increased memory are more than offset by the increased length of time required to achieve them. These methods are slow because students often do not have the desire to examine objects and phenomena to derive meaning from them and because most students need prodding to bring their prior learning to bear on the problem at hand. Thus, although discovery techniques have had their advocates since the nineteenth century, most science educators who support the concept of discovery today utilize a "guided discovery" technique whereby students are led by the teacher in a variety of ways to draw meaning from an experience. Students are provided with needed materials, are usually given a particular problem to solve, and are prompted with questions that lead them to "discover" some concept or relationship between concepts. This approach has the advantage of placing the students in direct contact with the richness of the relevant objects or phenomena in a controlled way without having to rely completely on their undirected and spontaneous insights.

READINESS FOR LEARNING SCIENCE CONCEPTS.   The second issue that has to do with notions of concept formation deals with the question of readiness for learning. Historically, children have been viewed as progressing toward increasingly abstract thought throughout childhood. When they are young, children need to work with concrete objects or with experiences that are familiar to them, and as they move toward adulthood their minds develop to the point that they are capable of thinking abstractly. This idea was used by nineteenth-century educators as part of the justification for presenting children with actual physical objects in science teaching and asking them to memorize concrete facts as opposed to teaching them more general principles of science. Later work by Piaget provided a refinement and elaboration of these stages of mental development that now help us predict more precisely when a child will be able to understand a particular type of concept.

No one, however, has yet to discover the actual mechanism by which the mind develops, nor the relative importance of physical maturation, personal experience, and organized instruction in that development. Differences between developmental theorists on these issues tend to focus on the question of whether the mind is organized as elaborated intact structures (schemata) that are dependent in part on physical maturation and that are similar from person to person, or whether the mind more simply reflects the unique arrangement of concepts that develop from the experiences of individual people. The idea that relatively stable mental schemata exist in the human mind has been popular in science education since Piaget's work was brought to the attention of American educators in the late 1950s by Bruner and others, and it has grown ever more popular over the years. It is popular not only among science education researchers but also among classroom teachers. It is one piece of educational research that seems to have a validity that is confirmed daily in the classroom. It is not universally accepted, however, largely because it is thought to represent a limiting view of the potential for individuals to develop mentally. If mind develops through the accumulation and integration of new concepts, then individuals have unlimited potential for mental growth and educators have unlimited potential to enhance that development. If, on the other hand, the development of the human mind is determined by a physiological process that is beyond their control, then educators are limited in how far they can move human understanding forward.

The Scientific Way of Thinking

Just as humans are by nature curious and have an irrepressible desire to understand their world, so too are humans by nature manipulators of ideas. We are thinkers. In addition to our ability to comprehend ideas, we distinguish ourselves from other living creatures by our ability to think rationally. Over our long history, we have developed a number of different approaches to thinking about the world so that we can make predictions about it and have some degree of control over it.

The natural sciences were built around a particular form of rationality that we know as inductive thought. By making·observations of the world, scientists are able to derive general principles to explain those observations. These principles in turn form the basis of organized knowledge in the science disciplines. Science also involves the rational process of deduction whereby the logical consequences of hypotheses are predicted by scientists. Although both induction and deduction are part of the scientific way of thinking, it is inductive logic that is most often associated with the scientific method. In addition to inductive and deductive logic, scientific thinking also involves a number of specific processes (making measurements and controlling variables) and attitudes (objectivity and tentativeness) that are considered important when conducting scientific research.

Why Teach Scientific Thinking?

A number of reasons have been offered over the years to justify the teaching of scientific thinking. First, especially during the nineteenth century, it was argued that the effort that is required to think in a disciplined, rational way can have an overall strengthening effect on the intellect that will lead to increased intellectual power. Second, it has been argued that the scientific way of thinking is transferable to nonscientific content and can, therefore, make people more effective in their everyday lives. Third, it is argued that future scientists must know how to think like scientists. Scientists have a particular way of thinking about the world, and it is essential that future scientists be initiated into this way of thought as early as possible.

SCIENCE STUDY TO DEVELOP MENTAL CAPACITY.   The first of these arguments for teaching the methods of science was the primary justification for the inclusion of science in the curriculum in the nineteenth century. Notions of disciplining the mind through an exercise regimen that included inductive thought were common before the turn of the century and were used to place science on an equal footing with mathematics and languages, which were thought to develop the mind through memory exercises and deductive thought. Although the idea of mental discipline was discredited in the early part of the twentieth century, it lingers on in various forms even today. It is often argued, for example, that the rigorous study of science and, even more so, the rigorous study of mathematics teaches people how to think—that is, it exerts a generalized discipline on the mind. This is a particularly popular conception among lay people, but it is also of interest to some researchers who have examined whether brain circuitry is permanently affected by use. As appealing as the exercise metaphor may be to some, we do not yet have the evidence that justifies teaching the methods of science as a way of strengthening the mind in a general way.

TRANSFER OF LEARNING TO EVERYDAY CONTEXTS.   We are similarly uncertain about the transferability of skills learned in one context to a new, unrelated one. Specifically, we are uncertain of the extent to which thinking skills learned in the context of science classes transfers to the rest of our students' experience. The potential for general transfer has fascinated researchers in education throughout the twentieth century. Thorndike's (Thorndike & Woodworth, 1901; Thorndike, 1924) work in the early part of the century cast doubt on general transfer. In his *Process of Education,* Bruner (1960), however, provided a modified notion of transfer that showed how general concepts can act to make the learning of new concepts easier. Recently educational researchers have tried to determine the extent to which knowledge can be transferred from one context to another, that is, how general the transfer is and how extensively a transfer can be made. This is important in a discussion of science education because it affects the legitimacy of the argument that the scientific way of thinking should be taught to everyone regardless of whether they are interested in science or not. If the only way people are going to develop skill in applying inductive thought to everyday problems is to teach those thinking skills in the context of those everyday problems, then using science classes to teach generalized thinking skills loses some of its appeal. On the other hand, if these skills are broadly generalizable, then teaching inductive thought in the context of scientific discovery accomplishes several aims at the same time.

Based on what we know about human potential for genius—for creativity and discovery—we know that transfer of skill and knowledge is possible, but we also know that individuals vary greatly in how far they apply what they know in new situations. Some people are highly bound by their immediate context and rarely see the application of skill or knowledge to novel contexts. For them, what is learned in science class is for science class and fails to change the way they operate in a nonscience experience. For these people, knowing how to control variables as part of a scientific investigation seems to have little if any impact on how they evaluate such things as advertising claims, unless perhaps those applications had been pointed out directly as separate concepts in themselves. Others seem to sense on their own the applications of skill to new contexts with little if any prompting. In its best representations, this insight into the applicability of familiar relationships to new contexts leads to the creation of new ideas, never before thought of in quite that way.

If many of our students do not make these applications on their own, then we cannot depend on the teaching of science processes to lead to rigorous thinking in everyday contexts. For some, the teaching of science process may affect general thought processes, but for many the specific links will have to be made for them and the applications taught directly. The problem with this *direct* approach, as Loud (1950) noted, is that the teaching of real-world applications takes time—time that must be taken away from the teaching of science itself. Loud discussed this issue in the context of a study he was involved with whose purpose was to create a general education program in higher education:

> There has been a growing body of evidence that even if students could learn a scientific method by studying the work of scientists, they would not transfer this method to problems in other areas without specifically being shown how to do it. In other words, the transfer of the method would have to constitute a major part of the study in science courses. (p. 292)

Another issue to consider when discussing the teaching of the scientific way of thinking for use in nonscientific contexts is that for many people the method is simply too rigorous and, in fact, a burden to apply. Even though good, clear thinking should be a joy to a member of a thinking species, the scientific method also has its onerous side in that it requires us to question everything, to be exasperatingly tentative in our conclusions, and to reject arguments based on authority or faith. It requires that all the links in an argument be valid, and it rejects conclusions that are based on insufficient evidence or weak arguments, no matter how appealing they may seem. Even if we could teach the scientific way of thought in our science classes for application in everyday life, we might find a good deal of resistance from people who prefer the pleasure that comes from thinking in less rational ways.

THINKING ABOUT SCIENTIFIC PROBLEMS.   The third argument for teaching the scientific way of thinking is that it helps prepare both scientists and nonscientists for thinking about *scientific* problems. Scientists need to be initiated into the ways of thinking that are used by members of the scientific community, and nonscientists need to learn how to think about scientific problems if they are to become contributing citizens in an increasingly scientific and technological world and if they are going to be sympathetic to the work of scientists. Knowledge of science processes leads to a fuller appreciation of the nature of scientific research and to the development of skills for conducting scientific research. Of the three justifications for teaching the scientific mode of thought, this is the most direct, the least controversial, and the easiest for most people to accept.

Teaching a Realistic View of Science Process

A persistent expectation of science educators over the years has been that students should acquire a *realistic* sense of the nature of scientific thinking. This means, for one thing, that the scientific method should not be taught as a series of steps that lead inevitably to new discoveries, but rather as a general form of inquiry that has many variations and a distinctly human character. A major contribution to the development of more realistic conceptions of scientific thinking was the replacement in the 1950s and 1960s of a stepwise scientific method with more extensive lists of science processes and attitudes, accompanied by the claim that science involves doing the best we can with these processes to arrive at an understanding of the world around us.

Another approach that has been used to present science more realistically is to teach the *history* of scientific discovery. To study how scientific knowledge has actually been generated is to see the scientific method in action. Students can observe from these historical studies the role that is played by intuition, luck, and hard work, and they can see that there is no simple formula that guarantees successful discoveries in science. A study of history is time consuming, however, and takes time away from the study of scientific knowledge as it is now organized. In addition, since this approach typically requires that students comprehend something that is no longer thought to be true (an outdated model of the atom, for example) in order to understand the logic behind the discovery, it leaves many science teachers wondering if it is worth the effort.

An examination of current science textbooks shows that not much more than lip service is paid to the use of history in teaching about the process of scientific discovery. Short biographical inserts describe past contributions to our present understanding of science, or brief synopses of past developments may be incorporated into the text itself. Although the use of history has been proposed by some as the primary basis for the teaching of science, it has not received widespread support among science educators. It may be that any extended study of the history of science would be best accomplished in a course by itself.

Still another attempt to present the methods of science more realistically has been the effort to replace older conceptions of scientific method, which focused on its inductivist and empiricist traditions, with more modern conceptions. Newer ideas about the nature of scientific investigation have emphasized the social construction of knowledge, the importance of teaching processes within a context of relevant concepts, and a view of the scientist as emotional and involved rather than coldly objective and detached. Although sometimes overemphasizing the emotional and personal dimension of scientific discovery at the expense of science as objective inquiry, critics of inductivist and empiricist approaches have presented many important insights into the nature of science.

The Role of the Laboratory in Teaching Science Process

Just as science educators have generally concluded that hands-on activity is needed for a full understanding of science *concepts*, they have also concluded that the best way to learn science *processes* is by practicing them in the laboratory. This is an idea that has survived with only minor challenges ever since laboratory instruction was introduced in the latter third of the nineteenth century, when it was considered by many to be the only effective way to teach the processes of science.

A threat to this emphasis on laboratory instruction came in the early twentieth century when educators concerned about educational efficiency used tests of scientific *content* to determine the effectiveness of laboratory instruction. Defenders of the laboratory at the time argued that laboratory instruction should be judged not on its contribution to the teaching of content but on its contribution to the teaching of process. The laboratory as a place to learn about and practice scientific inquiry received its greatest boost since the late nineteenth century when the inquiry-oriented curriculum projects sponsored by the National Science Foundation were introduced in the late 1950s and the 1960s. Since then, however, science educators have lost some of their enthusiasm for using the laboratory as a place for scientific inquiry, although the laboratory is still routinely used for demonstration and confirmation purposes.

A challenge facing science educators today is that of clarifying the role of the laboratory in developing science inquiry skills and determining the value that the laboratory has in developing an understanding of science. One of the things we have learned about laboratory instruction over the years is that it is easy to overestimate the ability of individuals to derive meaning from the empirical world on their own. This does not mean, however, that students should be denied all practice in trying to solve scientific problems in the laboratory as a scientist would do, although it does suggest that the method should be used sparingly, within the context of a reasonably well understood body of concepts, and certainly not as the primary means of acquiring knowledge or skill.

Similarly, we are beginning to realize that the mistake made by those who unwittingly tried to reduce the scientific method to a foolproof, stepwise process can also be made with respect to the lists of science processes. It is too easy to isolate the individual processes and to teach them as separated from the context in which they derive their importance in scientific research. Thus we may mistakenly try to teach the skill of observing as a generalized mental ability, sometimes through examples that have little to do with science. It was almost 90 years ago that Alexander Smith told us that an observation in science is not simply a sense perception but rather an interpretation of an event that is based on a particular conceptual context held by the observer. As Smith said:

> Observation in chemistry implies something much more complex and difficult than we sometimes appreciate. In its simplest terms it may consist in noticing the colour of a precipitate, or stating whether bubbles of

> gas do or do not appear, or perhaps, in describing the form of a crystal. . . . In many experiments, however, the use of experience and reasoning in observation so greatly predominates, that the part which the eyes or the sense of touch plays become relatively inconspicuous. . . . Ability to observe chemical phenomena is an attribute of the chemist and teaching observation consists really in teaching chemistry. (Smith & Hall, 1902, p. 87)

It is questionable, then, that we will make better observers (and thus better scientists) out of students by having them carefully examine some object and telling us everything they observe. Likewise it is important for us to realize that not every observation leads inevitably to a sensible inference, especially if the student does not have an adequate conceptual background in that area.

We also know now that hypothesis generation is as important an ability for a scientist to have as the skill of hypothesis testing. But hypothesis generation, too, requires a conceptual background in the area of investigation. We cannot expect students to generate meaningful hypotheses without a reasonably well-developed conceptual context within which to make them. Otherwise the hypotheses become either mere guesses on the one hand or statements of what they already know to be true on the other. Hypotheses should come logically out of a body of theory. At least some of the time students should be given the challenge of trying to generate hypotheses out of the content they are studying. This would take the form of determining the implications of some principle with which they are already familiar, and it should be done in a truly creative scientific atmosphere without the pressures of time and the knowledge that the student's performance is going to be evaluated. The little we know about creativity suggests that generating creative responses (such as generating innovative hypotheses) requires a thorough background in the area of investigation, as well as sufficient time and a certain degree of mental relaxation, without excessive external pressures.

When Are Students Ready to Think Like Scientists?

Another issue related to the development of scientific thinking is the issue of readiness. Piaget's stages of mental development (Inhelder & Piaget, 1958; Piaget, 1964) are closely related to the skills that are needed to think scientifically. The ability to control variables, to consider all possible combinations of events, to think correlationally, to reason probabilistically, and to generate hypotheses are all mental abilities that Piaget places in the formal operational category.

The development of formal operational thought is not believed by Piagetian researchers to begin until early to mid-adolescence and for some, at least, is not fully developed until late adolescence, if at all. What, then, are the implications of this for teaching science processes in elementary and junior high school, for example? Should fifth-grade students be expected to generate hypotheses or to conduct studies in which variables need to be controlled? What about seventh-graders?

These questions are not easily answered. Although Piagetian-based research has provided a way of explaining why students are unable to accomplish certain intellectual tasks at different stages of their development, the insights of classroom teachers are still needed to deal with the great disparities in abilities between children. This is a case in which the impressions gathered by teachers from actual classroom practice must come together with the findings of educational researchers. Teachers know from their own experience whether fifth-grade students can control variables, and they know whether those students can do so with understanding. If fifth-graders cannot control variables and seem to lack the ability to understand the concept of experimental control, then the teacher can find an explanation for that failure in the work of developmental researchers. In addition, viewing growth as the result of an intellectual challenge that requires students to stretch their minds to acquire new understanding is a metaphor that has served us well throughout our educational history, and Piaget's notion of the importance of disequilibrium as the energy that drives development fits nicely into this conception of mental growth. Teachers should teach the processes of science at any age they feel appropriate as long as they press for skill with understanding, driven by an appropriate level of challenge as a stimulus for growth. An appreciation for the limits of student understanding can come from the contributions of developmental theorists such as Piaget.

Science for Social Relevance

Socially relevant science education was promoted in one form or another by most science education leaders during the first half of the twentieth century. Social relevance experienced a brief lapse during the 1960s with the introduction of the NSF curriculum projects, which briefly turned attention away from technology and other social applications of science toward a study of the structure and processes of the science disciplines themselves. The focus on social relevance returned in the 1970s and 1980s with calls for scientific literacy and with the creation of a science-technology-society approach. Social relevance is an important and deservedly popular idea. It is curious, then, that science educators have had such a difficult time convincing classroom teachers of the merits of a socially relevant approach. If we examine the writing of advocates of social relevance since the early twentieth century, we see that so much of that writing has been directed at teachers, who were described as spending too much time on the study of science "for its own sake" and not enough time on socially relevant themes.

Related reasons for its limited use in the classroom are the perceptions of some that socially relevant science is not as rigorous as disciplinary science and its historical association with students who are less interested in learning about the organized disciplines per se. Thus it lacks the status needed to make it more popular with college-bound students, for example. A frequent claim made by critics of progressive education was that the emphasis on social relevance developed out of the need to provide easier subject matter for the new and supposedly less able students who flooded the secondary schools during the first several decades of the twentieth century. In more recent times, Shamos (1966) discussed the perception that social aspects of science are easier to learn and Yager (1985), in his advocacy of STS, said that the study of the disciplines might be appropriate for the brightest of our students, but not for everyone. In addition, college courses in "Science and Society" are typically aimed at nonscience students and often are less rigorous than traditional science courses.

Another reason for its limited application is a sense of confusion about exactly what socially relevant science is and what it means for the classroom teacher. Just as confusion about the nature of inquiry teaching has limited the integration of that aspect of science teaching into science classrooms, so has confusion about the nature of social relevance limited its incorporation. There are many justifications for teaching socially relevant science, and it is important that they be sorted out if this is to become an important aspect of science teaching.

Reasons for Teaching Socially Relevant Science

There are three reasons that have been suggested for teaching socially relevant science. The first is that by teaching science in the context of what is already familiar from daily experience—newspaper, television, and magazine accounts of nuclear power plants, environmental pollution, recycling, and the ozone layer, for example, or about objects in and around the house, such as electronic devices, the automobile, and household appliances—the student is motivated to learn the *science* that relates to those daily experiences. The second reason is that science, along with other school subjects, should inform and enrich the lives of individuals, something that is best accomplished by teaching about those things the individual experiences in everyday life. Included here is the ability to function as a citizen in a democratic society, to contribute to discussions on issues related to science, and to vote intelligently on those issues. The third reason is that the teaching of socially relevant science is important for the health and well-being, and perhaps even the survival, of the human race. In the early twentieth century the concern was for public health and the development of an industrial economy. Since the early 1970s the concern has centered more on the survival of and quality of life on our planet through education that is focused on such issues as environmental pollution, nuclear energy, and genetic engineering.

There is little disagreement among science educators about any of these reasons for teaching the social implications of science. The problem arises when we have to decide the extent to which the socially relevant issues become the focus of instruction. Technological accomplishments can themselves become the objects of study. Environmental pollution can itself become the subject of a science course. In the extreme form, these applications can essentially replace organized disciplinary science. Students may still learn some science, but only enough to understand the technological application. In this case the application becomes the determining and limiting factor in what science gets taught. Many critics of progressive education argued that window shade rollers, refrigerators, heating systems, smelting furnaces, and the automobile offered a diet that was light on science. In addition, the *organization* of science under such an approach is around socially relevant issues or problems, not around principles of science that have been developed and organized by scientists over the ages. Under such an argument we would not be taking advantage of the *logic* of science as organized by generations of our best minds. It also means that as new socially relevant problems emerge or as new technology is developed, the basic organization of science teaching must change as well. An alternative to this approach is for the individual science disciplines themselves to continue providing the organizational structure for the teaching of science while the applications of science are used to motivate students and to demonstrate how science functions in our world.

Much of the interest in switching from disciplinary science to a study of socially relevant issues is motivated today by what is perceived to be an impending environmental catastrophe. It is said that as much effort as possible in education should be redirected so that we can raise our collective environmental consciousness and avoid imminent disaster. Does this mean that it is time to abandon disciplinary science study? Have we reached the point where we should forgo the teaching of organized science to a generation of students so that their environmental awareness may be increased? This is an important question, one that needs to be answered quickly. What is our best hope for now and the future? Can we as science educators contribute to raising the social consciousness of our students at the same time that they are taught an understanding of the basic principles of science? Which, indeed, is more relevant, fundamental principles of science or a study of the issues themselves? This is a question that all teachers must answer for themselves, but for now, at least, some approach that combines the two seems to be the best course of action to most science educators.

Values Education

Another aspect of the recent emphasis on scientific literacy and social relevance is the inclusion of values education, decision making, and ethical problem solving in science classes. What limits should be placed on genetic engineering? Should the U.S. government lend financial support to overpopulated Third World countries for programs to control the birth rate through abortion? To what extent should industry be allowed to pollute the air for purposes of economic development? Should a higher gasoline tax be imposed on American automobile users in order to discourage driving? These are fascinating questions, and because of their obvious connection to science, they are of considerable interest to many science educators. Some, however, have wondered if these moral discussions are really science at all. If this is not science, then we need to ask if this kind of course content should replace organized science as we know it. And if it does replace conventional science instruction in whole or in part, a great deal of work needs to be done to establish standards by which these science-related social issues are analyzed. Some believe that current practices of "clarifying values" by sharing and discussing with others what one believes to be true may have a negative effect on ethical development by giving the appearance that any belief or opinion is as good as the next. On the other hand, agreeing on an ethical standard for the evaluation of social issues is going to be a difficult task indeed.

Why Socially Relevant Science Is Important

For reasons that have already been discussed in this chapter, it has been widely recognized by science educators over the years that it is important to link science concepts to those aspects of the everyday world to which those concepts relate. Virtually everyone accepts some form of social relevance in the science curriculum as long as it does not threaten long-held traditional values about the integrity of the science disciplines themselves. It is widely believed that all of education should relate to the present lives of students and, to the extent that we can determine it, their future lives as well. In fact, this was the argument that allowed science to enter the school curriculum in the first place. It was said that a world dominated by science could not leave a study of science out of its educational plans. Over the years some form of social relevance has become a standard by which we measure the quality of science education, for it is widely believed that education in every culture and at every time should relate to the basic needs and purposes of that culture.

A Composite Model of Science Teaching

After more than a century of organized science instruction in American schools, we can be secure in the realization that science education is firmly entrenched in the school curriculum at all levels. This is a world filled with science, and for science not to be a part of the curriculum would be strange indeed. Our task, as it has been for most of this century, is to continue to struggle with the question of what kind of science instruction should go on in elementary schools, in high schools, and in colleges. Before arguing for "more science," it seems that we need to make better arguments for the kind of science that should be taught. If we can offer something of obvious value, the demand for those courses should be great.

What should the program include? If we were to summarize the dominant thinking about science education over the past 150 years and use that as the basis for the science program, it would look something like this. First of all, science teaching would be organized around the science disciplines as those disciplines have been developed by scientists over the years. The logically organized disciplines are the product of the most thorough and rigorous examination of the physical world that humans have been able to create. The science disciplines represent a long history of contact with the natural world and attempts to derive meaning from that contact. The disciplines represent an ever-changing accumulation of organized knowledge and provide the starting point for future revisions of that knowledge. The science disciplines provide us with concepts for understanding our world, predicting probable outcomes of our interaction with our world, and deriving meaning and enjoyment from our world. An understanding of organized science empowers us in fundamentally important ways.

But to say that science study should lead to the formation of organized knowledge is not to say that science study is simply a vocabulary lesson. It is not at its root a linguistic study. It is not a study of words and their meaning. It is the study of natural objects and events. Although there has been a tendency over the years to allow science to become a book study, this practice has been widely criticized, and the dominant view has been that science study must involve as much direct contact with the physical world as possible. If the students have not had previous experience with the objects or phenomena that are essential for understanding the concept being taught, then the teacher should provide those experiences to the students. Without this, most science educators over the years have agreed, there is little hope that students will develop meaningful learning.

Unfortunately, as children grow older, there is a tendency to rely on their ability to form mental images or models to represent natural phenomena, even when direct observation or recall of the object or event is possible. Thus one may speak of wind, water, and glacial movement as causes of erosion without ever demonstrating those processes to the students or having the students reflect on previous experiences they may have had with those phenomena. Students may be told that conduction, convection, and radiation are three types of heat transfer without ever considering their own experiences with them. The distinctions are made, the categories are created, and the knowledge memorized for recall on a future test. Most science educators over the years have agreed that this vocabulary testing should not characterize science teaching. Learning in science involves reflecting on, discussing, and expanding on the experiences we have had with our physical world.

In a model of science teaching generated from the major historical ideas in the field, students would also learn the processes of science—the scientific way of thinking. For the most part, this would be accomplished by practicing many of the same skills that scientists use. Making linkages between theory and the physical confirmation of theory by means of experimentation would constitute the major part of teaching the processes of science. Usually, this would involve gathering data and comparing those data to what was expected from theory. Although some would attempt to add an element of "discovery" to these activities by having the laboratory work precede the discussion of the theory, many science educators have questioned the effectiveness of such an approach.

How much laboratory activities should be confirmations of what the students already know versus how much they should focus on the discovery of new knowledge has been a difficult question to answer and has led to considerable disagreement among science educators. Laboratory activities that are conducted in an area unfamiliar to the student can be virtually meaningless. A substantial prior understanding of the relevant content is generally a prerequisite for deriving meaning from an investigation, whether the investigator is a student or a practicing scientist. For this reason, laboratory activities would be, in large part anyway, confirmations of known or expected theory; that is, these activities would involve laboratory testing to see if what one thought was true was really true. Laboratory activities would enlarge and enrich the students' understanding of the theory because of their personal contact with the physical manifestation of that theory, and the laboratory activities would give the students practice in the processes of science within a context that was familiar to them. The key here would be to make sure students did not see themselves as trying to "prove" that something was true but rather that they perceived themselves as finding evidence for or against some claim.

Besides this seeking of evidence to support claims or predictions, many activities would be performed that were of a genuine inquiry, or "let's find out," type. Students might determine by experiment the effects of all kinds of conditions on growing organisms and draw conclusions from those observations. Plants could be grown in light and dark, with varying amounts of food and water. Mealworms could be subjected to moist and dry conditions. As their knowledge and experience grew, and as their motivation for making independent discoveries increased, students would be given additional opportunities to play the role of the genuinely inquiring scientist. Science educators over the years have seen the benefits of such opportunities, but they have also recognized the problems that can occur if students are placed in this situation without adequate preparation and support.

In a composite model of science teaching derived from the major

historical ideas in science education, students would be constantly re-
minded that the processes and products of scientific inquiry that they
are learning are about the world around them. They would master
the disciplines, yes, but not sets of unrelated facts associated with
those disciplines. What would be learned would represent the power
of the disciplines to explain the world they live in. They would realize
the potential that scientific inquiry has for affecting their lives and the
lives of their children. As such, there would be frequent discussions
about the relationships between the principles of science and the
events of the day. Nuclear power plants, recycling, birth control,
losses to the gene pool when species become extinct, the ozone layer,
and genetic engineering would be part of the daily interaction between student and teacher and between student and student. Students would be alerted to read about these issues in magazines and
newspapers and to discuss them with family and friends. As John
Dewey (1938) told us many years ago, isolation in all forms is the
thing to be avoided; connectedness is what we should strive for.

Conclusion

Science education, as all education, should lead to independent
self-activity. It should empower individuals to think and to act. It
should give individuals new ideas and investigative skills that contribute to self-regulation, personal satisfaction, and social responsibility.
Knowledge that is richly interconnected, intellectual skill that allows
individuals to work with what is known, and an awareness of the contexts within which that knowledge and those skills apply—all of this
should be part of science education.

There is, however, no one best science program for all. Students
differ, teachers differ, and local communities differ. Programs will
take into account these variations. The most important thing is that
we understand why we do what we do and the likely consequences of
that particular approach. There are so many legitimate reasons for
teaching science and ways to do it that it is probably unwise to try to
settle on one best way. The science education community would lose
a great deal of its vitality and enthusiasm if an attempt were made to
narrow the range of either goals or strategies. We need the advocates
of process, of social relevance, and of disciplinary study, and supporters of each need to make their arguments as convincingly as possible. What each individual teacher needs to do is to make decisions
about how much time to spend on each of the many worthy goals.

How much on the history of science? How much on process? How much on discovery? How much on social issues? How much on ethical decision making? Some programs will try to do many of these things, while others will focus on only a few. These are difficult decisions but ones that need to be made with intelligence and an understanding of the basis for each approach. A study of the history of ideas in science education is valuable in this regard because it can provide a context for developing a clearer sense of what is important and why. I wrote this book so that people associated with the science education enterprise could become better informed about their own ideas and their own practices. I trust that this effort will make us all more thoughtful about what we do and why we do it.

References
Index
About the Author

References

Adams, H. (1973). *The education of Henry Adams: An autobiography.* Boston: Houghton Mifflin. (Original work published 1918)

American Association for the Advancement of Science. (1967). *Science—A process approach.* (1967). New York: Xerox Division, Ginn & Company.

American Chemical Society. (1924). Correlation of high school and college chemistry. *Journal of Chemical Education, 1,* 87–99.

American Institute of Physics. (1964). Why is high school physics enrollment not keeping up with the school population? *The Physics Teacher, 2,* 389.

Applegarth, L. W. (1935). Comparison of the effectiveness of the single laboratory period and the double laboratory period in high school chemistry. *School Science and Mathematics, 35,* 627–633.

Aptekar, D. (1945). Can science courses be taught scientifically? *School Science and Mathematics, 45,* 33–37.

Armstrong, H. (1898). On the heuristic method. *Special reports on educational subjects, vol. II.* London: Eyre & Spottiswood.

Ausubel, D. (1968). *Educational psychology: A cognitive view.* New York: Holt, Rinehart & Winston.

Ausubel, D., & Ausubel, P. (1966). Cognitive development in adolescence. *Review of Educational Research, 36,* 403–413.

Babikian, Y. (1971). An empirical investigation to determine the relative effectiveness of discovery, laboratory, and expository methods of teaching science concepts. *Journal of Research in Science Teaching, 8,* 201–209.

Ballew, A. (1930). An analysis of biological drawing. *School Science and Mathematics, 30,* 490–497.

Barber, F. (1915). The present status and real meaning of general science. *School Science and Mathematics, 15,* 218–224.

Bestor, A. (1953). *Educational wastelands: The retreat from learning in our schools.* Urbana, IL; University of Illinois Press.

Biological Sciences Curriculum Study. (1963a). *Biological science: An inquiry into life* (BSCS Yellow Version). New York: Harcourt, Brace & World.

Biological Sciences Curriculum Study. (1963b). *Biological science: Molecules to man* (BSCS Blue Version). Boston: Houghton Mifflin.

Biological Sciences Curriculum Study. (1963c). *High school biology* (BSCS Green Version). Chicago: Rand McNally.

Biological Sciences Curriculum Study. (1963d). *Biology teachers' handbook.* New York: Wiley.

Biological Sciences Curriculum Study. (1966). *Patterns and processes.* New York: Holt, Rinehart & Winston.

Black, N. H. (1930). Better demonstrations in physics. *School Science and Mathematics, 30,* 366–373.

Boomsliter, A. (1936). *A selection of general science textbook material to meet the needs of junior high school children in an industrial community.* Unpublished master's thesis, West Virginia University, Morgantown.

Bradbury, R. (1915). Recent tendencies in high school chemistry. *School Science and Mathematics, 15,* 782–793.

Brandwein, P. (1955). *The gifted student as future scientist.* New York: Harcourt, Brace.

Brown, H. E. (1940a). The plight of high school physics, II. Peccant psychology. *School Science and Mathematics, 40,* 156–160.

Brown, H. E. (1940b). The plight of high school physics, III. Mismanaged mathematics. *School Science and Mathematics, 40,* 369–376.

Brown, H. E. (1940c). The plight of high school physics, IV. The languishing laboratory. *School Science and Mathematics, 40,* 457–462.

Bruner, J. (1960). *The process of education.* New York: Vintage.

Butts, D. (1964). The evaluation of problem solving in science. *Journal of Research in Science Teaching, 2,* 116–122.

Bybee, R. (1979). Science education and the emerging ecological society. *Science Education, 63,* 95–109.

Bybee, R., Harms, N., Ward, B., & Yager, R. (1980). Science, society and science education. *Science Education, 64,* 377–395.

Bybee, R., & Welch, D. (1972). The third force: Humanistic psychology and science education. *The Science Teacher, 39* (8), 18–22.

Caldwell, O. (1909). An investigation of the teaching of biological subjects in secondary schools. *School Science and Mathematics, 9,* 581–597.

Carlton, R. (1963). On scientific literacy. *NEA Journal, 52* (4), 33–35.

Carpenter, W. W. (1925) *Certain phases of the administration of high-school chemistry.* New York: Teachers College, Columbia University, Bureau of Publications.

Champagne, A., & Klopfer, L. (1977). A sixty-year perspective on three issues in science education: I. Whose ideas are dominant? II. Representation of women. III. Reflective thinking and problem solving. *Science Education, 61,* 431–452.

Chemical Bond Approach. (1962a). *Chemical systems.* New York: McGraw-Hill.

Chemical Bond Approach. (1962b). *Investigating chemical systems.* New York: McGraw-Hill.

Chemical Education Material Study. (1963a). *Chemistry: An experimental science.* San Francisco: Freeman.

Chemical Education Material Study. (1963b). *Laboratory manual for chemistry: An experimental science*. San Francisco: Freeman.

Chemical Education Material Study. (1963c). *Teacher's guide for chemistry: An experimental science*. San Francisco: Freeman.

Cleveland Schoolmasters Club: Committee Report on Science in Greater Cleveland, Ohio. (1925). Reports on biology, chemistry, physics and general science. *School Science and Mathematics, 25*, 462–474, 600–610.

Compayre, G. (1907). *Herbart and education by instruction* (M. Findlay, Trans.). New York: Crowell.

Conant, J. (1947). *On understanding science*. New Haven, CT: Yale University Press.

Cornog, J., & Colbert, J. (1924). A quantitative analysis of aims in teaching high-school chemistry. *School Science and Mathematics, 24*, 168–173.

Coulter, J. (1915). The mission of science in education. *School Science and Mathematics, 15*, 93–100.

Counts, G. S. (1926). *The senior high school curriculum*. Chicago, IL: The University of Chicago.

Cremin, L. (1964). *The transformation of the school: Progressivism in American education, 1876–1957*. New York: Knopf.

Cubberley, E. (1919). *Public education in the United States*. Boston: Houghton Mifflin.

DeGarmo, C. (1895). *Herbart and the Herbartians*. New York: Charles Scribner's Sons.

Dewey, J. (1916). *Democracy and education*. New York: Macmillan.

Dewey, J. (1938). *Experience and education*. New York: Collier.

Dexter, E. (1906). Ten years' influence on the report of the Committee of Ten. *School Review, 14*, 254–269.

DiVincenzo, R. (1976). Relative-certainty: A theoretical system for overcoming discovery-learning disabilities. *School Science and Mathematics, 76*, 469–492.

Downing, E. (1915). Some data regarding the teaching of zoology in secondary schools. *School Science and Mathematics, 15*, 36–43.

Dull, C., Metcalfe, H. C., & Brooks, W. (1951). *Modern physics*. New York: Holt.

Duschl, R. (1985). Science education and philosophy of science; twenty-five years of mutually exclusive development. *School Science and Mathematics, 85*, 541–555.

Earth Science Curriculum Project. (1967). *Investigating the earth*. Boston: Houghton Mifflin.

Easley, J., Jr. (1959). The physical science study committee and educational theory. *Harvard Educational Review, 29*, 4–11.

Educational Development Center. (1969). *Elementary science study*. Manchester, MO: Webster Division, McGraw-Hill.

Educational Policies Commission. (1944). *Education for all American youth*. Washington, DC: National Education Association.

Educational Policies Commission. (1952). *Education for all American youth: A further look*. Washington, DC: National Education Association.

Ehrle, E. (1971). If you teach the context who will teach the student? *The Science Teacher, 38* (6), 22–24.

Einstein, A. (1950). *Out of my later years.* New York: Littlefield.

Eliot, C. (1898). *Educational reform.* New York: Century.

Environmental Education Act. (1970). *Statutes at Large, 84,* 1312–1315.

Faraday, M. (1867). On the education of the judgement. In E. L. Youmans (Ed.), *The culture demanded by modern life* (pp. 191–230). New York: Appleton.

Feyerabend, P. (1975). *Against method.* London: Verso.

Feyerabend, P. (1981). *Problems of empiricism.* New York: Cambridge University Press.

Finlay, G. (1962). The physical science study committee. *The School Review, 70,* 63–81.

Finley, F. (1983). Science processes. *Journal of Research in Science Teaching, 20,* 47–54.

Fiske, J. (1899). Edward Livingston Youmans. In J. Fiske (Ed.), *A century of science and other essays* (pp. 64–99). New York: Houghton Mifflin.

Ford, L. A. (1940). Laboratory science. *School Science and Mathematics, 40,* 556–557.

Freundlich, Y. (1978). The "problem" in inquiry. *The Science Teacher, 45* (2), 19–22.

Gagne, R. (1977). *The conditions of learning* (3rd ed.). New York: Holt, Rinehart & Winston.

Gagne, R., Briggs, L., & Wager, W. (1988). *Principles of instructional design.* New York: Holt, Rinehart & Winston.

Gallagher, J. (1971). A broader base for science teaching. *Science Education, 55,* 329–338.

Garrett, A., Haskins, J., & Sisler, H. (1951). *Essentials of chemistry.* New York: Ginn.

Gauld, C. (1982). The scientific attitude and science education: A critical reappraisal. *Science Education, 66,* 109–121.

Gerry, H. (1925). The need and use of a scientific measure of the results of the teaching of chemistry. *School Science and Mathematics, 25,* 157–168.

Glass, B. (1962). Renascent biology: A report on the AIBS biological sciences curriculum study. *The School Review, 70,* 16–43.

Glass, C. (1983). Do we still need energy education? *The Science Teacher, 50* (9), 45–48.

Good, R., Herron, J., Lawson, A., & Renner, J. (1985). The domain of science education. *Science Education, 69,* 139–141.

Haiber-Sham, U., Cross, J., Abegg, G., Dodge, J., & Walter, J. (1972). *Introductory physical science* (2nd ed.). Englewood Cliffs, NJ: Prentice-Hall.

Harmon, M., Kirschenbaum, H., & Simon, S. (1970). Teaching science with a focus on values. *The Science Teacher, 37* (1), 16–20.

Harvard Committee. (1945). *General education in a free society.* Cambridge, MA: Harvard University Press.

Harvard Project Physics. (1968). *An introduction to physics.* New York: Holt, Rinehart & Winston.

Hawkins, J., & Pea, R. (1987). Tools for bridging the cultures of everyday and scientific thinking. *Journal of Research in Science Teaching, 24,* 291–307.

Helgeson, S., Blosser, P., & Howe, R. (1978). *The status of pre-college science, mathematics, and social science education: 1955–1975: Vol. I. Science education.* Washington, DC: U.S. Government Printing Office.

Herbart, J. (1893). *The science of education: Its general principles deduced from its aim.* (H. Felkin & E. Felkin, Trans.). Boston: Heath. (Original work published in 1806 as *General pedagogy, deduced from the purpose of education*).

Herbart, J. (1901). *Outlines of educational doctrine* (C. DeGarmo, Ed.; A. Lange, Trans.). New York: Macmillan. (Original work published 1835)

Hermann, G., & Hincksman, N. (1978). Inductive versus deductive approaches in teaching a lesson in chemistry. *Journal of Research in Science Teaching, 15,* 37–42.

Hofstein, A., & Yager, R. (1982). Societal issues as organizers for science education in the 80's. *School Science and Mathematics, 82,* 539–547.

Hopkins, L. T. (1925). A study of magazine and newspaper science articles with relation to courses in sciences for high schools. *School Science and Mathematics, 25,* 793–800.

Howe, A. (1971). A lost dimension in elementary school science. *Science Education, 55,* 143–146.

Hunter, G. (1910). The methods, content and purpose of biologic science in the secondary schools of the U.S. *School Science and Mathematics, 10,* 1–10, 103–111.

Hurd, A. (1925). Observations on factors determining success in physics. *School Science and Mathematics, 25,* 111–131.

Hurd, A. (1929). *Problems of science teaching at the college level.* Minneapolis: University of Minnesota Press.

Hurd, A. (1930). Present inadequacies and suggested remedies in the teaching of physics. *School Science and Mathematics, 30,* 539–546.

Hurd, P. (1953). The case against high school physics. *School Science and Mathematics, 53,* 439–449.

Hurd, P. (1958). Science literacy: Its meaning for American schools. *Educational Leadership, 16,* 13–16.

Hurd, P. (1970). *New directions in teaching secondary school science.* Chicago: Rand McNally.

Huxley, T. (1899). *Science and education.* New York: Appleton.

Inhelder, B., & Piaget, J. (1958). *The growth of logical thinking from childhood to adolescence.* New York: Basic Books.

Intermediate Science Curriculum Study. (1972). *Probing the natural world.* Morrisville, NJ: Silver Burdett.

IPS Group of Educational Services, Inc. (1967). *Introductory physical science.* Englewood Cliffs, NJ: Prentice-Hall.

James, W. (1899). *Talks to teachers on psychology: And to students on some of life's ideals.* New York: Holt.

Jones, H., & Russell, J. (1979). Hierarchical learning paradigm. *Journal of Research in Science Teaching, 16,* 489–499.

Karplus, R. (1977). Science teaching and the development of reasoning. *Journal of Research in Science Teaching, 14*, 169–175.

Kaufman, B. (1971). Psychological implications of learning in science. *Science Education, 55*, 73–83.

Kilpatrick, W. (1918). The project method. *Teachers College Record, 19*, 319–335.

Kinsey, A. (1930). The content of the biology course. *School Science and Mathematics, 30*, 374–384.

Klinge, P. (1950). Is biology a science course? *School Science and Mathematics, 50*, 379–383.

Koelsche, C. (1965). Scientific literacy as related to the media of mass communication. *School Science and Mathematics, 65*, 719–724.

Krenerick, H. C. (1935). A single laboratory period, a demonstrated success. *School Science and Mathematics, 35*, 468–476.

Kromhout, R., & Good, R. (1983). Beware of societal issues as organizers for science education. *School Science and Mathematics, 83*, 647–650.

Kuhn, T. (1970). *The structure of scientific revolutions.* Chicago: University of Chicago Press.

Lawson, A. (1979). The developmental learning paradigm. *Journal of Research in Science Teaching, 16*, 501–515.

Lawson, A. (1982). The nature of advanced reasoning and science instruction. *Journal of Research in Science Teaching, 19*, 743–760.

Lawson, A., Karplus, R., & Adi, H. (1978). The acquisition of proportional logic and formal operational schemata during the secondary school years. *Journal of Research in Science Teaching, 15*, 465–478.

Leker, W. R. (1925). The articulation of general science with the special sciences. *School Science and Mathematics, 25*, 725–739.

Linn, M. (1982). Theoretical and practical significance of formal reasoning. *Journal of Research in Science Teaching, 19*, 727–742.

Little, E. (1959). The physical science study committee. *Harvard Educational Review, 29*, 1–3.

Loud, O. (1950). Designing science courses for general education on the college level. *School Science and Mathematics, 50*, 289–296.

Luehamn, A. (1955). Science and mathematics for today's youth. *School Science and Mathematics, 55*, 725–730.

Malin, J. (1932). A brief survey of the mechanical fundamentals of high school chemistry taught in the United States. *School Science and Mathematics, 32*, 149–155.

Mallinson, G. (1955). The role of physics in the emerging high school curriculum. *School Science and Mathematics, 55*, 211–216.

Martin, W. E. (1945). A chronological survey of published research studies relating to biological materials in newspapers and magazines. *School Science and Mathematics, 45*, 543–550.

McConnell, W. R. (1920). What changes should be made in our methods of teaching high school geography? *School Science and Mathematics, 20*, 117–124.

McElroy, W. (1970). Point of view. *Science, 170,* 517.

McGee, J. (1935). A new look at the science laboratory. *School Science and Mathematics, 35,* 700–702.

Merrill, R., & Ridgway, D. (1969). *The CHEM Study story.* San Francisco: Freeman.

Metcalfe, H. C., Williams, J., & Caska, J. (1966). *Modern chemistry* (3rd ed.). New York: Holt, Rinehart & Winston.

Millikan, R. (1925). The problem of teaching science in the secondary schools. *School Science and Mathematics, 25,* 966–975.

Monahan, A. C. (1930). Science and its recognition in the high school curriculum. *School Science and Mathematics, 30,* 875–880.

Moon, T., & Brezinski, B. (1974). Environmental education from a historical perspective. *School Science and Mathematics, 74,* 371–374.

Moon, T., Otto, J., & Towle, A. (1963). *Modern biology* (5th ed.). New York: Holt.

Moravcsik, M. (1981). Creativity in science education. *Science Education, 65,* 221–227.

National Center for Education Statistics. (1981). *Digest of education statistics.* Washington, DC: U.S. Government Printing Office.

National Education Association. (1893). *Report of the committee on secondary school studies.* Washington, DC: U.S. Government Printing Office.

National Education Association. (1899). Report of the committee on college-entrance requirements. In *Journal of proceedings and addresses of the thirty-eighth annual meeting.* Chicago: Author.

National Education Association. (1911). Report of the committee of nine on the articulation of high school and college. In *Journal of proceedings and addresses of the forty-ninth annual meeting.* Chicago: Author.

National Education Association. (1918). *Cardinal principles of secondary education: A report of the commission on the reorganization of secondary education* (U.S. Bureau of Education, Bulletin No. 35). Washington, DC: U.S. Government Printing Office.

National Education Association. (1920). *Reorganization of science in secondary schools: A report of the commission on the reorganization of secondary education* (U.S. Bureau of Education, Bulletin No. 26). Washington, DC: U.S. Government Printing Office.

National Science Foundation. (1962). The role of the National Science Foundation in course content improvement in secondary schools. *The School Review, 70,* 1–15.

National Science Teachers Association. (1971). NSTA position statement on school science education for the 70's. *The Science Teacher, 38,* 46–51.

National Science Teachers Association. (1982). *Science-technology-society: Science education for the 1980's.* Washington: Author.

National Society for the Study of Education. (1932). *A program for teaching science: Thirty-First yearbook of the NSSE.* Chicago: University of Chicago Press.

National Society for the Study of Education. (1947). *Science education in Amer-*

ican schools: Forty-Sixth yearbook of the NSSE. Chicago: University of Chicago Press.

Newton, D. (1968). The dishonesty of inquiry teaching. *School Science and Mathematics, 68,* 807–810.

Noll, V. (1939). *The teaching of science in elementary and secondary schools.* New York: Longmans, Green.

Norris, S. (1985). The philosophical basis of observation in science and science education. *Journal of Research in Science Teaching, 22,* 817–833.

Novak, J. (1978). An alternative to Piagetian psychology for science and math education. *Studies in Science Education, 5,* 1–30.

Novak, J. (1979). The reception learning paradigm. *Journal of Research in Science Teaching, 16,* 481–488.

Novak, J., Ring, D., & Tamir, P. (1971). Interpretation of research findings in terms of Ausubel's theory and implications for science education. *Science Education, 55,* 483–526.

Otto, J., & Towle, A. (1965). *Modern biology.* New York: Holt, Rinehart & Winston.

Peabody, J. (1915). Preliminary report of the biology subcommittee. *School Science and Mathematics, 15,* 44–53.

Pella, M. (1967). Science literacy and the h.s. curriculum. *School Science and Mathematics, 67,* 346–356.

Physical Science Study Committee. (1960a). *Physics.* Boston: Heath.

Physical Science Study Committee. (1960b). *Physics, laboratory guide.* Boston: Heath.

Piaget, J. (1964). Development and learning. *Journal of Research in Science Teaching, 2,* 176–186.

Picton, H. (1899). The great shibboleth. *School World, 1,* 397.

Pieper, C. (1920). Fundamentals in method—old and new. *School Science and Mathematics, 20,* 409–415.

Pinloche, A. (1901). *Pestalozzi and the foundations of the modern elementary school.* New York: Charles Scribner's Sons.

Powers, S. (1924). *A diagnostic study of the subject matter of high school chemistry* (Contributions to Education No. 149). New York: Teachers College, Columbia University.

Powers, S. R. (1925). Achievement in high school chemistry—An examination of subject matter. *School Science and Mathematics, 25,* 53–61.

President's Scientific Research Board. (1947). *Science and public policy* (Vols. 1, 3, & 4). Washington, DC: U.S. Government Printing Office.

Quick, S. (1978). *Secondary impacts of the curriculum reform movement: A longitudinal study of the incorporation of innovations of the curriculum reform movement into commercially developed curriculum programs.* Unpublished doctoral dissertation, Stanford University.

Rachelson, S. (1977). A question of balance: A wholistic view of scientific inquiry. *Science Education, 61,* 109–117.

Ravitch, D. (1983). *The troubled crusade.* New York: Basic Books.

Rice, J. (1893). *The public-school system of the United States.* New York: Century.

Rich, S. G. (1925). Achievements of pupils in chemistry. *School Science and Mathematics, 25,* 145–149.

Richardson, J. S. (1945). Trends, deficiencies and challenges related to general science. *School Science and Mathematics, 45,* 202–210.

Roberts, H. F. (1913). Biology in the high schools. *School Science and Mathematics, 13,* 146–152.

Rousseau, J. (1979). *Emile, or, on education* (A. Bloom, Trans.). New York: Basic Books. (Original work published 1762)

Ruch, G. M. (1920). The general science of the future. *School Science and Mathematics, 20,* 423–432.

Rutherford, J. (1964). The role of inquiry in science teaching. *Journal of Research in Science Teaching, 2,* 80–84.

Sakmyser, D. (1974). Comparison of inductive and deductive programmed instruction on chemical equilibrium for high school chemistry students. *Journal of Research in Science Teaching, 11,* 67–77.

Sanford, C. (1950). High school science and mathematics—For whom and for what? *School Science and Mathematics, 50,* 307–319.

Schefler, W. (1965). A comparison between inductive and illustrative laboratories in college biology. *Journal of Research in Science Teaching, 3,* 218–223.

Schulman, L. (1968). Psychological controversies in the teaching of science and mathematics. *The Science Teacher, 35* (6), 34–38.

Schwab, J. (1962). The teaching of science as enquiry. In *The teaching of science* (pp. 1–103). Cambridge, MA: Harvard University Press.

Science Curriculum Improvement Study. (1970). Chicago: Rand McNally.

Secondary School Science Project. (1966). *Time, space, and matter . . . investigating the physical world.* Manchester, MO: Webster Division, McGraw-Hill.

Shamos, M. (1966). The role of major conceptual schemes in science education. *The Science Teacher, 33* (1), 27–30.

Sizer, T. (Ed.). (1964a). *The age of the academies.* New York: Columbia University.

Sizer, T. (1964b). *Secondary schools at the turn of the century.* New Haven, CT: Yale University Press.

Smith, A., & Hall, E. (1902). *The teaching of chemistry and physics in the secondary school.* New York: Longmans, Green.

Smith, M. (1949). *And madly teach: A layman looks at public school education.* Chicago: Regnery.

Smith, M. (1954). *The diminished mind.* Chicago: Regnery.

Smith, N. (1974). The challenge of scientific literacy. *The Science Teacher, 41* (6), 34–35.

Smyth, T. (1940). Problems associated with the high school science sequence. *School Science and Mathematics, 40,* 255–260.

Spears, B., & Zollman, D. (1977). The influence of structured versus unstructured laboratory on students' understanding of the process of science. *Journal of Research in Science Teaching, 14,* 33–38.

Spencer, H. (1864). *Education: Intellectual, moral, and physical.* New York: Appleton.

Stewart, A. W. (1935). Measuring ability to apply principles. *School Science and Mathematics, 35,* 695–699.

Strong, L. (1962). Chemistry as a science in the high school. *The School Review, 70,* 44–50.

Tanner, R. (1969). Discovery as an object of research. *School Science and Mathematics, 69,* 647–655.

Taylor, C. (1962). Some educational implications of creativity research findings. *School Science and Mathematics, 62,* 593–606.

Thomas, B., & Snider, B. (1969). The effects of instructional methods upon the acquisition of inquiry skills. *Journal of Research in Science Teaching, 6,* 377–386.

Thorndike, E. L. (1913). *Educational psychology.* New York: Teachers College, Columbia University.

Thorndike, E. L.(1924). Mental discipline in high school studies. *Journal of Educational Psychology, 15,* 1–22, 83–98.

Thorndike, E. L., & Woodworth, R. S. (1901). The influence of improvement in one mental function upon the efficiency of other functions. *Psychological Review, 8,* 247–261, 384–395, 553–564.

Toulmin, S. (1961). *Foresight and understanding: An enquiry into the aims of science.* Bloomington: Indiana University Press.

Toulmin, S. (1972). *Human understanding.* Princeton, NJ: Princeton University Press.

Tregoning, J. (1929). *Some of the items that should be included in a high school chemistry course.* Unpublished master's thesis, Colorado State Teachers College, Greeley.

Troy, T., & Schwaab, K. (1982). A decade of environmental education. *School Science and Mathematics, 82,* 209–216.

Twiss, G. (1920). The reorganization of high school science. *School Science and Mathematics, 20,* 2–13.

Tyndall, J. (1867). On the importance of the study of physics. In E. L. Youmans (Ed.), *The culture demanded by modern life* (pp. 57–85). New York: Appleton.

U.S. Bureau of the Census. (1975). *Historical statistics of the United States, colonial times to 1970, bicentennial edition* (Part 1). Washington, DC: U.S. Government Printing Office.

U.S. Bureau of Education. (1896). *Report of the Commissioner of Education, 1894–1895* (Vol. 1). Washington, DC: U.S. Government Printing Office.

U.S. Bureau of Education. (1911). *Report of the Commissioner of Education for the year ended June 30, 1910* (Vol. 2). Washington, DC: U.S. Government Printing Office.

U.S. Bureau of Education. (1912). *Report of the Commissioner of Education for the year ended June 30, 1911* (Vol. 1). Washington, DC: U.S. Government Printing Office.

U.S. Bureau of Education. (1924). *Statistics of public high schools 1921–1922*

(Bulletin, 1924, No. 7). Washington, DC: U.S. Government Printing Office.

U.S. Office of Education. (1950). *The teaching of science in public high schools. An inquiry into offerings, enrollments, and selected teaching conditions, 1947–1948* (Federal Security Agency, Bulletin, 1950, No. 9). Washington, DC: U.S. Government Printing Office.

U.S. Office of Education. (1951). *Life adjustment for every youth.* Washington, DC: U.S. Government Printing Office.

U.S. Office of Education. (1953). *Education for the talented in mathematics and science.* Washington, DC: U.S. Government Printing Office.

University of the State of New York. (1900). *Report of the committee of nine* (High School Report, Bulletin No. 7). Albany: University of the State of New York Press.

Von Bichowsky, F. (1913). Meeting new demands with high school chemistry. *School Science and Mathematics, 13,* 772–775.

Watson, C. (1926). A critical study of the content of high school physics with respect to its social value. *The School Review, 34,* 688–697.

Webb, H. (1915). Is there a royal road to science? *School Science and Mathematics, 15,* 679–685.

Weiss, I. (1978). 1977 national survey of science, mathematics and social studies education highlights report. In *The status of pre-college science, mathematics, and social studies educational practices in U.S. schools: An overview and summaries of three studies* (pp. 1–25). Washington, DC: U.S. Government Printing Office.

Welch, W., Harris, L., & Anderson, R. (1984). How many are enrolled in science? *The Science Teacher, 51* (9), 14–19.

Welch, W., Klopfer, L., Aikenhead, G., & Robinson, J. (1981). The role of inquiry in science education: Analysis and recommendations. *Science Education, 65,* 33–50.

Whitney, W. (1930). History of biology in the high schools of Chicago. *School Science and Mathematics, 30,* 148–152.

Wilson, S. (1940). The future of specialized science in high schools. *School Science and Mathematics, 40,* 115–118.

Wood, G. C. (1913). Practical biology, *School Science and Mathematics, 13,* 240–247.

Woodhull, J. F. (1915). Science teaching by projects. *School Science and Mathematics, 15,* 225–232.

Yager, R. (1983). Defining science education as a discipline. *Journal of Research in Science Teaching, 20,* 261–262.

Yager, R. (1984). Defining the discipline of science education. *Science Education, 68,* 35–37.

Yager, R. (1985). In defense of defining science education as the science/society interface. *Science Education, 69,* 143–144.

Yager, R., Bybee, R., Gallagher, J., & Renner, J. (1982). An analysis of the current crises in the discipline of science education. *Journal of Research in Science Education, 19,* 377–395.

Yale Corporation. (1961). The Yale Report of 1828. In R. Hofstadter & W. Smith (Eds.), *American higher education: A documentary history* (Vol. 1) (pp. 274–291). Chicago: University of Chicago Press.

Youmans, E. L. (Ed.). (1867). *The culture demanded by modern life.* New York: Appleton.

Young, V. (1965). Survey on enrollment in physics. *The Physics Teacher, 3,* 117.

Index

Abegg, G., 167
Academies, 21, 65
  role of, 18–20
  study of science promoted by, 20
Adams, Henry, 1–2
Adi, H., 194, 197–198
Age of the Academies, The (Sizer), 19
Aikenhead, G., 209
American Association for the Advancement of Science (AAAS), 158, 194
  Cooperative Committee on the Teaching of Science and Mathematics of, 131–134, 136–137
American Chemical Society (ACS), 105–106, 152–154, 156
  Ad Hoc Committee on Possible Organization of a High School Chemistry Course of, 153–154
  Report of the Committee on Chemical Education of, 105
American Geological Institute, 157
American Institute of Biological Sciences (AIBS), 149
American Institute of Physics, 147–148, 170
Amherst College, 20
Analytical problem solving, 195–196
Anatomy
  Committee of Ten on, 43
  Eliot on, 32
  Rice on, 36
Anderson, R., 104
And Madly Teach (Smith), 144
Applegarth, L. W., 112
Aptekar, David, 106, 119–120

Armstrong, H. E., 56
Arts, Spencer on, 13–14
Association for the Advancement of Progressive Education, 85
Astronomy, 42–43, 50, 72, 86, 142
Austin High School, 119
Ausubel, David, 191, 201–203, 206
Ausubel, P., 203

Babikian, Y., 211–212
Bacon, Roger, 198–199
Ballew, Amer, 119
Barber, Fred, 88–89
Bell, J. Carleton, 122
Berkeley, University of California at, 154
Bestor, Arthur, 144–145
"Beware of Societal Issues as Organizers for Science Education" (Kromhout & Good), 186
Binet, Alfred, 122
Biological Sciences Curriculum Study (BSCS), 149–152, 163, 166–169
Biology, 86, 108
  Bruner on, 159–160
  chemistry and, 92–93, 104
  Committee of Ten on, 45
  Committee on Science on, 69, 73–74, 77, 79–80, 95
  curriculum reform in, 149–152, 166–170
  development of scientific thinking in, 97–98
  in disciplining mind, 7
  at end of progressive era, 139, 141, 146

Biology *(continued)*
during first half of twentieth century, 92–98
general science and, 89, 91–93
in high schools influenced by colleges, 117–119
Huxley on, 9
magazine and newspaper coverage of, 125
physics and, 92–93, 99
Spencer on, 13
student vs. subject in teaching of, 94–97
tropisms in, 160
uncertainty concerning methods and content of, 93–94
and value of laboratory study, 115
after World War II, 131–133
Biology Teacher's Handbook, 163
Black, N. Henry, 111
Blosser, P., 167, 215
Boomsliter, A., 126
Boston English High School, 59
Botany, 72, 86, 118
biology and, 93
Committee of Ten on, 43–45, 49
Huxley on, 10
Boyle, Robert, 198–199
Boys' High School, 118
Bradbury, Robert, 81–82
Brandwein, Paul, 137
Brezinski, B., 184
Briggs, L., 204
"Broader Base for Science Teaching, A" (Gallagher), 178
Brooks, W., 167
Brown, Elmer Ellsworth, 88
Brown, H. Emmett, 102–103, 116
Bruner, Jerome S., 159–163, 191, 196, 200, 211, 227
Bureau of Education, 24, 87–88, 91, 93, 99
Bureau of the Census, 99, 104, 140
Butts, D., 194
Bybee, R., 180–182, 187

Caldwell, Otis W., 69, 82
Campayre, Gabriel, 25, 27
Campbell, J. Arthur, 154

Cardinal Principles of Secondary Education, 67, 69, 80, 85–86, 89
Carlton, Robert, 174–175
Carpenter, W. W., 111
Caska, J., 167
Central Association of Science and Mathematics Teachers, 135, 141
Century, 31
Champagne, A., 193
Chemical Bond Approach (CBA), 152–153, 156–157, 166
Chemical Education Material Study (CHEM Study), 154–157, 166, 170
Chemistry, 86, 108
analysis of student interest in, 126
biology and, 92–93, 104
central unifying themes in, 105–106
Committee of Ten on, 42–43, 49
Committee on College Entrance Requirements on, 53
Committee on Science on, 69, 73–76, 80
curriculum reform in, 152–157, 166–167, 170
at end of progressive era, 138–142, 146
during first half of twentieth century, 104–106
general science and, 87–89, 91–92
laboratory-based study of, 55–58, 115, 152–155
magazine and newspaper coverage of, 125
physics and, 99, 104
project method in, 110
Smith on, 54–58
Spencer on, 13
after World War II, 131, 133
Chicago, University of, 54, 80, 159
Chicago public schools, 117–118
Childrearing, Spencer on, 13
Classical studies
in disciplining mind, 5–6
Huxley on, 9–10
science vs., 1–17
Spencer on, 13
at turn of twentieth century, 39
Yale Report on, 3–4
Clergy, study of science for, 9–10

Cleveland Schoolmasters Club, 115
Cobb, Stanwood, 85
Colbert, J., 105
College Entrance Examination Board, 116
Colleges, 66. *See also specific colleges and universities*
    Committee on Science on differentiated courses for students bound for, 79–80
    CRSE on admission to, 68
    differing emphasis on applications of science in high schools and, 120–121
    high school curriculum dominated by, 116–121
Colorado, University of, 41, 124, 149
Columbia University Teachers College, 69, 99, 102
Commission on the Reorganization of Secondary Education (CRSE), 66–80, 82–84, 127
    on college admission, 68
    on curriculum, 68–69
    Science Committee of. *See* Committee on Science
    on testing, 123
Committee of Ten, 30, 37, 40–52, 62, 64, 66, 68, 78, 80, 86, 89, 93, 117, 153
    Conference on Geography of, 45–48
    Conference on Natural History of, 42–45, 47
    Conference on Physics, Chemistry, and Astronomy of, 42–43
    purpose of, 40, 42
    report of, 48–50
Committee on College Entrance Requirements, 50–53, 62, 64, 66, 117
    Chemistry Subcommittee of, 53
    final report of, 50–52
    Physics Subcommittee of, 59
    science subcommittees of, 52–54, 59
    Zoology Subcommittee of, 52–53
Committee on Science, 67, 69–80, 82, 84, 105–106
    on biology, 69, 73–74, 77, 79–80, 95
    on differentiated courses for college-bound students, 79–80
    on general science, 89–92
    on goals of science education, 72–74
    on importance of student interest, 78–79
    on physics, 74–76, 78, 80, 100, 102
    recommendations for science instruction by, 74–77
Conant, James B., 132
Concept formation, Herbart's theory of, 26–28
Concept learning, 200–206
Concrete operational stage, 197
Conditions of Learning, The (Gagne), 203–204
Content, scientific
    inquiry teaching of, 224–225
    learner and, 101–102
    methods for teaching of, 222–226
    readiness and, 225–226
    reasons for teaching of, 219–221
    uncertainty concerning methods and, 93–94
    what to include in, 221–222
Context-specific scientific thinking, 194–195
Cornell University, 202
Cornog, J., 105
Coulter, John M., 42, 80, 137
Counts, George S., 138
Cremin, L., 85
Cross, J., 167
Cubberley, E., 19, 21–23
Culture Demanded by Modern Life, The (Youmans), 4–5
Curriculum, 146
    Committee of Ten on, 48–49
    Committee on Science on, 69–70
    CRSE on, 68–69
    Eliot on need for science in, 30–31
    at end of progressive era, 140–141, 143–144
    Herbart on organization of, 28–29
    high school, college domination of, 116–121
    scientific study of, 121–127
    social relevance of. *See* Social relevance, science for
    spiral, 162
    why science is part of, 216–217
Curriculum reform, 147–173, 177, 185

Curriculum reform *(continued)*
analyses of projects introduced in, 170–171
in biology, 149–152, 166–170
Bruner's support for, 159–163
in chemistry, 152–157, 166–167, 170
commercial textbooks impacted by, 167–169
enrollment changes due to, 169–170
NSF support for, 147–158
in physical science, 157–158, 167
in physics, 147–149, 166–167, 169–170
research studies on impact of, 166–170
Schwab's support for, 163–166
success of, 166–171
theoretical support for, 158–166
and use of new programs, 166–167
Curtis, Francis, 114

Darwin, Charles, 150
DeGarmo, Charles, 24, 28–29, 37
Descriptive reasoning strategies, 196–197
Dewey, John, 37, 79, 109–110, 223, 240
Dexter, Edwin, 50
Diminished Mind, The (Smith), 144
Disciplines
Bruner on structure of, 159–162
social relevance and, 85–107
Discovery learning. *See* Inquiry teaching
DiVincenzo, R., 196
Dodge, J., 167
Downing, Elliot, 82, 96–98, 122
Dull, C., 167
Duschl, R., 200

Earlham College, 152
Earth Science Curriculum Project (ESCP), 157, 167
Earth sciences, 146. *See also specific earth sciences*
Committee of Ten on, 46–48
Easley, J., Jr., 148
Education
changes during nineteenth century in, 2
contributions of science studies to meeting goals of, 33–34

crisis in, ix
debate between science and classical studies in, 1–17
Eliot's constituents of, 33–34
Eliot's influence on, 30–34
environmental, 182–184
European influences on, 21–30
Herbartians on aim of, 29–30
Herbart's influence on, 24–30
humanistic, 179–180
life adjustment, 142–146
Pestalozzi's influence on, 21–24
Rice's influence on, 34–37
Rousseau on aim of, 21
Smith on contributions of science teaching to, 54–55
for social utility, 65–66
U.S. influences on, 30–37
values, 180–182, 236–237
Education: Intellectual, Moral, and Physical (Spencer), 12
Educational Development Center, 158
Educational Policies Commission, 132–134, 140–141
Educational Services Incorporated, 158
Educational Wastelands (Bestor), 144
Education for All American Youth, 132–133, 140–141
Education for the Talented in Mathematics and Science, 136–137
Ehrle, E., 179
Einstein, Albert, 200
Elementary Science Study (ESS), 158, 167
Eliot, Charles W., 30–34, 37–38, 40–42, 79, 137
Emile (Rousseau), 21
Energy and Man's Environment project, 184
Engineering, study of science in, 9–10
English Home and Colonial Infant Society, 23
Enrollment, 99–100
impact of curriculum reform on, 169–170
after World War II, 133–134
Environmental education, 182–184
Environmental Education Act, 183
Ethics, science, xi

Faraday, Michael, 8, 17, 32–33
Feyerabend, P., 199
Field trips
    Committee on Science on, 77
    general science and, 90
    in teaching chemistry, 58
Finlay, G., 148
Finley, F., 199–200
Fiske, J., 4
Fluid inquiry, 163
Ford, Leonard A., 115–116
Formal operational stage, 197
Forum, 35
Franklin, Benjamin, 18
Freundlich, Y., 194, 199
Froebel, Friedrich Wilhelm August, 21
Functional science, 139–140

Gage, A. P., 59
Gagne, Robert, 191, 201, 203–204
Gallagher, James, 178, 187
Garrett, Alfred B., 153, 156
Gauld, C., 192, 200
General Education in a Free Society, 132, 141
General Pedagogy (Herbart), 24
General science
    biology and, 89, 91–93
    chemistry and, 87–89, 91–92
    Committee on Science on, 89–92
    at end of progressive era, 140
    during first half of twentieth century, 86–92
    in high schools influenced by colleges, 119
    laboratory study in, 90, 115
    need for, 86
    reactions to, 91–92
    reasons for development of, 87–89
    recommended approaches for, 89–91
    after World War II, 133–134
General scientific thinking, 194–195
Geography
    Committee of Ten on, 45–49
    Eliot on, 32
    physical. *See* Physical geography
Geology, 86, 142, 175
    Committee of Ten on, 46, 49–50
Gerry, Henry, 123

Giftedness, identification of, 136–138
Gifted Student as Future Scientist, The (Brandwein), 137
Glass, B., 150
Glass, C., 184
Good, R., 186–189
Göttingen, University of, 24
Griscom, John, 21
Grobman, Arnold, 149

Haiber-Sham, U., 167
Hall, Edwin H., 54–63, 232
Harmon, M., 180
Harms, N., 181
Harris, L., 104
Harris, William T., 24, 40–41
Harvard Committee, 132–134, 141
Harvard Project Physics, 166–167
Harvard University, 30, 40, 45, 54, 111, 116, 159, 175
    Inglis Lectures at, 163
    laboratory study and, 59–60
Haskins, J., 156
Hawkins, J., 199
Helgeson, S., 167, 215
Herbart, Johann Friedrich, 21, 24–32, 37, 79, 158
Hermann, G., 212
Herron, J., 188–189
Heuristic method. *See* Inquiry teaching
Hierarchical learning, 203–205
High schools, 157. *See also specific high schools*
    college domination of curriculum of, 116–121
    college-style courses in, 117–120
    differing emphasis on applications of science in colleges and, 120–121
    NEA and. *See* National Education Association
    post-World War II science course enrollments in, 133–134
Hincksman, N., 212
Hitchcock, Edward, 20
Hofstein, A., 184–185
Holton, Gerald, 175
Hopkins, L. Thomas, 124–125
Howe, Ann, 179
Howe, R., 167, 215

Humanistic education, 179–180
Hunter, G., 82
Hurd, Archer W., 99–100, 120, 123
Hurd, Paul DeHart, 142, 150–151, 153,
    170–171, 174–177
Huxley, Thomas, 4, 8–12, 14, 17, 21, 55
Hygiene, 86
    biology and, 93
    Committee of Ten on, 43–44
    Committee on Science on, 76
    Eliot on, 32
    at end of progressive era, 140
Hypothetico-deductive reasoning strate-
    gies, 197

Illinois, University of, 92
    College of Education at, 143
    Committee on School Mathematics of,
        145–146
Illinois Secondary School Curriculum
    Program (ISSCP), 143–144
Indiana University, 42
Individual Science Instruction System
    (ISIS), 186
Inhelder, Barbel, 162, 232
Inquiry
    fluid, 163
    stable, 163
Inquiry teaching, x, 163–166, 206–214
    for chemistry, 56–57
    claims and criticisms of, 207–209
    comparisons of non-inquiry teaching
        and, 209–213
    descriptions of non-inquiry teaching
        and, 210–211
    for physics, 60–61
    research studies on non-inquiry teach-
        ing and, 211–213
    of scientific content, 224–225
Interest
    analyses of, 124–127
    Committee on Science on, 78–79
    Herbart's theory of, 25–26
Intermediate Science Curriculum Study,
    167
Intuitive problem solving, 195–196

James, William, 37, 79, 190–191
Jena, University of, 24

Johns Hopkins University, 42
Jones, F. T., 122
Jones, H., 204–205
Journal of Environmental Education, 183
Journal of Research in Science Teaching,
    196, 202–203

Kansas State Agricultural College, 118
Kant, Immanuel, 24, 26, 223
Karplus, Robert, 158, 194, 197–198,
    205–206
Kaufman, B., 210–211
Kent State University, 123–124
Kilpatrick, William Heard, 109
Kingsley, Clarence, 66–67, 69
Kinsey, Alfred, 94
Kirschenbaum, H., 180
Klinge, Paul, 94, 98
Klopfer, L., 193, 209
Knowledge, science as structured body
    of, 219–226
Koch, Robert, 97
Koelsche, C., 175
Königsberg, University of, 24
Krenerick, H. Clyde, 112
Kromhout, R., 186–187
Kuhn, T., 199

Laboratory study, 108–116
    BSCS on, 150–151
    in CBA, 152–153
    in CHEM study project, 154–155
    Committee of Ten on, 42–43, 45, 49
    Committee on Science on, 76–78
    debates on value of, 113–116
    demonstration vs. individual work in,
        110–112
    double vs. single periods in, 112
    Eliot on, 33, 38
    general science and, 90, 115
    Hall on, 60–63
    Harvard on, 59–60
    in high schools influenced by colleges,
        119–120
    Huxley on, 11, 14
    in NSF-developed physical science
        course, 158
    purposes of, 113–114
    Smith on, 55–58, 62–63

Spencer on, 14
in teaching science process, 230–232
use of project method in, 109–110
Lange, A., 28
Lawson, A., 188–189, 194, 196–198
Learning. *See also* Teaching, science
concept, 200–206
in developing scientific mind, 192–198
discovery. *See* Inquiry teaching
of general vs. context-specific scientific
    thinking, 194–195
heuristic. *See* Inquiry teaching
hierarchical, 203–205
of intuitive vs. analytical problem solv-
    ing, 195–196
and nature of science, 198–200
Piaget's analysis of, 196–198
of processes and products of organized
    science, 190–214
psychological principles of, 190–192
readiness for, 225–226
reception, 201–203
research focuses on, 191–192
of scientific method and scientific
    thinking, 193–194
transferability of, 227–229
Learning cycle, 205–206
Leker, W. R., 87, 91
"Liberal Education and Where to Find
    It, A" (Huxley), 55
Life adjustment education, 142–146
Lincoln School, 69
Linn, M., 198
Literacy, scientific
controversy about social issues as orga-
    nizing themes in, 184–189
definitions of, 174–176
environmental education and, 182–
    184
humanistic education and, 179–180
inadequate levels of, ix
new progressivism and, 173–189
STS theme in, 178–184
values education and, 180–182, 236–
    237
Little, E., 148
Loud, O., 228
Luehamn, Arno, 135–136
Lyell, Charles, 8, 17

McConnell, W. R., 86
McElroy, William, 179–180
McGee, Joseph, 115
Mackensie High School, 106, 119
Magazines, analyses of, 124–126
Malin, J., 138
Mallinson, George, 142
Mankato State Teachers College, 115
Martin, W. Edgar, 125–126
Massachusetts Institute of Technology
    (MIT), 145–146, 148
    Physical Science Curriculum Study at,
        146
Massachusetts Teachers' Association, 32
Mathematics, 66, 82, 128–129, 142, 161,
    166, 216
    Bruner on, 159–160
    Committee on Science on, 70–71
    in disciplining mind, 5–6, 10
    Huxley on, 10
    life adjustment education and, 145–
        146
    physics and, 99, 102–103
    after World War II, 131, 134, 137
Mayo, Charles, 22–23
Mayo, Elizabeth, 22–23
Meaningful reception learning, 202
Medicine, study of science in, 9–10
Mental development, Piaget's stages of,
    162
Mental discipline, 25
    Committee on Science on, 73
    contributions of science study to, 4–8,
        10–11
    in high schools vs. colleges, 120–121
    Huxley on, 10–11
    life adjustment education and, 145
    scientific thinking for, 227
    Smith on, 55
    Spencer on, 14
    and study of biology, 7
"Mental Discipline in Education" (You-
    mans), 4–5
Merrill, R., 153–156, 170
Metcalfe, H. C., 167
Meteorology, 50, 142
    Committee of Ten on, 46
Meyerhoff, Howard, 175
Miami University, 86

Michigan, University of, 40–41
Mill, John Stuart, 7–8, 220
Millikan, C., 91
Minnesota, University of, 120
Missouri, University of, 41
Modern Biology (Moon, Otto, & Towle), 167–168
Modern Biology (Otto & Towle), 167–169
Modern Chemistry (Metcalfe, Williams, & Caska), 167
Modern Physics (Dull, Metcalfe, & Brooks), 167
Monahan, A. C., 87, 99
Moon, T., 167–168, 184
Moral discipline, Spencer on, 14
Moravcsik, M., 195–196
Morris High School, 69
Harvey Mudd College, 154

National Academy of Sciences, 159
    Space Science Board of, 175
National Academy of Sciences-National Research Council, 149
    Division of Physical Sciences of, 147
National Aeronautics and Space Administration (NASA), 176
National Association for Research in Science Teaching, 95
National Center for Educational Statistics, 39, 64
National Commission on Life Adjustment Education for Youth, 143
National Education Association (NEA)
    Commission on Education Policies of, 132–134, 140–141
    Commission on the Reorganization of Secondary Education of. *See* Commission on the Reorganization of Secondary Education
    Committee of Ten of. *See* Committee of Ten
    Committee on College Entrance Requirements of. *See* Committee on College Entrance Requirements
    Committee on the Articulation of High School and College of, 66
    Conference on Natural History of, 80
    Department of Higher Education of, 50
    Department of Science of, 50–51

    Department of Secondary Education of, 50, 66
National Science Foundation (NSF), 130, 146–158, 166, 175–176, 179, 207, 209, 231, 233–234
    BSCS supported by, 149–152
    CBA supported by, 152–153, 156–157
    CHEM Study supported by, 154–157
    curriculum reform supported by, 147–158
    ESCP supported by, 157
    ESS supported by, 158
    PSSC supported by, 148–149, 158
    SAPA supported by, 158
    SCIS supported by, 158
    TSM supported by, 157
National Science Teachers Association (NSTA), 147–148, 174, 177–178, 184, 187
National Society for the Study of Education (NSSE), 121, 133, 193
    Thirty-First Yearbook Committee of, 90–92, 96–98, 100–102, 105–106, 111–114, 120
    Thirty-First Yearbook of, 176
    Forty-Sixth Yearbook Committee of, 139–140
National Survey of Science, Mathematics, and Social Studies Education, 166
Needs of students, analyses of, 124–127
Newspapers, analyses of, 124–126
Newton, David, 208
Newton, Isaac, 181, 198–199
New York, University of the State of, 56
Nightingale, A. F., 51
Noll, Victor, 126–127, 138–139
Norris, S., 199
North Division High School, 112
Novak, Joseph, 202–203, 210

Oak Park Township High School, 144
Oberlin College, 41
Object lessons, 22–24
Odishaw, Hugh, 175
Office of Education, 104, 136, 143
Ohio State University, 69, 153
"On the Study of Biology" (Huxley), 9
On Understanding Science (Conant), 132
Osborne, R. W., 69
Oswego Movement, 23

Otto, J., 167–169
Outlines of Education Doctrine (Herbart), 28

Francis W. Parker School, 69
Patterns and Processes, 166
Pea, R., 199
Peabody, James E., 69, 95
Pella, Milton, 175–176
Pennsylvania, University of, Department of Geology at, 175
Pestalozzi, Johann Heinrich, 15, 21–24, 31–32, 37
Philadelphia Academy, 18
Physical geography, 72, 86–87
    Committee of Ten on, 46–47
Physical science, physical sciences, 100, 146
    Committee of Ten on, 42, 49
    curriculum reform in, 157–158, 167
    in disciplining mind, 7
    after World War II, 131, 133–134
Physical Science Study Committee (PSSC), 148–149, 158, 166
Physics, 86, 108, 161, 216
    analysis of student interest in, 127
    approaches to laboratory instruction in, 60–61
    in attracting students, 99–100
    biology and, 92–93, 99
    Bruner on, 159–160
    chemistry and, 99, 104
    Committee of Ten on, 42–43
    Committee on Science on, 74–76, 78, 80, 100, 102
    criticisms of teaching practices in, 102–103
    curriculum reform in, 147–149, 166–167, 169–170
    at end of progressive era, 138–142, 146
    during first half of twentieth century, 98–104
    general science and, 87–89, 91–92
    Hall on teaching of, 59–62
    Harvard on, 59–60, 166–167
    Huxley on, 10
    learner vs. content in, 101–102
    mathematics and, 99, 102–103
    Spencer on, 13

and value of laboratory study, 115
after World War II, 131, 133
Physiology, 72, 86
    biology and, 93
    Committee of Ten on, 43–44
    Eliot on, 32
    Rice on, 36
    Spencer on, 12
Piaget, Jean, 162, 191, 196–198, 202–203, 205, 214, 225, 232–233
Picton, Harold, 56–57
Pieper, Charles, 110, 121–122
Pimentel, George, 155
Pinloche, A., 22
Pitzer, Kenneth, 155–156
Plato, 3
Popular Science Monthly, 4
Post-curriculum-reform period, x
Powers, S. R., 123
Powers Test of Chemistry, 123
Pre-curriculum-reform period, x
"Present Effectiveness of Our Schools in the Training of Scientists, The," 131
"Present Status and Real Meaning of General Science, The" (Barber), 88
President's Scientific Research Board, 129–136
Princeton University, 157
Problem solving
    intuitive vs. analytical, 195–196
    scientific thinking for, 229
Process of Education, The (Bruner), 159, 196, 227
Progressive Education, 85
Progressive Education Association, 85
Progressivism, 85, 106, 108, 127
    functional science and end of, 139–140
    life adjustment education and end of, 142–146
    role of specialized science and end of, 140–142
    science education and end of, 138–146
    scientific literacy and, 173–189
Project method, laboratory study and, 109–110
"Project Method, The" (Kilpatrick), 109
Prosser, Charles, 142–143
Public-School System of the United States, The (Rice), 35

Quick, Suzanne, 168–169

Rachelson, S., 195
Ravitch, Diane, 146, 174
Readiness
    for learning science concepts, 225–226
    for thinking like scientists, 232–233
Reception learning, 201–203
Reed College, 152
Remsen, Ira, 42, 137
Renner, J., 187–189
Reorganization of Science in Secondary Schools, 67
Rice, J. M., 34–37
Rich, Stephen G., 122
Richardson, J. S., 92
Ridgway, D., 153–156, 170
Roberts, Herbert F., 118
Robinson, J., 209
Rockefeller Foundation, 149
Rote reception learning, 202
Rousseau, Jean-Jacques, 21, 37
Ruch, G. M., 110, 122
Russell, J., 204–205
Rutherford, F., 207–208

St. Andrew, University of, 7–8
Sakmyser, D., 212
Sanford, Charles W., 92, 143–144
Schefler, W., 211
School Science and Mathematics, 82, 142
"School Science Education for the 70s," 177
Schulman, L., 211
Schwaab, K., 183
Schwab, Joseph J., 158–159, 163–166, 201
Science—A Process Approach (SAPA), 158, 167, 193–195
Science Curriculum Improvement Study (SCIS), 158, 167, 205
Science education
    components of, 7
    crisis in, ix
    definition of, 188
    goals of, xi, 72–74
    quality of, 31–33
Science Education, 193
"Science Literacy: Its Meaning for American Schools" (Hurd), 174

"Science-Technology-Society: Science Education for the 1980s," 178
Science-technology-society (STS) movement, 178–184, 234
    environmental education and, 182–184
    humanistic education and, 179–180
    values education and, 180–182, 236–237
Scientific method, learning scientific thinking and, 193–194
Scientific mind, development of, 192–198
Scott, Arthur F., 152
Seaborg, Glenn, 154
Secondary Schools at the Turn of the Century (Sizer), 49
Secondary School Science Project, 157
Seymour High School, 115
Shamos, M., 234
Sheldon, Edward A., 23–24
Simon, S., 180
Sisler, H., 156
Sizer, Theodore, 19–20, 49
Smith, Alexander, 54–63, 231–232
Smith, Mortimer, 144
Smith, Norman, 176
Smyth, Thomas, 95–96
Snider, B., 211
Social relevance, science for, 127, 173–174, 233–237. *See also* Science-technology-society movement
    biology and, 92–98
    chemistry and, 104–106
    controversy over, 184–189
    CRSE on, 67
    general science and, 86–92
    importance of, 237
    life adjustment education and, 145
    organized disciplines and, 85–107
    physics and, 98–104
    project method and, 109
    reasons for teaching of, 234–235
    Schwab on, 163–164
    scientific literacy and, 176–189
Social utility, education for, 65–66
Southern High School, 81
Soviet Union, 128–129, 173
    as threat after World War II, 135–136
    U.S. space race with, ix, 146–147, 159

Spears, B., 213
Specialized science, role of, 140–142
Spencer, Herbert, 4, 8, 12–17, 21, 55, 65, 67, 220
Spiral curriculum, 162
Sputnik, 146–147
Stable inquiry, 163
Standardized testing, 121–124
Stanford-Binet intelligence test, 122
Stanford University, 122, 174
Steelman, John R., 130, 134
Stewart, A. W., 123–124
Strong, Laurence E., 152
Studebaker, John, 143

Talent, identification of, 136–138
Talks to Teachers on Psychology (James), 37, 191
Tanner, R., 210
Taylor, C., 195
Teachers College of the City of Boston, 123
Teachers College Record, 109
Teaching, Herbart's four-step theory of, 25–30
Teaching, science. *See also* Inquiry teaching; Learning; *specific disciplines*
  in academies, 20
  composite model of, 237–240
  of content, 219–226
  as contributor to education, 54–55
  definitions of, 217–219
  goals of, xi
  Huxley on, 11–12
  influence of Pestalozzi on, 24
  laboratory-based. *See* Laboratory study
  origins of, xi
  recommendations of Committee on Science on, 74–77
  of scientific thinking, 226–229
  and socially relevant issues, 234–235
  student vs. subject in, 94–97
  total time assigned in schools for, 215
  after World War II, 134–135
Teaching of Chemistry and Physics in the Secondary School, The (Smith & Hall), 54
Terman, Lewis, 122
Tests, testing, 111
  standardization of, 121–124

Textbooks
  in BSCS biology course, 150–151, 167
  in CBA, 153, 156–157
  in chemistry, 56, 153, 155–157, 167
  in CHEM Study project, 155–157
  concept learning and, 201
  curriculum reform and, 149–151, 153, 156–158, 160, 163–165, 167–169
  Eliot on, 33
  general science and, 90
  Harvard and, 59–60
  in high schools vs. colleges, 121
  impact of curriculum reform on, 167–169
  in NSF-developed physical science course, 158
  in physics, 102–103, 167
  in PSSC physics course, 149
  Schwab on, 163–165
Thinking, scientific, 226–233
  acquiring realistic sense of nature of, 229–230
  in biology, 97–98
  general vs. context-specific, 194–195
  learning scientific method and, 193–194
  for mental discipline, 227
  readiness for, 232–233
  reasons for teaching of, 226–229
  and role of laboratory in teaching science process, 230–232
  about scientific problems, 229
  for transferring learning to everyday contexts, 227–229
Thomas, B., 211
Thorndike, Edward L., 96, 161, 191, 227
Time, Space, and Matter (TSM) project, 157
Toulmin, S., 199
Towle, A., 167–169
Tregoning, J., 126
Tropisms, 160
Troy, T., 183
Truman, Harry, 130
Twiss, George R., 69, 83, 110, 119
Tyndall, John, 3, 8, 17

"Unity of Educational Reform, The" (Eliot), 33–34

Universities. *See* Colleges
University High School, 110

Values education, 180–182, 236–237
Vassar College, 41
Verfication method, teaching physics
    with, 60–61
Von Bichowsky, Foord, 104–105

Wager, W., 204
Walter, J., 167
Ward, B., 181
Watson, C., 126–127
Webb, Hanor A., 80–81, 122
Weiss, I., 167
Welch, D., 180
Welch, W., 104, 209
West Tennessee State Normal School,
    80–81
"What Actions Ought to Be Taken by
    Universities and Secondary Schools
    to Promote the Introduction of the
    Programs Recommended by the
    Committee of Ten?," 50
"What Is a Liberal Education?" (Eliot),
    31
"What Knowledge Is of Most Worth?"
    (Spencer), 12, 55, 67
Whiting High School, 112
Whitney, Worralo, 117–118
Williams, J., 167
Williston Seminary, 20
Wilson, Sherman, 141–142
Wisconsin, University of, 175

Wood, George C., 118
Woodbridge, William, 21
Woodhull, John F., 69, 119
Woods Hole Conference, 159–162
Woodworth, R. S., 96, 161, 227
World War II, 128–138
    identification of gifted and talented in
        science after, 136–138
    low enrollments in secondary school
        science after, 133–134
    science for scientist and nonscientist
        after, 130–133
    science personnel shortages due to,
        129–130
    Soviet threat after, 135–136
    status of teaching profession after,
        134–135

Yager, R., 181, 184–189, 234
Yale Corporation, 3–4
"Yale Report, The," 3–4
Youmans, Edward Livingston, 4–8, 10,
    14, 17, 220
Young, V., 170
Yverdon, Pestalozzian institute at, 21–22

Zacharias, Jerrold, 145, 148
Zollman, D., 213
Zoology, 72, 86, 118
    biology and, 93
    Committee of Ten on, 43–45, 49
    Committee on College Entrance Re-
        quirements on, 52–53

About the Author

George E. DeBoer is Professor of Education at Colgate University, where he has been on the faculty since 1974. During that time he served as Director of the Master of Arts in Teaching Program, Chairman of the Education Department from 1982-1990, and Acting Director of the Division of Social Sciences. His main area of interest is science education. His research, which appears in numerous articles in the science education literature, has focused on the science course-taking patterns of males and females in high school and college and the reasons for their decisions to continue in science. He received his undergraduate education at Hope College, a Master's degree from the University of Iowa, and a PhD in Science Education from Northwestern University.